50 More Hikes in New Hampshire

50 More Hikes

In New Hampshire

Day Hikes and Backpacking Trips
from Mount Monadnock to Mount Magalloway

DANIEL DOAN AND RUTH DOAN MACDOUGALL

Fourth Edition

Backcountry Guides
Woodstock, Vermont

An Invitation to the Reader

Developments, logging, and fires all take their
toll on hiking trails, often from one year to the
next. If you find that conditions on these fifty
hikes have changed, please let the publisher
know, so that corrections can be made in future
editions. Address all correspondence to:
Editor, 50 Hikes
Backcountry Guides
PO Box 748
Woodstock, VT 05091

**Library of Congress Cataloging-in-
Publication Data**

Doan, Daniel, 1914–1993
    50 more hikes in New Hampshire : day hikes
and backpacking trips from Mount Monadnock
to Mount Magalloway / Daniel Doan and Ruth
Doan MacDougall. – 4th ed.
        p.   cm.
    Rev. ed. of: Fifty more hikes in New Hamp-
shire. 3rd ed. c1991.
    Includes index.
    ISBN 0-88150-407-6 (pbk. : alk. paper)
    1. Hiking–New Hampshire–Guidebooks.
2. Backpacking–New Hampshire–Guidebooks.
3. New Hampshire–Guidebooks. I. MacDougall,
Ruth Doan. II. Title.
GV199.42.N4D6 1998
917.4202'43–dc21   97-50014
                                        CIP

Published by Backcountry Guides
A division of The Countryman Press
PO Box 748, Woodstock, VT 05091
Distributed by W.W. Norton & Company, Inc.
500 Fifth Avenue, New York, NY 10110
Series design by Glenn Suokko
Trail overlays by Richard Widhu
Cover photograph of the summit of Mount
    Chocorua by Robert J. Kozlow
Frontispiece photograph "On Rogers Ledge in
    the Kilkenny" by Ruth Doan MacDougall
Printed in the United States of America
10 9 8 7 6 5 4 3

50 Hikes at a Glance

DISTANCE (in miles)	RISE (in feet)	VIEWS	GOOD FOR KIDS	WATERFALLS	NOTES
6.5	795	★	★		The Wapack Trail south
10	1640	★	★		New Hampshire's largest state park
2	60	★	★		The seashore
0.75	370	★	★		Wilderness near megalopolis
3.5	530	★	★		Wet-weather adventures
1.5	730	★	★		A quiet pleasure
2	660	★	★		An un-wild summit, Manchester view
4	755	★	★		A blueberry ridge
5.5	1480	★	★		2 summits: civilized & wild
9	2670	★	★		Everlastingly impressive
2.5	400	★	★		See historic central countryside
1	356	★	★		Vastest views for least effort
4.25	600		★		A woods walk
4.5	925	★	★		Once a mountain pasture
2	1105	★	★		Bare summit, panorama
3.5	1370	★	★		View of lakes & peaks
6	500		★		A main highway in 1850s
3	1200	★	★		Quartzite-frosted summit
6.5	1550	★	★		Woods, lake, ski slope
5	1452	★	★		Lake views!
3	950	★	★	★	Famous Crawford Notch view
3.25	1150	★	★		Spectacular summits
4.5	1200	★	★	★	Highest falls in New Hampshire
4.5	1860	★	★		A favorite for families
4	1770	★	★		2 summits; 1 perfect cabin

50 Hikes at a Glance

DISTANCE (in miles)	RISE (in feet)	VIEWS	GOOD FOR KIDS	WATERFALLS	NOTES
3.75	1800	★	★		Detour to see lime kilns
4.25	2000	★	★		A ski-slope descent
8.5	1780	★	★		Includes ancient Sandwich Notch Road
5.75	2469	★	★		Great view from Owl's Head
8.75	1600	★	?		Dramatic scenery
8.5	2100	★	★	★	Lovely cascades; virgin spruce
5.5	2633	★			Skyward in Crawford Notch
6 or 9.5	2265 or 3429	★	★	★	A short or long hike
8.5	2320	★	?	★	A compass-deceiving summit
6	2600	★	★	★	Majestic virgin spruce forest
9	2382	★	?		Full of surprises!
8.5	2605	★			Ponds & precipices
9.5	2740	★	★	★	Includes Diana's Baths
7	3400	★		★	Ice caves
8.75	2910	★			An individual mountain
9.75	3100	★	?		A sentinel
9.75	3250	★	★	★	Deservedly popular
11	3330	★			Best in October
12	3600	★		★	A spectacular route
2	1000	★	★		Northernmost views
8.25	2300	★	★	★	Bird-watching, too
7.5	2860	★	★		Adventures past & present
3	580		★	★	Bushwhack to bog-camping
16.5	3100	★	★		Leisurely but remote
21.25	5310	★	?	★	Includes Carter Dome

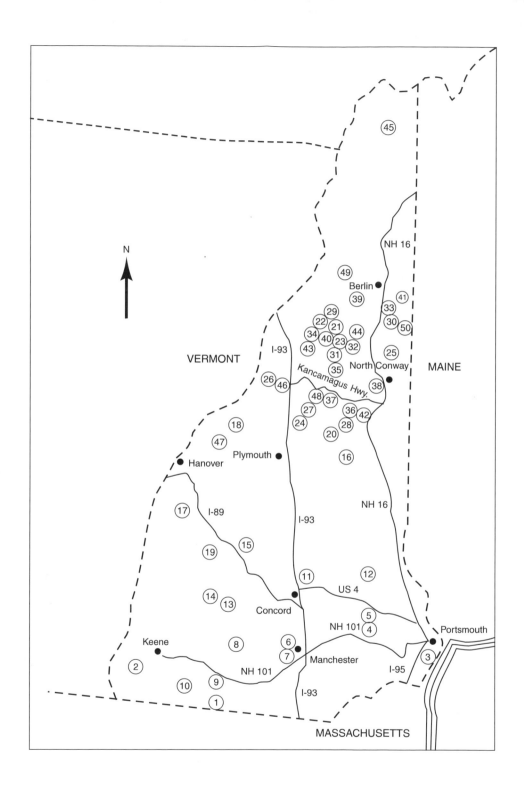

N

VERMONT

MAINE

MASSACHUSETTS

NH 16

Berlin

North Conway

Kancamagus Hwy.

I-93

Hanover

Plymouth

NH 16

I-89

I-93

US 4

Concord

NH 101

Portsmouth

Keene

Manchester

I-95

NH 101

I-93

Contents

Acknowledgments

From Ruth Doan MacDougall

My thanks to everybody who helped with this project, including: Donald K. MacDougall; Hal and Peggy Graham of Trailwrights, Penelope Doan, Marjorie Doan, Mary Kibling, Kirk Dougal, Amy Gumprecht, Steven D. Smith, Gloria and Larry Pond; Bill Appel of Friends of Pisgah; Jim Bearce, manager, Pisgah State Park; Rick Blanchette and John Flanders of Friends of the Wapack; and The Over the Hill Hikers of Sandwich, New Hampshire.

From Daniel Doan

I am indebted to many hiking friends, old and new, for their experience and companionship on these trails.

I have had many helpers. The impossibility of listing them all tempts me to a solution once used on old posters for farm auctions. These advertisements, detailing livestock, farm machinery, household furniture, and the cords of wood in the shed, always concluded with the words "and other items too numerous to mention."

I shall begin this list with Chris Lloyd, editor. His mountain experience, skill with computers, and editorial deftness provided acute filtering of revisions and cheerful tolerance of my jotted notes.

Next, my wife, Marjorie, for listening to my reviewing the hikes that she knows all about anyway.

Next our pal, Mary Kibling, who checked the southerly trails and summits that are a good distance from my home in Jefferson.

Now for friends and members of institutions who helped:

Bill Appel of Friends of Pisgah, Vera Smith for Pawtuckaway's North Peak, and Julia S. Mawson, former director of Odiorne Point Visitor Center.

Members of the AMC's New Hampshire Chapter—those I have not named, and AMC personnel at Pinkham Notch Visitor Center.

Members of the US Forest Service in all the Ranger Districts of the White Mountain National Forest.

Members of the New Hampshire Department of Parks and Recreation.

Hal and Peggy Graham of Trailwrights, Rob Nesham, Dave and Marita Wright, Roioli Schweiker, Peter Crane, Steve Smith, Ruth and Don MacDougall, Kirk Dougal, and The Over the Hill Hikers of Sandwich, New Hampshire.

Many names, I'm afraid, escape me. I extend to those people my gratitude, and conclude with the same for all others "too numerous to mention."

Preface to the Fourth Edition

I was born on a chicken farm in Belmont, New Hampshire.

This was the second farm that Dan and Ernestine, my parents, had owned. The first was in Orfordville, in the part of New Hampshire where Dan grew up learning the woods. He later wrote, "Orford had been a constant in my life because our house there was my summer home all through my boyhood. My maternal grandmother spent her first and last years in Orford. Aunts, uncles, cousins near or distant lived there summers or year-round. I thought the town was the most beautiful place in the world. Falling in love with a locality can be as powerful an emotion as falling in love with a person. In some form it lasts a lifetime."

Dan's father, Frank Carleton Doan, was a Unitarian minister and an author. In 1929, two years after his father died in Winchester, Massachusetts, Dan's mother moved to Hanover, and thus at age 15 Dan became a permanent resident of New Hampshire.

As Dan's graduation from Dartmouth drew nigh, he faced his future and realized that, as he later wrote, "life away from cities, business, professions, and society appealed to me. More than that, it possessed me. I could see no other route ahead for me. I formed the determination to settle in Orford, to learn farming for food (some of it) and writing for money (just enough), thus perhaps following the effects of reading *Walden* at age 17. Thoreau's different drummer is too often quoted. More importantly for youth, he says of his experiment in the woods, 'If one advances confidently in the direction of his dreams, and endeavors to live the life which he has imagined, he will meet with a success unexpected in common hours.' "

Dan enjoyed referring to the Orfordville farm as the first commune in New Hampshire, for he and Ernie, my mother, shared it with another young married couple, who happened to be Dan's sister and Ernie's brother. But eventually Dan and Ernie felt the need for a place of their own and bought the Belmont farm, where I was born and also my sister, Penny.

Chickens and short stories couldn't support the family, so Dan got a job at Scott & Williams, a company that manufactured circular hosiery machines, and we moved to Laconia.

"Walking to work!" Dan later wrote. "This was one of the advantages of Laconia, a good little mill town. I'm sure those walks relieved the tensions of earning a living as a time-study man and as foreman of the heat-treating department. I also fled problems by taking to the woods and mountains. Every street out of Laconia could be an escape hatch. And there was the White Mountain National Forest only a few miles north of the lakes."

Penny and I grew up with the woods an integral part of our lives; with Dan we went hiking and fishing and "camping out," as backpacking was then called.

Throughout these years Dan continued to write. His first novel, *The Crystal Years,* was a coming-of-age story about a boy who moves from Boston to New Hampshire. *Amos Jackman,* his second novel, was inspired by Quinttown, whose abandoned farmland he had discovered in his boyhood while fishing near Smarts Mountain.

Woods and writing were intertwined in my own life. By the time Dan took an early retirement at age 51 from Scott & Williams, my own first novel was being published and I was planning to return from England to my New Hampshire roots.

Retired, Dan could devote himself to writing and hiking, and the result was his two hiking guidebooks that have become classics, *50 Hikes in the White Mountains* and *50 More Hikes in New Hampshire*. Diabetes had struck him when he was 50, and he fought back with insulin and with exercises that he formulated into another book, *Dan Doan's Fitness Program for Hikers and Cross-Country Skiers*. During this time he also wrote a history of New Hampshire's north country, which was posthumously published in 1997, *Indian Stream Republic: Settling a New England Frontier, 1785–1842*.

After Ernie's death in 1982, Dan remarried, and he and my stepmother, Marjorie, went hiking in Scotland and then settled in Jefferson, New Hampshire. There Dan wrote *Our Last Backpack,* a memoir about a weeklong hike in the Mahoosucs.

At last his diabetes and a stroke crippled Dan. Under his supervision, I began updating his hiking books, checking the trails and inserting any changes into the new printings. Ever since I had given him my first story, written at age six, we had been in the same business, so to speak, sharing a passion for writing. And now I could make sure that his books would live on.

Amos felt quiet now, with a deep ease that made him aware of the life of his mind and body like a river in spring. It was as though he could grow and sustain himself from the earth and air.
—Daniel Doan, Amos Jackman

Dan died in 1993. I remembered how he once had summed up the writing life: "This thought emerges: Successful or not, the years devoted to the art, craft, trade, or hobby of writing may be looked upon as having been spent in a great tradition and enterprise. What did you do with your life? I tried to learn to write."

In this fourth edition of *50 More Hikes in New Hampshire* I have deleted two hikes and one backpack and substituted new ones—Mount Cube, Mount Magalloway, and Kilkenny Backpack. The others have been checked and updated.

Everybody develops a list of essentials to pack for a hike, and you will surely make up your own variation of Dan's suggestions in his Introduction. Mine includes, in addition to Dan's list, sunscreen, lip balm, a bandanna, and a plastic trash bag for a tarp. One reminder: Eat a square meal the night before a hike and a good breakfast that morning. Don't diet. Many of us forget that we need those calories and fat grams for energy and endurance on the trail.

As Dan used to sign his books: Happy hiking!

—Ruth Doan MacDougall
Winter 1998

Introduction

These day hikes, walks, and backpacks cover the territory from Mount Magalloway near the Canadian border to trails near the Massachusetts border. The book is divided into geographical sections: Southern New Hampshire, Central New Hampshire, the White Mountains, and the Far North. In the last section, Backpacking, all but one of the hikes are in the White Mountain National Forest, and that one, Smarts Mountain, is in the southwestern foothills of the higher ranges. Each section begins with the easier walks and climbs. Because of the natural contours of the state, the hikes in the southern and central sections take you to lower elevations or on simple woods walks.

I've included summits and places less known than those in my first book, *50 Hikes in the White Mountains*.

A word about maps. The composite maps in this book feature sections of government topographic sheets with the described trail superimposed on them. For a better understanding of the hikes and the country they pass through, you should consider buying the maps put out by the United States Geological Survey (USGS) or by the US Forest Service, which are based on the USGS contours, and by the Appalachian Mountain Club (AMC). The excellent AMC maps cover the White Mountains and Mount Monadnock. For central and other southern sections of the state, use the USGS maps. The USGS maps will also give you more topographical details than the AMC maps. The relevant maps have been listed along with the other basic data at the beginning of each hike.

In using the USGS maps, you should realize that those in the 15-minute series—and even some in the 7½-minute series—may be seriously out-of-date as to trails and roads, usually because routes have been abandoned or relocated since the original surveys. The topography, however, is reliable, because the earth's contours haven't changed. The 7½-minute series—much larger and more detailed than the 15-minute series—is generally accurate for the trails I have checked, but the forest service quads tend to be more up-to-date than their USGS counterparts. It should be noted that the government maps have their critics in the hiking community.

USGS maps are available at bookstores, outfitters, and sporting goods stores while the forest service quads can be bought at the headquarters of the White Mountain National Forest in Laconia. (See address at end of Introduction.) The forest service quads, unlike USGS, show the boundaries of Ranger Districts with names on either side of the designation along the dark dash, dash, and longer marks. Also, the forest service designates boundaries of wilderness areas and scenic areas by a band of solid gray. At times your trail will coincide with district boundaries for part of their lengths. These districts are for administrative purposes, are unmarked, and on the trails will not confuse you.

Remember to equip yourself with the *AMC White Mountain Guide* for complete details on White Mountain trails. Get it at the AMC's Pinkham Notch Visitor Center or at many retail outlets.

Pamphlets put out by the USGS are also helpful. From "New Hampshire and Vermont Index to Topographic and Other Map Coverage" and "New Hampshire and Vermont Catalog of Topographic and Other Published Maps" you learn which maps (called quadrangles) you'll need for different hikes. To learn the symbols and use of maps, get "Topographic Map Symbols." The pamphlets are free. They can be obtained at outfitters, bookstores, and sporting goods stores, or you can send to the USGS. (See address at end of Introduction.)

One of my aims in this book has been to describe some remote territory to both the beginning hiker and the experienced climber. Many of the hikes avoid the more popular trails where overuse is a problem. In the White Mountain National Forest the US Forest Service and the AMC are trying to deal with this increasing traffic—and are succeeding, too, in protecting and conserving the forest and trails.

This overuse, although bad for some of the more popular trails, is an indication of the joys of hiking and backpacking. Of course every hiker wants to see the famous peaks. But an infinite number of enjoyable, more remote hikes warrant your attention.

The ultimate goal of a program aimed at avoiding busy trails and campsites is hiking on no trails at all. That's commonly called bushwhacking. I've included in the backpacking section a simple bushwhack route to a remote beaver pond: Cheney Brook. There are miles and miles of New Hampshire forest without trails. Try them. I advise first that you follow streams and go with companions experienced in the use of maps and compass. You'll discover another world.

The hiking season on southern and central trails runs from March to December. In the White Mountains it's shorter: May to October. These arbitrary dates vary from

➤ Balance

For outdoor practice, I think there's nothing like rough, trailless, woods walking, both uphill and down. Without a path through the woods you're so busy deciding where to go—if you're new at it—that you haven't time to concern yourself with balance, and you improve before you know it. In contrast, following an open trail through the woods, you're inclined to hesitate, teeter from rock to rock, and grab for nearby trees and bushes.

Such grabbing, however, is good if you can learn to keep moving as you do it. It's particularly helpful when you're descending a steep trail, where trees and branches provide handholds that give you security and confidence.

—Daniel Doan, Dan Doan's Fitness Program for Hikers and Cross-Country Skiers

year to year depending on the arrival and melting of snow. On higher elevations, especially in the White Mountains, you can expect snow on the ground through May and storms of sleet and snow in any month.

Snowshoes can make you a winter hiker. Cross-country skiing is also a great way to extend the hiking season. For either sport (when you have learned to travel on snowshoes and skis and have the proper winter gear, clothing, and experience), I suggest you try Pisgah State Park, Fox State Forest, Old Croydon Turnpike—to name only a few almost-level routes.

Except for the bushwhack, the hikes follow maintained trails, paths, or old roads. In the White Mountains the majority of the trails are maintained by the forest service and the AMC, although some are kept up by smaller clubs. To the south various clubs, conservation groups, and public organizations look after the trails. In state parks the New Hampshire Division of Parks and Recreation does the job, sometimes assisted by volunteers such as Friends of Pisgah.

Old logging roads appear often in the hike descriptions, because many trails follow these routes, which were once used to sled out timber. They usually lead to rougher mountain trails farther up steeper slopes. Of similar vintage are the abandoned old logging railroads. The tracks are gone but the grades make for good walking. You may encounter logging operations south or north of the White Mountains, but in the national forest the forest service supervises the cutting to leave wide bands of trees on either side of the trails.

Many of the trails traverse private property to reach the national forest. The forest service posts signs at the boundaries where trails cross from privately owned land. Through private property you hike on sufferance. Needless to say, behavior should be that of a considerate guest. Otherwise there'll be closed trails and NO TRESPASSING signs.

The trails change from year to year because of natural causes such as erosion, landslides, beavers flooding low ground along streams, and windstorms blowing down trees. Yet many have remained virtually unchanged for generations. For the latest information, check with the US Forest Service, the AMC, or the New Hampshire Department of Resources and Economic Development.

Distance, Walking Time, and Vertical Rise

Each hike description begins with gauges by which you can decide the hike you want, depending on the time and amount of energy you have to expend and your physical fitness. The distances are for a round-trip unless otherwise noted.

The times are based on moderate climbing speed—the pace at which a moderately fit hiker can walk and still talk to a companion without gasping for breath. This is the only sensible pace to use. The times do not include stops for snacks, observing nature, eating lunch, or viewing scenery.

The vertical rise is the actual amount of upward climbing. If you start at a 1000-foot elevation and climb to a 2500-foot summit, no matter how far you walk or for how long, you'll climb an equivalent of 1500 feet straight up. In general, if the climb contains only 750 feet of vertical rise, it is half as difficult as one with 1500 feet of vertical rise. I must add that this is not always so. If the 750 feet go up difficult boulders, ledges, gullies, and rock slides, they may be more of a challenge than 1500 feet on a gradual trail. There are too many variables for a useful rating system, and I've not included one.

The White Mountain National Forest

Because over half of these hikes are partially or completely within the White Mountain National Forest, you should know a bit about the history of its more than 770,000 acres. Many of these acres had not been logged until the 1880s and 1890s, when railroads built by lumber barons such as J.E. Henry of Lincoln penetrated the rugged valleys. By 1905 the spruce and pine had largely fallen to ax and saw. Logging continued through World War I, with pulpwood for paper and hardwood for veneer a large part of the operations as late as the 1930s. During the peak years of logging and immediately after, fire consumed thousands of acres. When lightning struck in tinder-dry branches left by loggers, the remains of the forest exploded like a giant torch. Sparks from wood-burning

Nancy-Jane Jackson

Bristly club moss (Lycopodium annotinum) *is often found above tree line.*

locomotives also were a danger. So were careless smokers and campers who touched off some devastating fires.

Concern by conservationists resulted in the founding in 1901 of the Society for the Protection of New Hampshire Forests. To this day it is active and effective in the state. The society led the fight to save the mountains and succeeded with the Weeks Act of 1911. The federal government began to purchase land for a national forest in the White Mountains the next year.

The national forest is managed by the forest service. Its directives are based on a "multiple-use policy," which provides for timber production, watershed protection, recreation development, and wildlife protection. Ten scenic areas and five wilderness areas protect for posterity the wild environment of thousands of acres within the national forest.

Ruth's note: IMPORTANT. PARKING PASSES REQUIRED. In 1997 the White Mountain National Forest began participating in a "national recreation fee project." These user fees help pay for services, recreational facilities, and trail maintenance in national forests across the country. There are four types of passes. The "annual," "annual household" (two vehicles), and "weekly" passes can be bought at local stores, at all WMNF ranger stations, at the WMNF office in Laconia, or by mail. "Daily" passes are available at the self-service pay stations you'll find in many parking areas in the national forest. For more information, including prices, phone the Androscoggin Ranger Station at (603) 466-2713 or visit the WMNF website at www.fs.fed.us/r9/white.

Trees and Animals

Since about 1850 the New Hampshire forests cut down by the early settlers have been growing back. In the southern and central sections mile after mile of fields and hilltop pastures returned to woods as families migrated west, as men never returned from the Civil War, and as young people sought wages in city mills. This natural reforestation is continuing.

The forest is composed of diversified conifers and deciduous trees. The evergreens populate the high elevations and the swamps, the leafy trees fill in between, and mixtures of both varieties are common everywhere depending on soil and exposure. Of course some peaks like Monadnock still remain bare after more than 100 years since early fires denuded their slopes.

In the White Mountains proper, the division of tree types is more marked. Beech, maple, yellow birch, and white birch took over after the cutting of the original spruce on the lower slopes. From an elevation of about 3000 feet up to tree line, evergreens—red spruce, black spruce, and balsam fir—are better adapted; they cover the mountainside and many summits. (The alpine zone, treeless, at about 5000 feet and up, cannot support trees because of the elevation's climate, which resembles that of Labrador and Greenland.) White birch is often dominant on burned land. The evergreen hemlocks and white pines blend with the deciduous forests. Twisted white birches and small mountain ash trees commonly grow with the highest spruce and fir.

Scrub spruce at tree line deserves special mention because it closes in the trails with impenetrable thickets. Don't try to travel in this scrub.

New Hampshire animals are almost invariably shy or nocturnal or both. Red squirrels, gray squirrels, and chipmunks are exceptions. I've never seen a bobcat. There are no problems with poisonous snakes. Each year a rattlesnake is reported in the southern and central sections, usually in a newspaper account, but I have yet to meet

anyone who laid eyes on one.

Black bears can be a problem at campsites, so take careful precautions to keep from attracting them. Do your cooking at least 100 feet downwind of the campsite, and keep your food and cooking utensils separate from your sleeping area. Put food scraps in closed containers. Hang the food at least 10 feet off the ground and 5 feet out on a limb that won't support a bear. A more elaborate method of hanging food, to outwit bears who have learned to bite through a rope, is to divide your food into two bags and counterbalance them 20 feet above the ground and 10 feet from the tree trunk.

Like all mice, the New Hampshire woods resident known as the white-footed mouse, or deer mouse, will chew your pack if you leave it on the ground. Hang your pack by a cord from a tree to discourage them. Raccoons will raid food containers you leave unattended for the night.

Porcupines aren't dangerous, but don't fool with one; their quilled tails move faster than lightning.

You'll see white-tailed deer in the evening or morning. Most moving hikers make too much noise to see deer along trails. Deer stay off the high peaks. Moose have become much more common, but you'll probably see only their oxlike tracks. Stillness is important, if you would see animals. If you remain silent as you step out on a pond's shore, you might see a moose belly deep feeding on roots of water lilies.

The eastern coyote has become an important member of our wildlife, although mostly invisible. They are not dangerous.

Skunks, foxes, hares, and small rodents such as mice forage mostly at night. Beavers are also active then. In daylight sometimes a beaver will swim about his pond apparently checking on the water level and the dam. Fishers are as scarce as bobcats. Mink and otter frequent ponds and streams.

One dangerous species is *Homo sapiens.* Ironically the "wild" woods and mountains seem to have a civilizing effect on most people. Trailheads and parked cars, however, do invite theft and vandalism. Don't leave anything you value in your car. A locked trunk can be an inducement to force it open on the theory that you've used it for a strongbox.

Clothing and Equipment

Start with comfortable underwear (including perhaps a synthetic-blend T-shirt that wicks perspiration away from the skin), a long-sleeved shirt of cotton-polyester blend, and fully cut walking pants of the same material. (I think blue jeans are an abomination in the woods. They are cold when wet, take forever to dry, and are cut like tights. You have to be a contortionist to get into the pockets, from which you lose valuables when you lie down. Besides, they remind me of work.) Shorts are great in warm weather. Up high, if rain threatens or if it's early or late in the season, pack warm pants, too.

Boots should be leather, ankle high, and need weigh no more than 3 pounds per pair. Rubber lug soles are best. For hiking in the early spring or in the first fall snow, leather-topped rubbers with an innersole keep your feet drier than leather boots. I've tried the ankle-high lug-sole sneakers—again, good woods footgear.

After the above conservative advice, however, I will add a more up-to-date suggestion. Modern lightweight hiking boots, which incorporate designs and materials from jogging shoes, may be right for your purposes and feet. During a long hike, such boots, compared to some of the monstrosities on the market, can save you from lifting literally tons. I use a pair that weighs 2 pounds but would not recommend them for backpacking unless your feet are tougher than mine.

Inside your hiking boot wear a light inner sock of wool and nylon and an outer all-wool (or nearly so) heavy sock. Hikers favor the ragg-knit type.

Rain or shine, a hat is a necessity. It stops insects from crawling through your hair and protects you from both rain and sun. The brim shades your eyes.

What about the knapsack or rucksack and its size, style, and contents? If you buy a small one, you'll want a bigger one. Mine is made of waterproofed nylon. It's 14 x 18 inches, with side pockets and a pocket in the flap. I use it year-round.

Carry in your rucksack a heavy wool shirt, sweater, or insulated jacket, and a poncho or rain suit with hood. A nylon parka or "shell" is a must above tree line and a comfort for hiking the lowlands on cool, windy days. Over a wool shirt it's better hiking garb in showers than a rain suit in which your own sweat and condensed vapor wet you as much as rain would. Wool is still the basic fabric for hiking in the rain, especially cold rain; it's warm even when it's wet. Pack extra wool socks. If you don't wear them on your feet, they'll be welcome as mittens some cold, wet day when you've forgotten to pack gloves.

You should consider a parka made of a laminated material that is microporous, making it both breathable and waterproof. Many equipment companies produce such parkas for a wide choice of styles and conditions. There are also rain pants. Boots utilize it for uppers in lightweight hiking footwear. Although expensive, this material could, however, eliminate your other raingear for active use, but don't expect a miracle of total sweat evaporation. Such a parka will at times substitute for a windproof shell.

Besides suitable clothing you should have matches and firestarter in waterproof containers within your rucksack's side pockets. Compass, map, and guidebook should be there also. I pack a flashlight but seldom use it.

Here are pants and shirt pocket items: pocketknife with can opener and screwdriver; sunglasses; insect repellent in a small squeeze bottle.

In your rucksack you should have a quart of water in a canteen or plastic bottles. Besides the day's lunch and whatever trail snacks you like to munch on, carry spare food for two meals and extra water. A simple first-aid kit and elastic bandage for sprained ankles or knees should be in a waterproof bag.

Backpackers will need a tent, sleeping bag, pad to sleep on, and cooking equipment. Freeze-dried food is excellent, and there are less expensive dehydrated and dried foods at supermarkets. You should have the latest water-purifying method; investigate tablets and filters. Of course you'll need a large pack to put all this in.

Such a sketchy summary of equipment is only an introduction to vast and varied choices. I suggest you read a book on the subject, study catalogs, visit outfitting stores, and talk to other hikers. Renting from outfitters is a good way to avoid making mistakes in permanent purchases. Equipment should be simple, lightweight, and practical. Try it out before you go on an extended day hike or backpack.

This last piece of advice applies particularly to new boots. They should be well broken in. Even so, your boots can give you blisters. Carry moleskin in your first-aid kit.

Rules and Regulations

In general, sensible behavior keeps you within most rules and regulations. There are certain specifics, however. If you are hiking on private property, no wood or charcoal fires may be built without the landowner's permission and a fire permit from the district fire chief. Use a portable stove; it's a simpler solution. Furthermore, there's no overnight camping allowed on private property without the landowner's permission. Carry out all your empty containers, wrappers, and other trash. Don't litter. Don't cut trees or boughs; don't destroy plants. Park your car completely off traveled roads. Don't park in any opening into the woods, any gateway, or any logging road. A state law prohibits obstruction of a right-of-way.

For the White Mountain National Forest the long-standing requirement of fire permits was discontinued in 1985. There are, however, special regulations about camping and fires. You should get the latest seasonal information from the Laconia headquarters or from district ranger stations in Conway, Gorham, Plymouth, Bethlehem, and the visitors center in Bethel, Maine. The forest service also maintains information centers located near I-93 at Campton and Lincoln and at the Lincoln Woods Visitor Information Center on the western end of the Kancamagus Highway.

The AMC offers information at the Pinkham Notch Visitor Center, at Lafayette Place in Franconia Notch, and the Crawford Notch Visitor Information Center at the former depot near the Crawford House site just north of Crawford Notch.

New Hampshire State Parks, Reservations, and Forests have other rules and regulations. In general no camping or wood or charcoal fires are allowed outside designated campgrounds. Regulations are posted. For a brochure, write the New Hampshire Division of Parks and Recreation. (See address at end of Introduction.)

Although in the White Mountain National Forest no fire permits are required, this does not reduce the danger nor your responsibility. You must obtain and abide by the forest service publication "Backcountry Camping Rules," which provides detailed listings of current camping regulations. In Forest Protection Areas (formerly called Restricted Use Areas), overuse has compacted the soil and damaged plants, trees, and water. Natural recovery is encouraged by Forest Protection Areas, and future harm is prevented.

Here are some examples of restrictions: Camping and fires are not allowed within 200 feet of certain trails and within 0.25 mile along some roads and around various huts, shelters, tent platforms, and lakes. No camping is allowed above tree line (which has been set at the altitude where trees are less than 8 feet high), except where snow is 2 feet deep or more.

There are five Wilderness Areas mandated by Congress: Great Gulf, Presidential–Dry River (both on Mount Washington), Pemigewasset, Sandwich Range, and Caribou-Speckled. I should point out that various structures and shelters may be removed in accordance with the policy set forth in the Wilderness Act. Check when you get your forest service publication. All five Wilderness Areas are open to day hikes. If you are planning to hike or camp with a group, the limit is 10 people.

To avoid confusion as regards the name "Wilderness" applied to the Pemigewasset, you should know that this drainage of the East Branch has been known since about 1880 as the Pemigewasset Wilderness, or, to the numerous hikers who enjoy it, The Pemi. A federal Wilderness Area there begins at Franconia Brook. You should be aware that the access trail, from the parking area off the Kancamagus Highway, long known as the Wilderness Trail, received a new name in 1991 for the first 2.75 miles. This section is the Lincoln Woods Trail, which leads to the boundary of the official Pemigewasset Wilderness.

Huts and Shelters

In the White Mountains, the forest service and the AMC provide shelters and accommodations of various sorts. The AMC's mountain huts have bunkrooms and serve meals. Make reservations at the Pinkham Notch Visitor Center. Log or board shelters, whose open fronts face stone fireplaces, are maintained by the forest service, the AMC, and several other clubs. At some AMC shelters and campsites, tent platforms for backpacking tents have been built. A caretaker supervises the site and collects a modest fee per night per person.

Safety

Surely you've seen the annual headlines about some hiker dying on the trail. Storms above tree line can be fiercer than you believed possible when you were down in the forest, and they can be sudden. When you reach tree line, make a judgment of the weather; if clouds or winds foretell a storm, turn back. Indeed, if the forecasts have indicated possible bad weather, don't go to tree line at all. If you must hike regardless of weather (and when you're as hooked as I am you sometimes feel that way), hike on a forest trail to a pond or a low wooded mountain.

Storms above tree line always get worse. Fog and winds will shove you, semiblinded, from rock to rock in a dangerous, teetering gait. Don't try it. Turn back into the trees.

You should hike with a companion. Loners invite trouble (and cause it for their rescuers) if they twist an ankle or move off the trail and fall.

Drinking water purity is a consideration you should bear in mind. A clear stream might contain *Giardia lamblia*, a common intestinal parasite that causes delayed diar-

Not drink water from brooks and streams? Ridiculous! We knew enough about pollution not to drink from the Connecticut River, though we swam in it. But at watering boxes for horses along the roads, such as the one on the way to Orfordville, we relished the cool sweet water running in along the gouged-out log that conducted it from the sidehill spring. If there was giardiasis then, nobody warned us. And of course the beavers had not returned.

–Daniel Doan, Our Last Backpack

rhea and other, worse symptoms. Animals as well as humans are carriers. Beavers can infect streams and ponds. Boiling and disinfecting are standard precautions. The forest service offers a pamphlet, "Is the Water Safe?" If I must drink woodland water I look for a small spring trickling from a steep slope. Not absolutely safe, mind you. Also note that mention of water herein does not mean *safe* water.

Before a hike, study your maps and guidebooks. Estimate the time needed to get back before dark. Carry a compass and learn how to use it. Carry enough emergency clothing and food so you can spend a night in the woods if you have to.

Getting lost happens to even the best hikers. The standard advice is to sit down and think about your predicament. It does work. Very likely you will remember where you missed the trail or took a wrong turn. Study your map and orient it with your compass. Distances out to roads are not great in most of New Hampshire. When you are really confused, follow a stream. If injured, build a fire (assuming you can). Throw on ferns and leaves to make a smudge that will

signal above the trees. Someone will spot it and come looking for the fire if not for you. Even if you can't build a fire, someone will come looking if you have left your itinerary with a responsible person and have adhered to it. Leave word at home and with rangers or other officials.

It's best to have an alternate hike for unpredictable bad weather and to leave word of this. Go to one or the other. You'll probably never need to worry about being searched for, but it's a good feeling to know you'll be found if something happens. Cares have no place on hikes. Leave them all behind; enjoy the forests and the mountains.

Addresses
Appalachian Mountain Club
5 Joy Street
Boston, MA 02108
or
Pinkham Notch Visitor Center
Gorham, NH 03581

White Mountain National Forest
719 Main Street
Laconia, NH 03246
(603) 528-8721

New Hampshire Division of Resources and Economic Development
PO Box 1856
Concord, NH 03302-1856

New Hampshire Division of Parks and Recreation
PO Box 1856
Concord, NH 03302-1856

Society for the Protection of New Hampshire Forests
54 Portsmouth Street
Concord, NH 03301

United States Geological Survey
Washington, DC 20242

For USGS maps by mail, order from:
USGS Information Services
Box 25286, Denver Federal Center
Denver, CO 80225
To order by fax, call 303-202-4693
For information about USGS maps, call
1-800-USA-MAPS

Key to Map Symbols

■■■ main trail

● ● ● side trail

Ⓐ Appalachian Trail

Ⓣ shelter

Ⓟ parking

Southern New Hampshire

Out of the corner of one eye he caught a glimpse of a scarlet flash and turning his head he saw in the open woods beyond the white blossoms of the hobblebush a tanager flitting like a spark through the trees. Almost before he was sure what he was looking at, almost before he realized the flame of scarlet and black was a bird, it had gone.

The ecstasy of the moment flooded over him and he remained kneeling there among the wildflowers, entranced, hopefully and then almost prayerfully awaiting the return of the bird. At last he came back to himself and had some vague inkling that beauty is swift and brief. The knowledge did not make him sad for that was the way it should be. He got to his feet and strung the trout on a twig and went on with his fishing while a glowing happiness filled him and brightened the day more than the spring sun.

—Daniel Doan, The Crystal Years

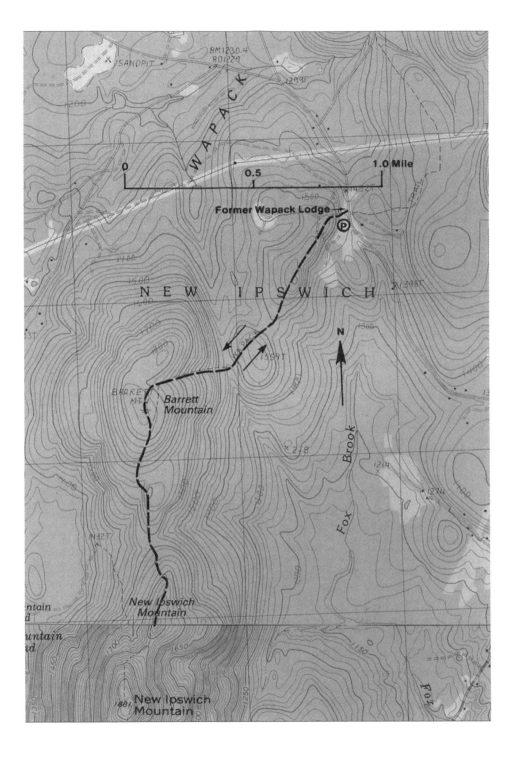

1

Barrett Mountain

Distance (round trip): 6½ miles

Walking time: 4½ hours

Vertical rise: 795 feet

Map: USGS 7½' Peterborough South

Blueberries in June? Sometimes they ripen then on New Ipswich Mountain, which is part of the long ridge south from the summit of Barrett Mountain and is the final goal of this hike. To a man from northern New Hampshire, June is early for blueberries. Although he's accustomed to extending the season into September by going upward in the White Mountains, he thinks finding blueberries during the strawberry season is too much luck for his own good. Nevertheless, I ate blueberries on New Ipswich Mountain one June 22 and at home the same day picked strawberries for supper.

The route of this hike is simple. It's a section of the Wapack Trail. Your destination can vary. I have chosen to approach from the north and pick up the Wapack Trail off NH 123. (In this area NH 123 and NH 124 coincide.) The hike follows the trail to and from an arbitrary point of no return and lunch spot at the lookoff ledges on the north side of Middle Barrett Mountain.

The Wapack Trail's 21 miles extend over Watatic Mountain in Massachusetts and into New Hampshire for Barrett Mountain, Kidder, Temple, and Pack Monadnock. It is maintained by the Friends of the Wapack. (For more information, write Friends of the Wapack, PO Box 115, West Peterborough, NH 03468.)

How to Get There

Driving east on NH 101 out of Peterborough, turn south on NH 123. About 0.5 mile after NH 123 joins NH 124, watch for a sign on the right: WAPACK ROAD, PRIVATE DRIVE, DEAD END. Park off the highway.

Daniel Doan on the Barrett Mountain trail around 1978

Jacqueline Donegan

The Trail

Walk up Wapack Road past the site of the historic Wapack Lodge, built by Marion Davis and her first husband, Frank Robbins, who together also built the Wapack Trail. Marion Davis, a farmer, cattle drover, and 1935 Women's World Champion Wood-chopper, coined the name "Wapack" from

the mountains at the trail's start and finish, Watatic and North Pack Monadnock.

The section of the Wapack Trail leading south over Barrett Mountain begins at a sign and a yellow triangular marker on a big oak tree, near the corner where the road past the lodge site turns left to a house.

The trail immediately angles uphill and to

the left. Signs will caution you about private property. You are in the Windblown Ski Touring Center, where winter hiking is not permitted. Wapack Trail maps are posted. Follow the Wapack Trail's yellow blazes amid the intersecting ski trails. Junctions are marked, and reasonable care will keep you on the Wapack Trail.

Be alert for a sharp left turn. Straight ahead lies a ski trail. The Wapack Trail remains on high ground.

About 10 minutes from the start, you step out on an open ledge with a dramatic and unique view cleared by the Friends of the Wapack trail crew and the property owners. This spot is known locally as Stony Top, and the view includes Mount Monadnock through the trees to the west, Barrett, New Ipswich, and Watatic Mountains to the south, and the Boston skyline to the southeast. You are still on private property; no camping or fires.

The mountain is all forested except for rocks similar to those found at this viewpoint. As on most mountains of southern New Hampshire, trees have taken over the old pastures, which once provided summer grass for cattle and sheep. The cattle were often driven up from Massachusetts farms.

The Wapack Trail slabs through older woods, ascends a slight grade under hemlocks, and dips into a narrow ravine. The damp shade favors the lichens and moss growing on the rocks that stud the opposite steep mountainside. The upper branches of tall maples and beeches provide a perfect home for that patient, unobtrusive flycatcher, the wood peewee, whose plaintive notes are also his name. The ravine in 1753 became a route for the "Boston Road" several years after New Ipswich was settled.

The trail crosses the ravine and faces up the mountain for your first steep climb. An ascent of a few yards brings you to a rocky

trickle at your left, which in late summer may be a line of dry rocks. You climb to its source in a shallow basin.

Climbing on, you soon top out on Barrett's north shoulder. The Wapack Trail heads south. You walk into a spruce forest. Meadowsweet, the high bush similar to hardhack but with a white flower spike instead of pink, borders the trail. It obviously can survive for a time in woods after its chosen habitat, a sunny pasture, is gone. Open rocks contain enough soil to support northern bush honeysuckle. Fifteen minutes beyond the north shoulder you reach the wooded summit of Barrett Mountain at 1853 feet.

In the next 0.75-mile section the trail crosses two stone walls, surmounts two minor knobs, and takes shade in two declivities before rising toward the daylight shining over a crude wall and through a cluster of mountain ash trees. The open ledge, which turns out to be the light source, offers no striking view but invites you to return in autumn to admire the red berry bunches.

Proceeding higher, the trail winds to partially wooded rock, where extensive vistas spread north and west as far as Pack Monadnock and Grand Monadnock. The tower you see rises from the south summit of Pack Monadnock. (The two peaks are known to hikers as South Pack and North Pack. See Hike 9.) To the west Grand Monadnock's pyramid rises into the sky alone and is unforgettable.

Directly ahead of you to the north, Barrett's summit presents a green, rounded contour. To the right and more in the distance, Kidder Mountain and then Temple Mountain show you the terrain that the Wapack Trail traverses north of NH 123 beyond your car.

Although you are at a pleasant lunch spot, continue along the trail, ascending gradually, for another 20 minutes (about 0.5

mile) to this ridge's most interesting elevation, New Ipswich Mountain, and wider views from open ledges.

Now turn your back on the mountains and exchange the views for the blueberries I mentioned earlier. Wander off the trail into the small patches of low bushes. After sandwiches, the tart-sweet little morsels make a delicious dessert.

I like to pick a handful instead of eating them one at a time. This procedure satisfies my need for a little (very little) postponed gratification, which doubtless I inherited from Puritan ancestors. Better still, I like to have a companion more avid to pick them than I am and also generous. I've decided there's no comfortable blueberry-picking position, except maybe kneeling, and in time that gives me a crick in the back. Besides, it stains the knees of my pants. Still, the berries are worth any inconvenience. If I can't wangle a gift of a half cup, I'll pick my own quick enough.

The return retraces the morning hike.

2

Pisgah State Park

Distance (round trip): 10 miles

Walking time: 6 hours

Vertical rise: 1640 feet

Maps: USGS 7½' x 15' Keene; USGS 7½' x 15' Winchester; Pisgah State Park Summer Trails Map

This forested state park spreads southwest of Keene across 13,500 acres of low ridges, ponds, and marshes. The ponds and streams drain south to the Ashuelot River, and Broad Brook in the eastern section runs through a valley once cleared for farms. This inviting spot could well have been the Promised Land for a pioneer arriving with his ax and Bible; naming the overlook Mount Pisgah would have been natural.

In the park's northwest section, where this loop hike is set, there are few remnants of earlier farming. These steep ridges were probably better suited for logging and pasturing. The New England Box Company once logged the area extensively, but the forest has renewed itself, and the land is rough and wild.

While the Winchester Metric Quad is accurate and as reproduced here interprets for you the contours and ponds and streams, you should supplement this with the "Pisgah State Park Summer Trails" map. (A winter trails map is available for winter use.) It will help you to locate yourself during the progress of the hike. A mailbox near the Horseshoe Road Parking Area, at the start and end of this hike, contains copies of the park map.

The park headquarters at the end of the Old Chesterfield Road in Winchester has been constructed under the sponsorship of the Friends of Pisgah. For more information, write Pisgah State Park, PO Box 242, Winchester, NH 03470, or phone (603) 239-8153.

to NH 63

0   0.5   1.0 Mile

N

P 24

ROAD

306

HORSESHOE

278

C H E S T E R F I E L D

392?

Hubbard Hill
421?

x 293?

x 406?

WL
291   Lily
Pond

w/
206   Fulla
Pond

Baker
Pond

x 38?

258
W/20

x08

WL
317   North
Round Pond

BM 20
Hd/20

x 37?8?

Pisgah

P I S G A H   S T A T E   P

Dogwood
Swamp

Mt Pisgah

Brook

Chestnut
Hill

M
O
U
N
T
A

4WD

How to Get There

From the Keene junction of NH 9 and NH 101, drive 9.2 miles to NH 63 south and turn east at Chesterfield. You can't miss the stone library, town hall, and post office. The way to the park begins with the Old Chesterfield Road opposite the post office. After driving a short distance, turn right onto Horseshoe Road, which becomes gravel and winds up and down through the woods. At about 1.75 miles from the village, you reach the parking area at the memorial to Chief Justice Harlan F. Stone, and the granite foundation of the house where he was born.

The Trail

From a field east and south of the road you have a sweeping view across the park's wooded ridges. The panorama begins to take on meaning when you get out your maps and orient them. Mount Pisgah lies 2.5 miles to the south and slightly west. Out of sight behind the ridge is the trail you will descend to the northern arm of Pisgah Reservoir, also known as Pisgah Pond. Hidden, too, is another attraction you'll visit, Fullam Pond, but you can acquire from this view a general picture of the country you'll be walking down into, up and down, and back up again to this lookoff place.

Set out down the continuation of Horseshoe Road. At the bottom of the hill bear left across an old field now covered by sumac growth. (Horseshoe Road bends right here for its return back to NH 63.) Beyond the old field you pass above an active beaver flowage on your right and join a dirt road branching southwest from Horseshoe Road. Turn left downhill. Almost at once you come to a fork. Take the right fork up an incline for a short distance. You come to another fork. An iron gate has been installed here. You are now on the

Pisgah Reservoir Trail and at the point where you will complete your loop.

Keep to the right uphill. As you climb you pass two forks on your left and one on your right. Some of these roads do not appear on your maps, so pay close attention and make notes about junctions, forks, and bearings. With these observations, this hike can be a base for later explorations of the park.

As the road begins to level, it brings you to an opening cut in the tall oaks and maples to your left. You are about 40 minutes from your car. Eastward, the green forested ridges running north and south set off a distant view of Mount Monadnock almost due east.

Now the way is downhill past mountain laurel and maturing hardwoods and hemlock trees. After about 0.5 mile, watch for a trail to the right. Leave the Pisgah Reservoir Trail here and take the Baker Pond Trail (formerly the Baker Trail), which crosses a bridge over a seasonal brook. The trail winds up in S-curves into hemlocks. After 15 minutes you come to the Hubbard Trail, and you see a glimmer of Baker Pond ahead. Notice a wide trail forking left marked by orange tabs on the trees. You will take this to the Pisgah Mountain Trail, but first you should continue straight ahead to see Baker Pond.

There is a path to the shore about midway on the east side. Beside it, sprouts of chestnut trees may attain a height of 15 feet before the blight kills them. Another stranger to the northern woods is the black birch, here quite at home. A variety of water brush lines the shore, and out in the pond a rounded rock "island" gives rootholds to bushes.

After a rest, and perhaps a snack, return to the fork at the wide trail you passed earlier. Follow the Baker Pond Trail marked by the orange tabs for about 5 minutes. The trail makes a sharp turn to the left and narrows and follows the east side of a ridge.

You climb out of these woods to the first rocky outlook along this ridge trail. About 10 minutes later, another rocky outlook opens up a vista to the southeast. Beyond it you descend into a ledgy ravine where the trail keeps parallel with the jumbled rocks that suggest dens for porcupines, bobcats, and fishers. You climb out of this craggy glen to the left, over a ridge, and down to a trail junction and signs. You are about 40 minutes from the start of this trail if you walk as I do, to enjoy the scenery.

The signs orient you. To the right (west) a trail leads to Kilburn Pond. To the left (east) the yellow-tabbed Pisgah Ridge Trail (formally the Pisgah Mountain Trail) continues. A sign points behind you to Baker Pond.

Turn left. After a short descent, you climb uphill to a rock summit. Views east and west have been opened to Monadnock and the Connecticut River valley. Keep straight south between these two outlooks, staying on the rocks and then entering the woods where the trees are again plainly marked with yellow tabs. You descend and climb two more knolls before reaching the crest of Mount Pisgah.

Again the bedrock forms an outlook to your left, although the trail stays along the top at the edge of the woods. Directly ahead and not far from the cliff, which drops off more than 300 feet, a beaver dam forms a pond in Pisgah Brook. Monadnock contin-

ues to dominate the horizon in that direction. To the south you see an arm of Pisgah Reservoir extending toward you.

You pass one more outlook, then descend past an enormous boulder on the right. In a little valley, a brook bed may contain water. Turn left along it to an old logging road, which you follow down to the head of Pisgah Reservoir. Here the trail swings left and passes once more through the woods. As you follow the pond's shoreline, watch for ducks and herons. Checking the Pisgah State Park map, you can see that you are on a hooklike curve and heading northeast.

A footbridge takes you across Pisgah Brook. Walk a few yards, and you come to the junction of the Pisgah Reservoir Trail. Signs have been installed giving mileages and directions. Turn left onto the Pisgah Reservoir Trail and follow the wide trail (it is also used by snowmobiles) for about 0.5 mile. You pass through hemlock growth and beaver flowages.

You pass a beaver pond on your left. You saw it an hour earlier from Mount Pisgah, and there far above you is the rounded rock cliff where you stood. The trail bears right from the beaver pond. Five minutes in fine hemlock woods bring you to the Parker Trail forking right toward Fullam Pond. Turn onto the Parker Trail and follow the yellow tabs. You walk over a low ridge into a young forest of white birches.

Beyond this you descend to an old logging road and to a junction with the Chestnut Hill Road Snowmobile Trail. Turn left and soon you are at the Old Chesterfield Road parking area. You have been walking about 45 minutes since the beaver pond.

On your left the Old Chesterfield Road crosses a bridge over an inlet to Fullam Pond. Turn right and stride along this dirt road above swampy ground for 10 minutes to the junction of the road leading into

Fullam Pond. Go left past a big pine tree for another 5 minutes to the pond.

Like all woodland ponds, Fullam is a fine habitat for ducks, herons, and the insectivorous birds who feast on some of the pests you've warded off with bug repellent. A rest under the pines on the shore gives a sense of aquatic and forest wilderness.

For the return to your car, allow an hour's walk when you turn right onto the Old Chesterfield Road from the junction with the Fullam Pond road. You pass the parking area at the Chestnut Hill/Parker Trailhead, continuing on the Old Chesterfield Road, cross the bridge, and start uphill. You'll be climbing steadily most of the way as you pass the junction of the North Ponds Trail on the left. You then continue for almost a mile and take the left fork up an incline, leaving an old road that is level with old beaver flowages on the right, and complete the loop at the junction of the Pisgah Reservoir Trail just beyond the crest of the incline. Continue on the Old Chesterfield Road to the fork at the old beaver flowage, bearing right on the trail across the old sumac growth, passing the junctions of the Nature Trail, and continue uphill on Horseshoe Road to the parking area.

Note: If you prefer a shorter hike, consider the possibilities at the Kilburn Road Trailhead. From NH 63, drive 4.6 miles through Chesterfield to the signs for Pisgah State Park, Kilburn Road Trailhead, and turn left into the parking area. A mailbox at this trailhead contains copies of the "Pisgah State Park Summer Trails" map.

For an introductory hike of about 5.5 miles, do the Kilburn Loop around Kilburn Pond. Or take the Kilburn Road and part of the Kilburn Loop to the Pisgah Ridge Trail up to the Mount Pisgah outlooks and return the way you came, a total of about 6 miles. For a longer hike, you could make a loop from the Pisgah Ridge Trail to the Pisgah Reservoir Trail to the Baker Pond Trail.

3

Odiorne Point

Distance (round trip): 2 miles

Walking time: 1 ½ hours

Vertical rise: 60 feet

Map: USGS 7 ½' Kittery

This is a seashore state park. Waves and tides reach across the stony shore toward marsh grass and bayberry bushes; the everlasting fascination of the ocean holds you. Even when you wander in woods of oaks and pines, the mewing gulls coasting overhead and the smell of seaweed remind you that salt water is near. I have outlined a walk to many attractions. Anyone choosing to alter the route will not get lost and will be equally rewarded.

Odiorne Point State Park's 330 acres extend along NH 1A in Rye for about 2 miles, taking in the shoreline from Odiorne Point on the south to the salt marshes of Witch Creek on the north. Once a farming settlement and later a summer colony, the area was bought by the federal government in 1942 and became a military reservation for coastal artillery. Fort Dearborn, as it was then named, guarded the entrance to Portsmouth Harbor and navy yard. The government dismantled it after World War II but concrete casemates still remain as reminders of the park's wartime function. They look out over picnic tables, trees, shrubbery, marshes, rocky shores, and sea as far as the Isles of Shoals. I suppose I'm pointing out the obvious (I can't resist the irony of the park's origin) by stating that a world war, in effect, preserved this unique bit of New Hampshire's exploited coastline. Shut behind its chain-link fence for many years, the land became a state park in 1972.

Unlike nearby Wallis Sands or Hampton Beach, this is not a park for sandy lolling or saltwater bathing, although there is sand at

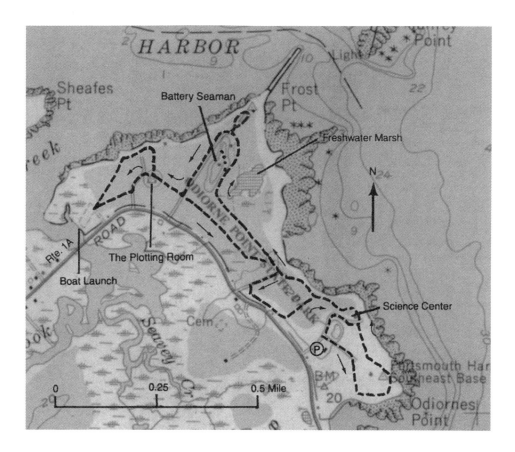

low tide off the northern rocks that form Frost Point. The park is primarily a place to enjoy the ocean setting and study the related ecology.

How to Get There

At the Portsmouth traffic circle, take the exit for "Beaches and Hampton," and drive the US 1 Bypass and US 1 south for about 2 miles. Just beyond Yoken's Restaurant on your right, turn left at the stoplights onto Elwyn Road. Drive about 1.4 miles to NH 1A at Foyes Corner and follow that route south about 1.8 miles, passing the Odiorne Point State Park boat launch and north parking area, to the main entrance to the park, where a gatehouse attendant collects the admittance fee and gives you a park brochure, which includes a little map.

The Trail

Park in the central parking area beyond the gatehouse. The smell of the sea comes to you from beyond the brushy flat. A cool breeze sweeps out of the sunny spaciousness, which extends over the water to the horizon. The adventurous English landed here in the spring of 1623. They built a stone manor house, smithy, cooperage, fort, and racks for drying fish.

Before you begin the hike, visit the Seacoast Science Center (a small additional fee), pick up a more detailed trail map at the information desk, and look at the orientation

Odiorne Point

Donald K. MacDougall

map near the entrance. You'll also want to see the various habitat and history exhibits and reach into the "tidepool touch tank." (For information about the center's programs for adults, families, and organizations, phone 603-436-8043.)

Now return to the main parking area. The route of this hike shows you first the southern area of the park including Odiorne Point. Walk along the paved path, keeping west of the rest rooms; continue past a fine grove of Scotch pines on the left to a stony beach and a tremendous view of the ocean.

At the cove beyond the point the wave-lapped shingle rises to heaped seaweed deposited by the highest tides. Beach peas extend their vines over the pebbles, and the common nightshade thrives in the unpromising habitat. Poison ivy in places will probably keep you from taking close-up color photos of the *Rosa rugosa* bushes and their dark pink blossoms.

Above the shingle, where there's enough soil, tansy grows. It's common all over the park. When you walk through it, the pungent odor, suggesting thyme to me, draws into your nose.

In this cove, stumps of trees that grew here 3500 years ago are visible at low tide. The now Sunken Forest once stretched to the Isles of Shoals.

Walk on along the shore past a round concrete foundation on the left. Look for the ledges extending beyond the scattered rocks and pools. At low tide you can walk out to the metamorphic bedrock of the ledge. A basaltlike trap dike forms a grayish black band through the pressure-folded sandstone.

Continue on the shoreline rocks, or take the dirt path inland past the Group Use Area. Skirt the seaward side of the Seacoast Science Center. Turn right in a sumac grove onto the sheltered dirt path that leads toward Frost Point. You'll see informal paths to the shore along the way; explore these if you like. Gulls sail over the bayberry bushes and the *Rosa rugosa,* or they slant gracefully out to sea. At the shore, close to the coarse sand, three-toothed cinquefoil, often seen on barren mountains, displays white flowers and the notched leaf that gives the name. Back from the shore, arrowwood blooms white in June. This shrub's straight sprouts provided arrow shafts for the Native Americans who camped near here and lived well in summer on fish, clams, crabs, and seabirds.

The paths to the left, narrow enticing alleys through the woods, will be explored on your return trip.

At about 0.5 mile from the Seacoast Science Center, bear right at a fork. You are passing a freshwater marsh glimpsed through the trees on your right. Next you come to a major fork in a stand of maples. Continue right. The path leads under the scowl of the concrete watchroom that caps a 40-foot knoll. This is the Battery Seaman, a 16-inch gun casemate.

Climb the ramp in front of the battery to the high point of the park. You can walk to the right or left along the top. In spots the path is closed in by sumacs, but elsewhere there are fine views. You watch ships at sea, observe the Isles of Shoals, and admire white gulls gliding and black cormorants skimming the waves. You can also see the freshwater marsh and its winged inhabitants: red-winged blackbirds in the cattails; killdeer nesting on hot sand; swallows skimming above blue flag clusters; kingbirds on guard against crows and hawks; and, in the brush, yellowthroats calling *witchery, witchery, witchery.* Binoculars are helpful.

Retrace your steps down the ramp. To help prevent erosion, don't use the paths at either end of the Battery Seaman.

Continue along the path to Frost Point. In calm weather the granite jetty accommodates fishermen. Farther at sea you look across into Maine beyond the entrance to Portsmouth Harbor. Near at hand the shore's ledges include a pegmatite dike extruded through the metamorphic layers and containing large crystals of glinting mica and gray-yellow feldspar. The rock is worn and scratched by the glacier.

Follow the loop along past the view toward boats moored in Little Harbor, the once-grand old Hotel Wentworth, and New Castle Island. Here is the sandy beach. Continue back toward the Battery Seaman, this time taking a path to the right behind it. Now you will head for the northern end of the park, the salt marsh and boat launch, by taking the second right. At a junction, bear right. At the next junction, go straight. You pass another World War II remnant, the plotting room, filled with jumbles of rocks.

Bear right onto an old paved path that soon becomes a trail. You step out at the salt marsh. In the pastels of the scene, you may see a bright red cardinal. Turn right along a stone wall and follow this shore path until it ends at Little Harbor's rocky shoreline. Keep following the shore path right, into the woods. Turn right through a gap in a stone wall and continue through sumacs, back to the wartime plotting room. Turn left, the way you came, past shagbark hickories. Bear left at a fork. You are returning to the vicinity of the Battery Seaman, but this time you will veer left across the wide path and go straight on past another World War II structure, which may have been a commissary. You'll recognize the next junction; you came in on the left-hand path. Keep straight, on the right. At the next junction, rejoin the path on which you walked north from the science center.

As the path nears the shore, turn right into a shaded alley, bordered on both sides by stone walls. At its end, bear left, and almost immediately take another left to avoid the bike path.

Take a left to the dolphin fountain on your right, and continue back to the ocean on the path to the left. The rock work is the site of the Marvin-Straw home. Here as elsewhere in the park, shrubs and trees and plants from homes have gone wild.

Once again you rejoin the shoreline path. Turn right, retracing your route back to the Seacoast Science Center.

You may want to linger at a picnic table to look some more at the sea, the *Rosa rugosa,* and the wide sky.

4

Pawtuckaway: The Tower

Distance (round trip): ¾ mile

Walking time: ¾ hour

Vertical rise: 370 feet

Map: USGS 7½' Mt. Pawtuckaway

Among the rolling hills of southeastern New Hampshire, a wooded park shelters wilderness as it might have looked not long after human beings first penetrated it. Yet the 5500 acres of Pawtuckaway State Park were cultivated and pastured for more than a century. Now oak, pine, and hemlock have reclaimed the hills and valleys.

The stone walls that border beaver ponds and narrow dirt roads are about the only remainders of man's presence. You can find solitude and forested isolation among marshes, ponds, and high cliffs that rise above immense boulders.

All this awaits you near creeping megalopolis (represented by Manchester and Concord to the west, Durham and Portsmouth to the east). From the fire tower atop South Peak you can see—on clear days—from Mount Washington to the sea.

But you *are* in a state park, whose rules and regulations should be observed. Camping and fires are permitted only at places provided or designated.

How to Get There

The road into the park heads eastward from NH 107 between Deerfield and Raymond. Approaching from the north, you'll come to a junction of NH 107 and NH 43. Continue south on NH 107 for 4.2 miles. Watch closely for two signs on the left, a street sign for Reservation Road and a small brown sign for New Hampshire Forest Fire Service, Pawtuckaway Lookout Station. If you're coming from the south, the signs are 3.2 miles from the junction of NH 107 and NH 101 Business Loop.

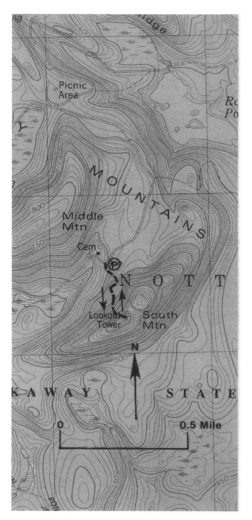

mer or fall to reach the trailhead.

You'll soon find yourself in the midst of marshes and old beaver ponds. At 2.5 miles comes a junction where signs on the right say STOP and NOT A THROUGH STREET. Turn left across a small bridge.

For 0.7 mile beyond this corner, the road winds up and down through the forest. Then it curves to the right up a longer hill. You'll see the parking area on the right.

The Trail

A blazed trail enters from downhill at the right end of the parking area, but you will take the blazed wide path to the tower that begins at the upper end and quickly turns left.

Under pine boughs you climb quite steeply over pine roots in the aisles between the tree trunks. You may hear ovenbirds sing with ascending emphasis, *teacher, TEAcher, TEACHER!* The mountainside exposes its foundation of imposing, rounded bedrock. The small cliff supports fine growths of rock tripe, a leathery, large, gray-green lichen.

Rock tripe is edible if boiled long enough, but consult books and lichen experts first. It was the famine food of Native Americans. Ernest Thompson Seton, the naturalist-artist-writer whose books I pored over as a boy, advises drying rock tripe to prevent its purging effect, and then boiling it for 3 hours to produce a sticky liquid that's slightly sweet and tastes of licorice. Thus encouraged, although wary of eating rock tripe for years, I've discovered he's right. His report is somewhat exaggerated about the licorice, but the glutinous porridge is indeed as he says in his *Book of Woodcraft:* "Far from unpalatable at any time, and to a starving man, no doubt, a boon from heaven." I admit to avoiding a full meal.

The plants near the ledges, growing not on harsh stone but in soft forest duff, in-

The distance from this turn to the trailhead is about 3.2 miles. The road changes from asphalt to gravel after 0.9 mile. At the first intersection, bear right. The road continues past an old cemetery on the right. At a left fork, keep straight on this south half of the park's loop road.

Drive slowly and watch out for rocks and ruts. In spring mud season, if your car is low, you'll have to pull off the road, park on solid ground, and start walking. If you have a truck or sport-utility vehicle, use it even in sum-

clude the fringed polygala, which blooms in May showing tiny pink flowers with fringed "tongues" among the ferns and lady's slippers' leaves. Conscientious hikers regard picking as a form of vandalism.

The ledges take on the smooth shapes typical of the Pawtuckaway Mountains. They look like grazing elephants. The level stretch below the rock changes to a curve left uphill. Oaks and maples continue to shade the trail until you climb to the open rock and reach the tower.

The nearby water to the east, indented with bays, divided by peninsulas, and dotted with islands, is Lake Pawtuckaway. (There the park, off NH 156, offers swimming, camping, fishing, and picnicking.) Your distant views of sea and northern mountains are most likely to appear on a clear fall day.

Smog from the Manchester area may obscure Mount Monadnock off to the southwest. Smog from other cities also to the south—Nashua, Salem, Haverhill, Lawrence, Newburyport, Boston—won't improve visibility. But here at least are trees, skies, birds, and primeval verities that existed long before population centers.

Unless you seek out the Indian Steps, 15-odd shelves in an igneous rock dike northwest of the summit, you'll need only 20 minutes for the descent to your car.

5

Pawtuckaway: Rainy-Day Hike

Distance (round trip): 3½ miles

Walking time: 3 hours

Vertical rise: 530 feet

Maps: USGS 7½' Mt. Pawtuckaway; USGS 7½' Northwood

Every hiker should set aside a forest for a rainy-day hike. Sometimes you feel you must get out, get away, take off, yet the heavens open upon you for a week, and the weather forecaster sees only clouds and rain ahead. Then your rainy-day hike saves you from utter frustration.

I specify the forest because it shelters you. For this purpose I like Pawtuckaway State Park and North Peak. As well as release, you'll find that the ridge can provide varied experiences for the days when you are inadvertently caught in rain midway of a hike.

Although the route is blazed in white and marked occasionally with cairns, you should take the USGS Mt. Pawtuckaway quad and your compass, if only for practice. The ability to use map and compass is essential in the rain and fog.

The tall oaks, pines, and hemlocks along the lower section of trail filter the raindrops into a fine mist. If the wind shakes down big splashes of rainwater, ponchos easily shed them or you can wear wool and get wet but stay warm. On top, you will come to no harm if you stay off the wet and slippery rocks.

Remember, state park rules and regulations apply at Pawtuckaway and should be kept in mind whenever you hike there. Camping and fires are permitted only at places provided or designated.

How to Get There

The entrance road to the park heads eastward from NH 107 between Deerfield and Raymond. Approaching from the north, you'll come to a junction of NH 107 and NH

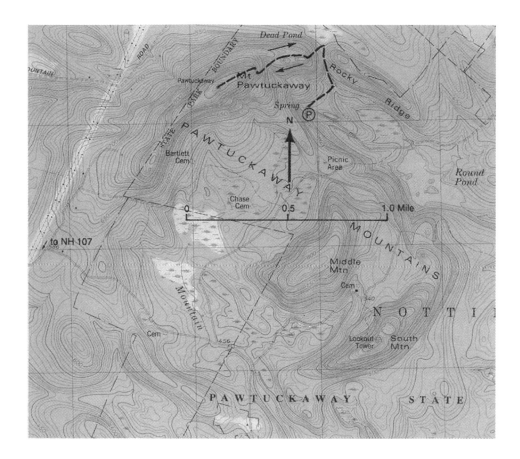

43. Continue south on NH 107 for 4.2 miles. Watch closely for two signs on the left, a street sign for Reservation Road and a small brown sign for New Hampshire Forest Fire Service, Pawtuckaway Lookout Station. If you're coming from the south, the signs are 3.2 miles from the junction of NH 107 and NH 101 Business Loop.

The distance from this turn to the trailhead is about 4.6 miles. The road changes from asphalt to gravel after 0.9 mile. At the first intersection, bear right. The road continues past an old cemetery on the right. At a left fork, keep straight on this south half of the park's loop road.

Drive slowly and watch out for rocks and ruts. In spring mud season, if your car is low, you'll have to pull off the road, park on solid ground, and start walking. If you have a truck or sport-utility vehicle, use it even in summer or fall to reach the trailhead.

You'll soon find yourself in the midst of marshes and old beaver ponds. At 2.5 miles comes a junction where signs on the right say STOP and NOT A THROUGH STREET. Turn left across a small bridge.

The North Peak trailhead is 2.1 miles from this junction. The road winds up and down through the forest. A steep hill leads up past the parking area for the trail to South Peak's tower. Continue over the hill. Keep right at the next junction. Watch on the left for a small sign high on a tree: BOULDER TRAIL. Park off the road.

The Trail

White blazes lead down to massive boulders—out of sight at first in the woods. The trail becomes plain as it slants down to a seasonal brook, while a ridge to the right hides the road. The first of the enormous boulders appears after 5 or 6 minutes. On your right among tall pines and hemlocks, its top rises 30 feet into green boughs. A split in the rock has heaped pieces into a cave tunnel through which you can crouch and step toward the light.

Nearby are similar rocks of almost equal size. You may find your attention divided between the extraordinary boulders and the curious (to me) nutshells on the ground. Shagbark hickories, parents of the nuts, are not common farther north where I do most of my hiking. Long strips of bark flake from the mature trunks.

A few yards north of the boulders a sign points left to the North Mountain Trail. (Beyond this corner a trail offers a loop back to the road.) The path rises slightly among pines and hemlocks and more hickories. White blazes on the big trees continue ahead. Another scattering of huge boulders appears to the left below a wooded cliff. About 20 minutes from the first group of boulders, the gleam of Dead Pond lightens the shadowy, wet woods. The trail turns left just before the pond, which lies at the base of the ridge forming North Peak.

If you approach the pond you will see that the boggy water extends out of sight into areas of brush and marsh. The low shore is host to sphagnum moss, goldthread, young hemlocks, and leatherleaf bushes. Where the rootless sphagnum moss extends into the bog, it supports cranberries. The plants with spear-shaped leaves and single white "petals" are water arum or wild calla. They grow in open water. Pitcher plants and sundew prey on insects,

The rain dappled the surface of the brook. He baited the hook and tossed out his line, playing it so the drift of the slow current would carry it down beyond him. He didn't expect to catch many fish, but he knew there were some good ones in the channel. Maybe he'd get two or three. He lost track of the time he waited, for he wasn't thinking or worrying about the rain, just fishing with the patience of a heron hunched on the shore.
—*Daniel Doan,* Amos Jackman

as do the swallows overhead.

Rejoin the trail to the left of the pond. After a brief descent it becomes abruptly uphill. You scramble over rocks and past big pines. A grip on a small striped maple could help. Note that their broad leaves suggest webbed feet of a giant goose. Black birches are common. The twigs have a strong wintergreen flavor.

As you approach the cliff on your left you see the jumble of rocks called the Devil's Den. The trail bears to the right, avoiding ledges suitable only for experienced rock climbers with their gear. Along here a pair of ravens may protest your proximity to their nest up among the stone projections. At one time this nesting site was said to be the southernmost for ravens in New Hampshire during their expansion of territory from Canada.

Keep climbing, and soon the steep trail takes you to a flat ledge overlooking Dead Pond, all misty below you this rainy day. Face about and follow the blazes and cairns up the slope.

You are bypassing the rock-climbers' challenges to your left, and find that you are taking a curved route around and above that dangerous area for specialists. You enter an open growth of leverwood (also known as ironwood or hop hornbeam), as the trail gradually levels at the top of the east shoulder of North Peak.

Here for practice you may consult your map, compass, and watch. In rain and fog this will train you for real emergencies, when no white blazes show you the way. Also observe the indications of a path, or the mere passage of other boots. Your eyes will learn to register stretches of trodden leaves, sometimes called a "herd path," if no trail work has been done. You'll notice with sharper vision that a small pile of stones for a cairn is not a natural formation. Old random blazes in yellow or blue paint will appear faded compared to the newer white.

All these skills of observation improve with practice. An aptitude in woods travel should be yours for pleasant and knowledgeable hiking. For instance, once you're off a trail, whatever the reason, finding a trail is difficult without the experience of a woodcrafter as opposed to a sports enthusiast. Because of constant attention to earth, trees, plants, and skies, I thought I had a habit of automatic observation, yet more than once, bushwhacking through the woods to another trail, I have stepped right across it.

Now this rainy day you're observing all indications of the route, so naturally you keep west along the ridge. The open woods change to gloomy hemlocks as you descend into a col. You soon face a sudden height of jagged ledges contrasting with the soft duff underfoot from fallen hemlock needles.

Keeping to the right, you slab this rugged height under the hemlocks. The path leads you upward in a north circuit under the crest on your left. You arrive at a clearing and a big scaffolding of steel girders set on concrete posts. The frame supports a khaki-colored wallboard construction—a reflector of the Public Service Company of New Hampshire.

(If the day happens to be clear and you like a view with your meal, have lunch here.)

At a rainy-day pace you require 0.5 to 0.75 hour to get here from the east shoulder above the cliffs. Now turn right and climb higher into the clouds and rain. Entering open woods again, you'll see the trail keeping to the crest of the ridge. Check your compass and map to orient yourself to the lay of the land invisible around you in the mist. Someday, caught in a mountain storm, you could be glad of this training.

North Peak's topmost ledges once supported a small, dilapidated wooden tower for a view toward Concord and the capitol's golden dome. Fortunately the dangers of that flimsy lookoff are gone, but unfortunately the trees now hide the view.

About 15 to 20 minutes from the Public Service reflector, you come to a big cairn and two USGS markers in the ledge. Lunchtime has arrived.

The blazed trail continues west from the 1011-foot summit but is not for a through hike without two cars. It leads down into a forest of hemlocks and deciduous trees with good views when the foliage is off. Joining an old woods road, it follows this to the west trailhead at the Reservation Road, which you followed to your start at the boulders. This west trailhead is only a short distance inside the park boundary.

The simplest return to Dead Pond is by the same route you took up, remembering to bear left above the cliffs. At the pond, keep to the right along the trail through those fine woods. A right turn at the boulders soon takes you out to your car.

6

The Uncanoonucs: North Peak

Distance (round trip): 1 ½ miles

Walking time: 1 ¼ hours

Vertical rise: 730 feet

Map: USGS 7 ½' Pinardville

On the North Peak of the Uncanoonucs nature is busy reforesting an old pasture. On the South Peak man asserts himself with relay towers and an auto road. The consequent environments on these twin hills west of Manchester provide complete contrast for the hiker; yet from a distance their rounded contours present the same silhouettes. The close physical resemblance no doubt provided the Native American name *Uncanoonucs,* which is said to mean "the Woman's Breasts." Preserving the vastly different zones on the two summits, no trail connects them.

Both can be climbed in a long afternoon. I suggest choosing North Peak first, to prepare yourself spiritually for the exploitation you'll see later on South Peak. Other hikers may prefer to climb South Peak first and recover faith in the future on North Peak.

How to Get There

Take NH 114 to Goffstown. Near the center of town, turn south onto Mountain Road. After 0.9 mile, the road forks. Turn left. You will soon pass a farmhouse and a large barn on the right. Just beyond, 1.5 miles from NH 114, part of the way up a wooded hill, watch on the right for a break in the stone wall. White blazes mark the start of the White Circle Trail. Park across the road.

The Trail

The White Circle Trail climbs immediately under hemlocks. White circles appear on trees, as do white dots. The steep grade gives you the feeling that on this miniature

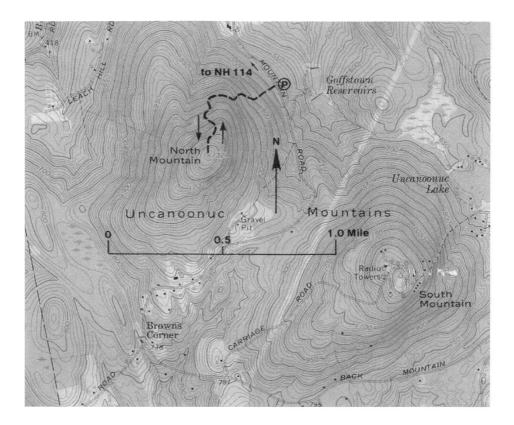

mountain you'll reach the 1324-foot summit quickly. But you'll use the better part of an hour.

Time passes easily, however, as you ascend the varied slope. Leafy trees and bushes have taken root among the ledges, where frisky lambs probably once gamboled on the greensward. Hemlocks spread their green branches to the sun. They shade their seedlings, which thrive in this protection. Due to this affinity for shade, hemlocks may in time take over the land of the leafy trees—except for beeches, whose seedlings also love shade.

The trail bears left and then right. You climb steadily to a remarkable rock overhang, which forms a cave in which you can almost stand upright. Part of the overhang has been closed by a neat wall of laid-up stones. The cave reminded me that phoebes in their natural habitat attach their nests under sheltering rocks. One forgets that there were phoebes in New Hampshire before house eaves or bridges came along to shelter their nests.

The outside rock holds lichens, mosses, and ferns. They are rapidly (geologically speaking) breaking down the rock in combination with weather and making earth for trees to grow upon.

The trail swings above the cave in a left curve that takes you to a ledge slanting upward and wooded just enough, on its several shelves, to suit pink lady's slippers. I stopped there one May 27 and quickly counted 16 flowers. (Nobody seems to call them moccasin flowers anymore.)

Among other trees on North Peak black

birch thrives here, although it cannot do so 50 or 60 miles north. Along with the black birch, whose dark brown bark resembles that of black cherry, striped maple and hornbeam appear. These two varieties of trees also occur farther up North Peak; trees of the latter variety form a grove through which the trail winds to the summit.

There oaks shade flat rocks, blueberry bushes, grass, moss, ferns, and junipers. A frame of green leaves sets off South Peak and causes the distance to seem greater than the mile it is. Above South Peak's rounded summit and scanty trees, openwork steel needles bristle and relay cones gleam.

Although views here are now somewhat blocked by trees, they are still worth seeking. For a view of Mount Monadnock, go southwest through oak woods, where Canada mayflowers form a mosaic in hues of green.

The twin leaves are cleftlike hearts at the stem and taper to points. Flowers resemble tufts of white foam; later they yield whitespotted berries that turn red in the fall. You descend the gradual slope. There's Monadnock, and a breezy spot for lunch as well.

To the south you may see Joe English Mountain, shaped like a bulldozed gravel pile. Eight miles or so beyond, the Souhegan River cuts east and west through the town of Milford. The wooded flatland is dotted with ponds. The scene may not be as dramatic as it is on other mountains, but it's a quiet pleasure that should not be underrated.

Descend to your car by the same White Circle Trail. Paint marks are scarce on the summit. If you have wandered far enough to be uncertain of the summit, look for the rock fireplaces drawn together by picnickers near the top ledges. The trail leads down from the northern corner of the clearing.

7

The Uncanoonucs: South Peak

Distance (round trip): 2 miles

Walking time: 1 ¼ hours

Vertical rise: 660 feet

Map: USGS 7 ½' Pinardville

Of the twin Uncanoonucs, the South Peak for its view overlooks the city of Manchester. This seems fitting because the summit bears the effects of civilization and progress. I've mentioned the towers and auto road in the hike to North Peak (see Hike 6). I should say again that South Peak's contour and elevation (1321 feet) bestow on it a startling similarity to North Peak. But the ambience is totally different when you climb them. On North Peak it's natural forest regrowth. On South Peak it's careless commercialism.

The removal of the fire tower has done away with views of all southern New Hampshire and Mount Monadnock. Looking north to Mount Washington is no longer possible, and sad to say in recent years haze and smog have often hidden the White Mountains altogether. Communication towers and a chain-link fence have replaced the 62-foot fire tower and cab. The easterly terrace once opened wide over the city and surrounding countryside; trees are now obscuring some of these views. To the south on a clear day you may see the silhouettes of tall buildings in Boston. On the horizon to the east several summits are the Pawtuckaway Mountains, which you can explore by Hikes 4 and 5.

One true improvement does not exploit the mountain. The Goffstown Conservation Commission maintains a nature trail to the summit.

How to Get There

To reach the South Peak trail, turn off NH 114 south about 0.5 mile east of Goffstown onto Wallace Road. You are still within the

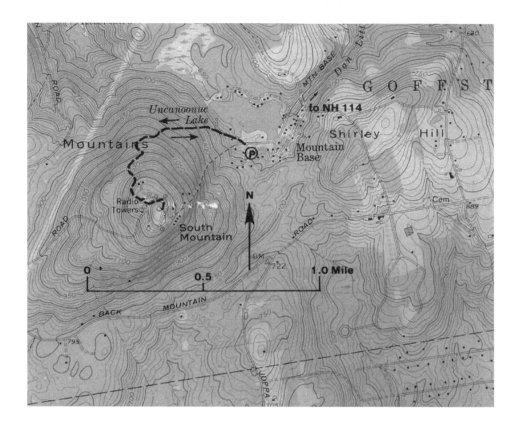

town's residential district. Just after the turn onto Wallace Road you will see a right fork. Don't take it. Bear left along Wallace Road and keep driving 1.4 miles. Turn right onto Mountain Base Road. This takes you—after 1 mile through a neighborhood of small houses and trailers—to the south side of Uncanoonuc Lake at a beach. The mountain rises to your left.

Park in the beach parking area. You'll see a nature trail sign directing you toward the trail, ahead along the road.

The Trail

Before you begin your hike, first face toward the mountain. A concrete foundation partially hidden in bushes is visible between a house up on the slope to the left and a cottage in the trees on your right. This was the lower base for the mountain's unique cable cars, two of which operated on a trestle and rails from 1904 to 1938. The downward weight of one car helped the ascent of the other. A hotel on the summit was an added attraction. If you have heard about the "snow trains" out of Boston in the 1930s you may imagine skiers swooping down trails from the summit, the experts demonsrating the Arlberg technique—stem-christie turns and a crouch for rough bumps. A crude footbridge and steep path up the old grade can be a descent route from the summit. More about this soon.

Follow the dirt road around the edge of the lake. At the woods a sign notifies you of the nature trail. About 40 yards farther into the hemlocks a map sign shows the trail swinging around a westerly arc to the summit.

The route includes descent by the grade of the vanished trestle and rails. I seriously advise against it. From the summit to reach the grade you may not be a trespasser on property adjacent to the houses below, but warning signs and barking dogs make it a concern. Aside from this, the steep grade is littered with ankle-threatening rocks the sizes of jagged baseballs and angular golf balls. A more pleasant and less dangerous descent is a return by the trail you climb, and this is the directive here.

But now walk up from the sign, bearing left from a driveway to a cottage. The path is wide. About 5 minutes from the nature trail sign, the trail forks. The way to the summit is left uphill. (The right fork is a spur leading to hemlock woods and a marsh—well worth a visit and return to this junction, but the time and distance are not included in this hike.)

Now you climb up steadily along a curving trail in a forest of trees that become larger as you ascend. You'll notice that beech trees begin to predominate. Their smooth, pewter-colored bark glows when the western sun flashes under green branches. Thrushes proclaim a peaceful afternoon. Ovenbirds stridently declare they own a patch of forest. After a shower, red efts appear like magic from beneath stones and bark. Terrestrial for a year or more, they return in their older age to water as the familiar olive green newts you find in ponds.

A great hemlock, left of the trail, remains as a memento of an earlier forest. It is so large that an arm hug—6 feet, let's say—reaches only halfway around the rough bark. Beyond the hemlock the trail tops the steepest rise and passes among more hemlocks and again into open woods. When you come to a fork at a footpath sign, take the right. The trail soon leads you to the asphalt auto road.

Turn left up the auto road a few yards, and then leave it by a dirt road to the right before you come to a cluster of towers and service buildings on the left. The dirt road circles the summit, but first takes you past more towers inside a chain-link fence to the eastern terrace and a view of Manchester about 5 miles away.

Binoculars bring details closer. The city's bridges span the Merrimack River. A brick mill with many windows extends along the falls of the river. Waterpower built Manchester. The Amoskeag Mills, now divided into various businesses, once were among the world's greatest spinners and weavers of cotton goods. Throughout the city church spires pointedly contrast with square commercial structures and modern high-rise buildings and the cubes of houses with angled roofs. The flatland outside the city extends southward to Massachusetts and east to the coast.

Nearby in front of you and below a section of asphalt you can see rooftops. To the left was the upper terminal for the cable cars.

You may retrace your steps along the dirt road or complete its circle of the summit. Then descend the way you came. The unspoiled forest seems to surround you with nature's beneficence. Don't let the mood lead you down a trail to the left. Keep to the right on the nature trail, to the lower signs and your car.

You have come down from one of New Hampshire's most interesting un-wild summits and perhaps have decided to help preserve others, still wild, from a similar fate.

8

Crotched Mountain

Distance (round trip): 4 miles

Walking time: 2¾ hours

Vertical rise: 755 feet

Maps: USGS 7½' Peterborough North; USGS 7½' Hillsboro; USGS 7½' Deering; USGS 7½' Greenfield

Crotched Mountain is typical of many New Hampshire blueberry ridges. The southern approach to the summit treats you to wide views long before you reach the topmost ledges. Spread out behind you lies all the country between Pack Monadnock on the east and Mount Monadnock on the west. During a summer day the heat distills fragrances from the open turf, bushes, and seedling pines. Sparrows and towhees flit close to the ground or sing from gray birches. Hawks sail the windswept skies.

How to Get There

The access road to the Greenfield Trail up Crotched Mountain branches northeast from NH 31 at 1 mile north of Greenfield and 4.25 miles south of Bennington. A large sign identifies this road to the Crotched Mountain Rehabilitation Center.

Drive past the Greenfield swimming beach and up the winding asphalt for 1.75 miles. On the right you pass a drive that leads to the center. Then at the top of the hill watch on the left for a gate. This blocks access only to vehicles, not to people. Park off the road near the gate. There may not be a trail sign.

The Trail

Beginning as a gravel road to the blueberry ridge, the trail takes a left fork almost at once and soon another. A reasonable grade lifts you to wide views, which include the summit partially hidden by spruces. It appears remote, and the hike to it will be an adventure into vast territory that was once pastureland for cattle or sheep. Look behind you often. In the southwest the light and shade on Mount Monadnock change each time you turn your head.

The service road becomes a grassy jeep track curving through the blueberry bushes. One of the fragrances the heat brings out originates in a knee-high shrub called sweet fern. Its misleading name refers to leaves that resemble—but are not—fern fronds. Their aromatic odor may suggest bayberry, which is a member of the same family.

At the top of the ridge, walk straight ahead, keeping the radio tower on your left. You come quickly onto a narrow trail through woods, which you follow until you reach a good gravel road. Turn right onto this road. It leads downhill. Watch carefully for a wide, grassy road about 70 yards on your left. Take this road upward through blueberry bushes. You will soon be at the entrance to another woods trail. An arrow on a tree points left, showing the way down into woods of spruce and birch. The broad, firm path enters a little valley.

Soon the trail crosses the upper reaches of a seasonal brook on a crude bridge laid across the mud and trickles. You'll probably prefer to cross on rocks. Then upward you go. Eventually you step out of the woods into thick junipers and scattered trees. If you wear shorts and brush against the junipers carelessly, you'll learn that their evergreen needles can prickle. The purple berries help flavor gin. Another pasture pest, steeple-bush, blossoms in August. The pink cones or spires exhibit the reason for the name. The derivation of its other common name, hardhack, must go back to the first farmer who attempted to stop with a scythe its invasion of his pasture. The stems are woody and tough.

Now the trail curves more steeply to the left. You climb out on a ledge for an overgrown view of Pack Monadnock, Temple

Crotched Mountain

Mountain, and Barrett Mountain in a diminishing series. To the southwest Monadnock lives up to its old name, Grand Monadnock.

Now the trail winds into spruces. In 1.4 miles from the gate you pass the Bennington Trail coming in on your left off NH 31. You are 0.4 mile from the summit. The route is an S-turn much eroded. Tree roots grip the rocks as though determinedly tenacious, and perhaps in a sense they are thus motivated in a way unknown to mere humans. The red spruces frame an open rock shoulder, which is the summit.

The north–south alignment of the bare ledge drops off eastward sharply. The relay tower beyond aims two big disks off the mountain.

The summit at 2055 feet is the center of the trio of heights that form Crotched Mountain. The "crotched" or twinned silhouette cannot be made out from all approaches. Seen from Mount Monadnock, it's very plain.

Exploration of the summit to the east reveals upper sections of Crotched Mountain Ski Area in Francistown. South of the summit brushy woods have taken over some of the ledges, once open, and hide rocks forming a massive wall, a relic from 19th-century pasturing.

In 1976, when I first climbed Crotched Mountain, the wall provided a fine lunch site and a panorama south and west. My companion and I had been fascinated watching a storm pass over Mount Monadnock and deliver a shower to Pack Monadnock. Dark clouds, seething and rising, had formed spectacular anvil shapes. We were so occupied with the fine show of weather (and our sandwiches) that we didn't notice a threatening black cloud sneaking up behind us. It let go with a flash of lightning. We grabbed rucksacks and lit out for the spruces. I think the next bolt bounced off the rocks.

The sheltering spruces and raingear were necessary for only 20 minutes. We walked down the mountain admiring another weather display. This time sunlight in long shafts illuminated distant woods and fields, as though celestial spotlights had been switched on through holes in the clouds.

After your lunch, you'll begin the rewarding descent of Crotched Mountain. When you reach the vicinity of the radio tower, the wide views open before you, and now you don't have to turn around to see the mountains and the rolling countryside.

Pack Monadnock Mountain

Distance (one way): 5½ miles

Walking time: 4½ hours

Vertical rise: 1480 feet

Maps: USGS 7½' Peterborough North; USGS 7½' Greenfield; USGS 7½' Peterborough South; USGS 7½' Greenville

This high ridge east of Peterborough has two summits: civilized, 2300-foot South Pack and wild, 2278-foot North Pack. There is no resemblance to Grand Monadnock, although the Native American meaning of *pack* is said to be "little." An auto road up South Pack leads to a fire tower, relay towers, a stone shelter, picnic tables, and a northern viewpoint, from which North Pack's barren crags urge you to get away from it all.

How to Get There

To visit both summits requires either an across-and-return trek (7.25 miles) or two cars. This hike description is for two cars. Pack Monadnock, traversed by a northern section of the Wapack Trail (see Hike 1), should be hiked from south to north so your final impression is of an unspoiled mountain. This means leaving a spare car at the northern end of the trail.

To do this, drive two cars from the blinker in Greenfield southeast on NH 31 for 2.8 miles to Russell Station Road. Turn right. You soon cross railroad tracks. Keep on for 0.8 mile from NH 31. Here the road branches to the right uphill. This is the Old Mountain Road leading to the termination of your hike on the Wapack Trail.

Turn right on the Old Mountain Road. Check your mileage. You have 1.9 miles to drive before the trailhead. As you approach the total 1.9 miles, watch the woods to your left. The trail at first follows a wide old woods road up a slope. There's a WAPACK TRAIL sign high on a tree. The yellow triangular Wapack blazes also identify the trail. Park one of your cars off the right shoulder. This will be the endpoint of your hike.

After you've left off your pick-up car here, drive the second car west, straight ahead, toward Peterborough. At 1.4 miles from where you left your pick-up car, turn sharply left onto East Mountain Road. There's a steel post topped by a street sign. Drive the hilly road for 2.8 miles. You will pass a parking place and trail sign on your left for the Raymond Trail up South Pack. This is NOT your trailhead. Continue to a T-fork. Turn left. (A street sign identifies the right fork as Cunningham Pond Road.) Your left turn leads up a long grade and in 0.6 mile delivers you to NH 101. Turn left uphill on NH 101 for 0.3 mile to the sign on the left for Miller State Park. Turn left into the extensive parking at the base of the auto road up South Pack. (There is a fee.)

Confused by the multiplicity of roads? I was. Maybe you should search out the route before the actual date of the hike.

The Trail

So now you have your two cars arranged and your party gathered at the parking area. To reach the start of the hike, walk to the east corner of the parking area. Entering the woods, you immediately come to a trail junction. You have a choice of routes to the South Pack summit: the Marion Davis Trail with its blue blazes or the Wapack Trail with its yellow blazes. (A large map at the parking lot and bulletin board will outline trails.)

The Wapack Trail to the left ascends over rough ledges that require some scrambling, so it is more challenging and interesting than the Marion Davis Trail. Your attitude toward rocks and cliffs should decide your choice.

I'll assume you elect the older, easier Marion Davis Trail by bearing right at the junction near the parking area and following the blue blazes.

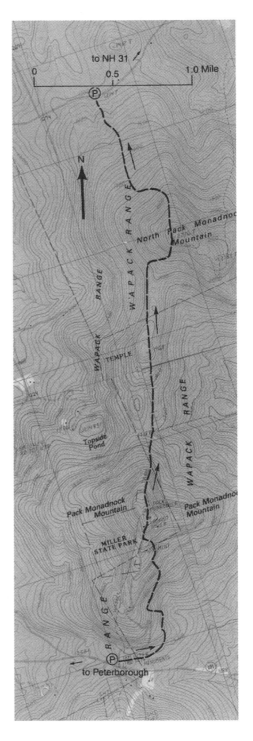

Checking out the view on North Pack

After a stone wall and birches, the trail curves steeply left up past huge rocks and under large red oaks. You walk down into a little ravine among spruces and then into the light of leafy trees. You climb once more. You cross another stone wall. You are alternately slabbing the mountainside and climbing abruptly. This is the trail's method of ascent for the hour or so required to reach South Pack's summit. The upper part of the trail has been relocated, and instead of joining the auto road it now enters the summit parking lot. (The Wapack Trail's summit approach has also been moved; the trail now enters the parking lot from the west.)

Southern New Hampshire spreads out all around you. Grand Monadnock's unique, shouldered pyramid dominates the west. The popularity of South Pack, however, does nothing to encourage lingering. Auto fumes, families of sightseers, and noise are sufficient incentive to take up the trail again. But first, inspect the shelter. A solid structure of mortared flat stones, open front, based against a ledge, it faces a large fireplace.

Your route north is the Wapack Trail to the left of the shelter. It slants into a little depression among spruces and leads to the lookoff rocks.

You can see North Pack and a massive cliff to the right of the summit. Spruces grow along the ridge. The topmost ledges are barren. Although 22 feet lower than South Pack, they seem on a greater mountain. An obvious spruce-grown knob about midway between you and North Pack is 1942 feet. I should add that the descent from South Pack to the col is more than 500 feet. The traverse of Pack Monadnock is no ridgepole walk.

Continue following the yellow blazes of the Wapack Trail, which falls away from South Pack's ledges into spruce woods. When the trail takes a sharp turn left, watch for an OVERLOOK sign; a short side trail leads to a good view to the east. After the spruces, you encounter small-scale deciduous woods. You are entering an area of former pastures. Trees have slowly but surely taken over heights cleared by settlers with ax and fire. These same tough pioneers and their descendants also laid up the unbelievable distances of stone walls.

You now are hiking in the Wapack National Wildlife Refuge, a 1672-acre wilderness preserve managed by the US Fish and Wildlife Service.

The trail over the middle knob crosses ledges where you may want to stop for lunch, although the view is limited. Then continue walking toward North Pack. As you approach the base of the peak, you may note on your right the Cliff Trail, an alternate, rugged route to the summit. The Wapack's yellow blazes lead straight ahead for the abrupt final climb to the summit. Follow these blazes, thus bypassing cliffs on your right. Over there, however, ravens may entertain you with their barking calls and seemingly playful cavorting on wind currents. The steep ascent of North Pack takes you to open ledges and the bare summit with its cairn.

Directly ahead, north across the valley and past the town of Greenfield, you see Crotched Mountain rising as a three-summit ridge. Beyond, if the day is blessed with crystal atmosphere, you see the distant White Mountains. South, the towered summit you first climbed seems far away, perhaps because, except for Monadnock on the west, flat countryside stretches all around it.

North Pack's summit drops off from ledges on the west. A rocky perch near the cairn is a great place to watch storms out of the west in the making. Exploration of the summit eastward reveals an interesting little bog surrounded by scrub spruces, blueberry bushes, and brush much frequented by warblers and sparrows.

The Wapack Trail departs the summit northward from the cairn. It leads across several rocky outcrops before curving down to the left into a stand of spruces.

The descent of 1.5 miles avoids eroded gullies. A spread of wild rhododendron is outstanding among brushland of birches, rhodora, bracken, and high-bush blueberries. Then hemlocks shade you for the final yards to the road and your car.

10

Mount Monadnock

Distance (round trip): 9 miles

Walking time: 7 hours

Vertical rise: 2670 feet

Maps: USGS 7½' x 15' Monadnock Mountain; USGS 7½' x 15' Marlborough

Traditionally known as Grand Monadnock, and rising from the mists of the past as it now rises from the morning mists in southwestern New Hampshire, Monadnock's rocky crest entices or challenges multitudes of hikers. Although a small mountain—3165 feet—Monadnock is everlastingly impressive.

The first recorded ascent was on July 31, 1725. A party of rangers from Lancaster, Massachusetts, scouting and hunting Native Americans and under the command of Captain Samuel Willard, camped on top. It was then forested but, as now, it stood alone, which is the meaning of its Native American name.

The earliest date chiseled into the rocks is 1801. Between that year and 1815, forest fires laid waste the slopes and summit.

Climbing to the newly barren crags became more popular. During the summer of 1815 several parties made their way to the top. There came to be a path. Famous men felt the spell of the mountain. The sage of Concord, Massachusetts, Ralph Waldo Emerson, wrote a poem about his experience, and his eccentric friend Henry David Thoreau made camp below the upper rocks.

As popular interest in the mountain grew, so did a concern for its preservation. Now the area includes a reservation of some 5000 acres under the cooperative guardianship of the New Hampshire Parks Division, the town of Jaffrey, and the Society for the Protection of New Hampshire Forests. The latter has been a prime mover for years in Monadnock conservation.

The town of Jaffrey has long been the southern takeoff to many trails. On that side are the state park and nature center. I think, however, you'll enjoy a lesser-known, northern, and longer route—the Pumpelly Trail.

Prepare for above-treeline weather by carrying suitable clothing and equipment in your pack. Take plenty of food and water and the AMC Monadnock map.

How to Get There

To reach the Pumpelly Trail, drive on NH 101 to the east end of Dublin Lake and turn south on East Lake Road. You follow it less than 0.5 mile. As soon as you come to the lakeshore on your right, watch for the trail. It's a woods road and bridle path opposite a shorefront log cabin. There may not be a sign. Park off the shoulder of the road farther along.

The Trail

You walk up a wide path into the woods. Move quietly and with respect for the people in the houses set among the trees. This is private land.

About 350 feet from East Lake Road your route leaves the path at a sharp right turn onto a trail; a sign points the way. The trail curves left under ancient pines, hemlocks, and oaks.

You shortly come to another woods road about 5 minutes from East Lake Road. Turn left uphill. This is an abandoned farm road. A stone wall borders it on the left. You come to a spring, also on the left. In early summer the overflow trickles across the old road.

Beyond the spring you walk up Oak Hill through a growth of hardwoods and down to a little valley. Climb out of the valley, noting an old path off to your left. Watch for an arrow that points you to the right onto a true trail. Although other paths will join yours, keep to the main trail. You're now on a winding footpath, eroded and rocky, and you're really headed for the mountain. The

trail is named for its originator, the geologist and conservationist Ralph Pumpelly, a summer resident of Dublin. He laid out the route in 1884.

About 0.75 hour from the Lake Road you pass another spring on the left. Now you begin the serious climb. No longer following a woods path, you're at last on a mountain trail. Part of the enjoyment and interest comes from noting the changes in vegetation and the season as you climb beyond the 2000-foot elevation. By the second week in June blueberry bushes may be past blooming below but up here they will be displaying massed, creamy flowers.

Several lookout ledges on spur trails to the left give views of Crotched Mountain's saddled ridge, Mount Kearsarge farther north, and the Uncanoonucs on the northeast horizon. Pack Monadnock arises to the east, identifiable by north and south summits with a low ridge between.

On the main trail you come to a slanting ledge with scattered evergreens. Keep to the crest and you'll find the cairns marking the way. A westerly view opens and shows you a sharp triangle of mountain over in Vermont. That's Mount Ascutney.

Then there's the summit ahead but far away. It's attached to your Dublin Ridge by a long eastern shoulder. The trail continues upward and southwest among rocks and evergreens. Yellow paint marks the Cascade Link on your left among spruces. (The Cascade Link drops to the state park via the White Dot Trail.) A dome of rock on your left turns the trail west around its base.

Here, as you cross the Dublin town line into Jaffrey, mountain cranberry puts on a vivid display if you happen to be climbing in mid-June. The modest, dark pink flowers on the creeping vines somehow manage to be spectacular.

Time for lunch. The rounded knob on

Mount Monadnock in winter

Jacqueline Donegan

your left gives wide outlooks.

After your repast, the way along the trail for 20 minutes traverses open ledges alternating with corridors through scrub spruce. Watch for the cairns as you cross the bare rock. You reach the top of Dublin Ridge. The trail bears left and descends into woods, then turns right, up into cranberry territory again. The Spellman Trail, identified by white letters and blazes on the rock, forks to your left. (The Spellman Trail is a steep route down to the Cascade Link.)

At the Spellman Trail junction, your Pumpelly Trail turns abruptly right and dips into a little wooded ravine. Climbing out of this you approach a rectangular rock left by the glacier. Named the Sarcophagus, and also called the Boat, it makes me think of a whale.

A few minutes beyond the Sarcophagus (you've swung westward toward the summit now) there's a large cairn surrounding a high ledge. The Red Spot–Old Ski Trail is marked with paint to the left of the ledge. (The Red Spot–Old Ski Trail descends to the Cascade Link.) From beside the cairn you have an excellent view of the summit, which is still 0.75 mile away by trail.

Blossoming mountain sandwort grows at the foot of the ledge. White flowers on leafy stems cluster above shorter clumps of leaves and decorate the shallow soil from mid-June till frost. From here on you'll be watching for cairns, which are far apart. You'll see at the same time the low plants of goldthread and three-toothed cinquefoil. In bogs surrounding two pools are plant communities that include sheep laurel and cotton grass.

You at last approach the topmost rocks and begin the final climb. The smooth, billowed schist shows glacial striations here and there, which stones embedded in ice scratched 30,000 years ago. Marks made by humans consist of names, initials, and dates. Tapping hammers and clinking chisels annoyed Henry Thoreau when he camped on the mountain.

Although you may be in fine physical condition and not winded at all on the summit rocks, you'll catch your breath, I'm sure. The whole of New England extends around you, or so it seems. The distant mountains fade into the afternoon haze, and your stand on the summit seems remote—despite the company of many other hikers. That's the magic of Monadnock.

Beginning the descent you can easily miss the way unless you locate the large white letters proclaiming PUMPELLY TRAIL and an arrow painted on the rocks. Then you must make certain you pass the first cairn and several more to insure your picking up the trail. After about 20 minutes you reach the Red Spot—Old Ski Trail and the big cairn atop the ledge. You are well on your way to the upper end of Dublin Ridge. The trail winding past the Sarcophagus and through the little ravine could almost be new as seen from these return angles. There's the Spellman Trail, the knob where you ate lunch, and the Cascade Link. You are on the narrow ridge heading down into the woods. But first, face about for a last look to the summit. Yes, you were indeed there 1½ hours ago.

Central New Hampshire

At last he pulled himself out into sunlight on a shale slope directly below the cliff and made his way across to a weathered slide which led to the top of the sheer ledge. He was out of breath when he reached the topmost rock but he could look across all the forest he had hunted on the east side of Quartz and Cobblestone. It gave him a wild lift of excitement. He knew the contours beneath the trees and now he could study it from above, as a bird might see it.

—Daniel Doan, Amos Jackman

11

Oak Hill

Distance (round trip): 2½ miles

Walking time: 1¼ hours

Vertical rise: 400 feet

Maps: USGS 7½' Loudon; USGS 7½' Penacook

Like most of middle New Hampshire, the forested land sloping up Oak Hill in Loudon and Concord was once field and pasture. Now the jeep road to the fire tower is bordered by a forest of white oaks, red oaks, and maples. The road begins as a farm lane leading about 0.5 mile to a cellar shown on the 1927 USGS 15' map as a house at the end of the lane. No fire tower then existed on top of Oak Hill from which to survey the rolling forest.

How to Get There

At the junction of NH 106 and NH 129, note your mileage and drive into Loudon village. Bear right across the bridge over the Soucook River. Take the first left, onto School Street. Drive past a school on the left to a four-corner intersection. Turn left onto Oak Hill Road. Going uphill, the road takes you past houses and woods. Drive slowly because no landmark identifies the fire warden's jeep road up Oak Hill.

At 1.7 miles from NH 106, you'll see the gated jeep road on the right, just as Oak Hill Road makes a wide right turn downhill. Park across the road on the narrow shoulder.

The Trail

The jeep road is your route to the hilltop. As a grade for walking, the road allows effortless observation and enjoyment of the woods. The fields were first taken over by deciduous trees, but white pines are now thriving. White pines are the climax forest in this area. The pines form a green line suggestive of a hedge beyond the stone walls.

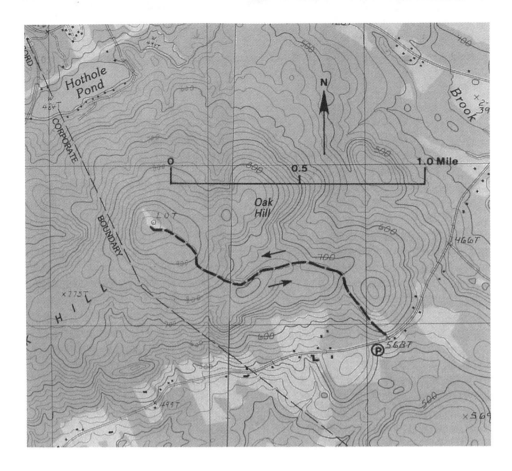

In a dead stub you may see annual nest holes—one above the other—of pileated woodpeckers. The red-crested black and white birds as big as crows will use the same stub for several years, but will chisel out new nest holes with their powerful bills. The nest holes are round, whereas the holes chiseled in search of grubs are elongated and wide open.

At the cellar the tremendous hand-split granite slabs for the foundation appear as the tower road bears left. An older, less used way continues uphill beside the cellar hole.

Keep on the jeep road. The earth becomes drier at a slight upward pitch. Low blueberries line the road. Canada mayflowers, also called wild lilies-of-the-valley, grow so thickly that you can squint your eyes and blend the little leaves into a green rug.

When you reach the summit, you find sky-high transmitters cluttering up the place. But the fire tower is still there, and it is still staffed, depending on weather and fire conditions. Its steep stairs zigzagging up from landing to landing may discourage anyone troubled by heights, but the railings will steady the most timorous hiker. If the cab is open, you can look out from this glassed-in room; if not, gaze from the top landing. You are rewarded with a view of New Hampshire's historic central countryside and its scattered mountains.

The twin Uncanoonucs near Manchester stand out prominently to the south. Farther away and to the west you see Pack Monadnock and Crotched Mountain. To the south-

Old stone walls in the woods are a sign that this land was farmed once.

west you can't miss the crags of Monadnock. Directly west, Sunapee Mountain extends a long shoulder from the summit. To the north-west there's Mount Kearsarge. Next comes a ridge, which is Ragged Mountain.

A scant 5 miles away toward the south-west the state capitol's dome glistens golden in the sunlight. Below the dome New Hampshire's General Court, as our legislature is known, meets in Concord, if not in concord.

If you're lucky, an about-face from the capitol view will show you another distinc-tive New Hampshire sight: one of the world's windiest mountains, Mount Wash-ington. Clouds through the 70 miles usually intervene.

This reminds me: Haze reduces the ef-fectiveness of the panorama from the tower. Visibility is usually better in the morning. Oak Hill requires distant vision to be entirely successful. Perhaps it should be an early-morning hike.

12

Blue Job Mountain

Distance (round trip): 1 mile

Walking time: ¾ hour

Vertical rise: 356 feet

Map: USGS 7½' Baxter Lake

Pronounce it Job, as in "the patience of . . ."

How can a 1356-foot hill open up the vastest views for the least effort in New Hampshire? The isolated location helps. So does the fire tower on top. Blue Job's elevation is much higher than the surrounding countryside in the east-central townships of Farmington, Barnstead, and Strafford. As for the effort, you drive to an elevation of 1000 feet before you begin the climb.

How vast is the view? To the north you see Mount Washington and other White Mountain peaks cutting the horizon. To the south your binoculars may pick out Boston's John Hancock Tower. East beyond Portsmouth the Atlantic Ocean encircles the Isles of Shoals. To the west you look into Vermont.

Save little Blue Job for a day when the weather forecaster predicts visibility limited only by the earth's curve. Otherwise you'll be disappointed. I suggest May or October. At either time Mount Washington could be capped with shining snow.

How to Get There

In Rochester, take Exit 13 off NH 16 (the Spaulding Turnpike) onto US 202 West. Drive 1 mile to Estes Road. Turn right onto Estes Road and drive 1.5 miles to Meaderboro Corner. (If you are coming from downtown Rochester, take NH 202A west to Meaderboro Corner.)

Note your mileage at the junction. At about 0.4 mile on NH 202A, you'll see a CROWN POINT sign as NH 202A swings left. Keep straight onto Crown Point Road. At 2.5 miles from Meaderboro Corner, Crown

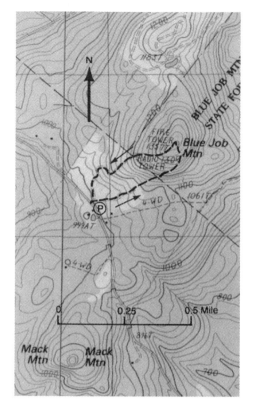

The well-worn trail leads directly toward the hillside. You enter the oak woods. The trail seems to bear left, but this is a route for blueberry pickers. Keep to the right and walk up a slanting ledge. From here to the top the trail is plain enough. Stone steps ease your climb. The trail circles east, so the steeper slopes are on your left.

An open ledge on the right gives the first views. Soon the oaks blend with spruces and pines. You climb left and emerge upon a grassy clearing with scattered trees, the tower ahead, and the warden's cabin on your right.

The tower is open in the summer and staffed. Approach its stairs with caution. A steel crossbeam is set at the correct height to deliver a blow on your head—if you're 5'10" as I am.

From the tower, in addition to the points of interest already mentioned, others will claim your attention, including the former Pease Air Force Base, the University of New Hampshire, and to the north any number of mountains.

The Belknap Mountains, near to the northwest, present unusual outlines. They hide Lake Winnipesaukee, from whose shores and waters the angular silhouettes and rounded ridges are more often seen. The Belknaps also hide several summits on the western edge of the White Mountains, but if you look closely between Mount Major and Mount Belknap, you'll see Mount Moosilauke's barren dome on the horizon.

Return the way you came. Or, for variety, walk past the fire tower to the service road and descend past a transmitting tower. Views open up, and you'll see a large marsh that collects meandering streams at the source of Big River. On ledges, blueberrying paths veer off the road. Keep on the road; you'll arrive down at the gate in about the same time as the descent by the trail.

Point Road joins First Crown Point Road in Strafford Corner. There's a grange hall on the left and then a church on the right. Bearing right, continue on First Crown Point Road through farmland and woods. You'll see the rounded knob on your right that's Blue Job topped by its tower. At 6 miles from Meaderboro Corner, opposite a house on your left, turn to park beside a locked gate leading into an overgrown blueberry field. A service line strung on poles extends up into Blue Job's oak forest.

The Trail

The gate is for the service road, which you might like to use to descend from the summit. To ascend, look for the trail to the east from the gate—that is, to your right as you face the mountain.

13

Fox State Forest

Distance (round trip): 4¼ miles

Walking time: 3 hours

Vertical rise: 600 feet

Map: USGS 7½' Hillsboro Upper Village

In 1922 Caroline A. Fox of Arlington, Massachusetts, gave the state her 348-acre farm with its fine house and barn. Since then the state has expanded this holding north of Hillsborough to 1445 acres, most of them abandoned farmland where woods have taken over the fields. The house is now the headquarters for Fox State Forest and the South Region of the Division of Forests and Lands.

To fulfill the conditions of the original trust, the state combines forestry practices and related experiments with education and nature trails. The environmental center, built in 1972 for ecology classes and conservation meetings, contains a forestry museum. (For more information, write the New Hampshire Division of Forests and Lands, PO Box 1175, Hillsborough, NH 03244, or phone 603-464-3453 or 603-271-3456.)

More than 20 miles of well-marked trails wind through the forest. The simple day hike I'll describe, over the loop path named the Ridge Trail, conducts you through the eastern part of the forest. It includes a detour to a glacial "kettle" with the inevitable name of Mud Pond and a return down Hemlock Ravine. The western part of the forest and a lookout tower are attractions for another day.

How to Get There

From US 202 and NH 9 in Hillsborough, turn north at the stoplights toward Hillsborough Center. Drive through a residential section and on along Center Road past two splendid farms. After 2 miles turn in, to the right, at the FOX FOREST sign.

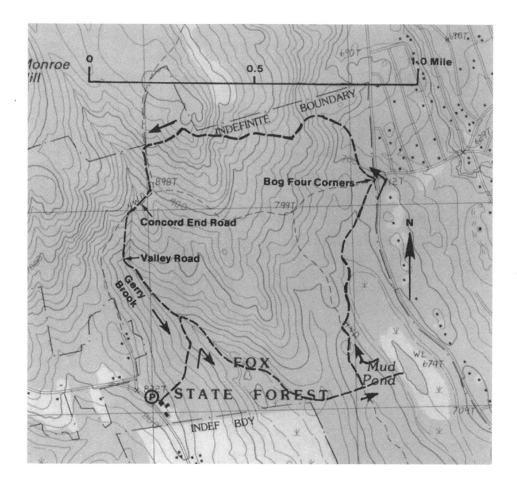

The gray and white house with its side porch suggests leisurely summer days and rocking chairs. The mailbox in front contains copies of the trail guide. Pick up a copy and drive on to the parking area ahead.

The Trail

The Ridge Trail begins at a sign on a tree at the right-hand corner of the parking area. Coinciding with Valley Road, it curves downhill, past the Tree Identification Trail and the Mushroom Trail. You walk down into a growth of hemlocks and pines, following the Ridge Trail's red-on-white blazes.

At the bottom of the hill the road turns sharply left. In 100 yards you cross Gerry Brook on a footbridge to a junction. Valley Road continues left up to Gerry Cemetery on Concord End Road. (It will be your return route.) Turn right at the MUD POND sign and continue following the Ridge Trail's red-on-white blazes.

Pines and hemlocks grow on the higher ground to your left as the trail parallels a sunny swamp and the remains of a beaver pond on the right. Tangled alders, grasses, and ferns partially hide Gerry Brook. Warblers are at home in this green jungle. During June, myriads of mosquitoes command attention. The trail rises beside a stone wall on your left and then enters an impressive grove of virgin hemlocks and beeches, probably the oldest in Fox Forest.

Here the Ridge Trail veers left. The Mud Pond Trail forks right, blazed with white dots; take this detour. After several minutes the Mud Pond Trail crosses a woods road, the intersection marked by signs for Mud Pond Boardwalk. The trail continues a short distance to Mud Pond. You'll return to the woods road after seeing this bog.

The boardwalk provides dry access to the sphagnum moss and shrubs that float out from the west shore. *Stay on the boardwalk.* Further investigation might harm rare plants, and it also means wet feet and a moment of trepidation when you first see and feel the bog's mat undulating beneath your weight. You realize the origin of the term "quaking bog."

The rootless sphagnum moss has the capacity to spread out and grow across water. It forms a mat that becomes a seedbed for other plants. Eventually the bog will fill the pond with peat. Present-day sphagnum bogs are relicts, having survived from the glacial era. Because the chemistry of sphagnum moss makes its environment acid, other plants must be able to thrive in such a condition. Various members of the heath family can do this. In Mud Pond's bog you see blueberry bushes, bog rosemary, sheep laurel, cranberry vines, and leatherleaf. There are two insectivorous plants: sundew and pitcher plant. Two pink orchids, pogonia and calopogon, bloom in late June. (I'm sure you know they're not to be picked!) The bog supports stunted tamarack and black spruce.

Retrace your steps on the Mud Pond Trail as far as the woods road and turn right. In dry pine woods the Ridge Trail soon joins the road from the left and follows it a short way before branching right. Continue along the Ridge Trail, which winds through a

Then he saw, exactly at the spot where he had been staring, a tiny frog no bigger than his thumb. It looked like the tree frogs he had seen in the summer woods. It blew out its throat and called, "Knee-deep, knee-deep." The little feet grasped a blade of grass, the head and back were out of water. Ray could see the St. Andrew's cross on the back. Now that his eyes were focused on the frog he wondered how he could have failed to see it at once. He moved his eyes in search of another, but found none and when he sought the first again, it seemed to have disappeared, blending with the water and grass and weeds. Then he saw it in the same place.

He was pleased and excited to learn what made the chorus from the pool. He felt that he had discovered the answer to an important mystery. It seemed miraculous to him that these little frogs should suddenly appear in a pool of water which a few weeks before had been ice and snow. He stood for a long time on the edge of the pool and did not notice that his feet had sunk into the moist ground and were soaking wet.

—Daniel Doan, The Crystal Years

younger hardwood forest. Less than a half hour from the pond you come to the east edge of the forest at the Bog Four Corners.

You are in a logging clearing on the eastern end of the Gould Pond woods road. Traffic may be speeding past on the paved highway. Directly across the clearing is the cellar of the Davis farmhouse.

Just to the left of the cellar, the Ridge Trail leaves the woods road northward under lofty trees. You climb a moderate slope

Ruth Doan MacDougall pauses at Mud Pond in Fox State Forest.

among scattered boulders. Then you climb on steadily for about 0.5 mile, up Jones Hill. Beeches replace the oaks, maples, and birches. A blue post near a T-junction of stone walls marks the forest's boundary.

Over the hill you go, as the trail curves left and levels. You come to Concord End Road. (Beyond Concord End Road the Ridge Trail continues into the western part of Fox Forest.) Turn left and follow this graded dirt road down past the junction with Gould Pond Road.

A few yards farther on the right you may visit the large cellar hole of the Gerry-Kimball farmhouse, which was built in the early 1800s. You can see that the farm had a form of indoor plumbing: a well inside the house. But because this water was deemed unsafe, a well across the road was used for drinking and cooking. The house burned in 1908. Birches and poplars took root inside

the walls of rock.

Continue down Concord End Road. Under it Gerry Brook flows through an impressive stone culvert. Farther along on the left you come to the family cemetery. Headstones show different early spellings of the later "Gerry."

At the cemetery, turn left off Concord End Road onto a woods road downhill. This is the north end of Valley Road and leads down Gerry Brook to Hemlock Ravine. You first enter leafy woods. In the trees' shade, through royal ferns, you cross Gerry Brook and arrive at the hemlock woods. They grow so close along the brook that the name Hemlock Ravine is appropriate indeed.

You descend to the junction where you turned onto the Ridge Trail southward. Again cross the footbridge. You climb curving to the right until light ahead proves to be the parking area.

14

Lovewell Mountain

Distance (round trip): 4½ miles

Walking time: 3¼ hours

Vertical rise: 925 feet

Map: USGS 7½' x 15' Lovewell Mountain

Lovewell Mountain makes me think of a blunt galleon boring south into a forested green sea. The prow points toward Mount Monadnock. The foredeck is the open ridge below the upper deck of the summit's spruce woods. The sails are clouds.

At other times I try to imagine how Lovewell must have looked as a treeless mountain pasture during the 1800s, when surrounding farms in the town of Washington turned out sheep and cattle for the summer grazing on its broad slopes. Now all but the south ridge is forested. The stone walls exist as relics without a purpose. The old road at the mountain's south base was once a thoroughfare between the village of Washington and the farm community at East Washington. It still is suitable for horse-drawn wagons but that's about all. Modern logging trucks have disrupted it. You'll walk, so it's included in the distance for this hike.

As in earlier days, the present village of Washington with its store, , brick library, old white church, town hall, and fine houses, remains spick-and-span, unspoiled in its high isolation on NH 31 northwest of Hillsborough.

The gazetteer notes that Lovewell Mountain "received its name from Captain Lovewell, who was accustomed to ascending it to discover the wigwams of Indians, and who, on one occasion, killed seven Indians near its summit." There are other legends and theories about its name and a question about the name itself, which perhaps should be "Lovell."

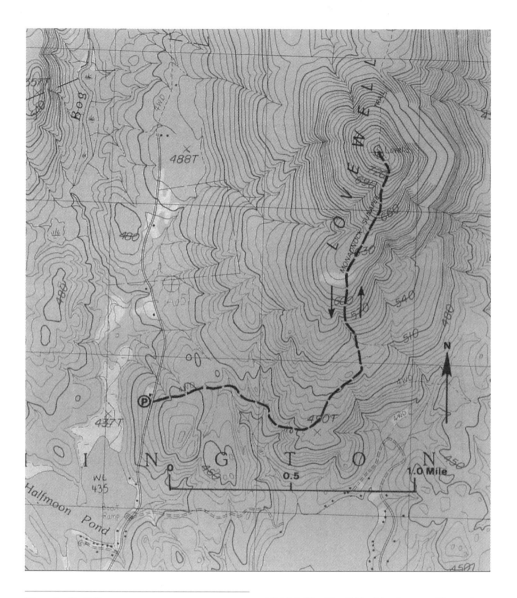

How to Get There

Take a road that forks southeast from NH 31 opposite the store and post office in the center of Washington. You immediately pass the church and town hall on your left. After 0.5 mile a left turn around a big house takes you to Halfmoon Pond. Shorefront cottages appear on your left. Continue past Halfmoon Pond for a total of 2 miles from NH 31. The East Washington road branches off to the right. Here you should select a parking place off on a shoulder. Or if the road is passable a few yards for low-slung cars, there's a smooth, broad ledge a little ways in. Use cautious judgment.

The Trail

Rectangular white blazes on the trees will

indicate that you're on a section of the Monadnock-Sunapee Greenway. Along this old road between stone walls, evergreens and leafy trees blend around larger hemlocks and oaks. The gradual ascent consists of ups and downs leading to a level height-of-land at 1620 feet.

A glaciated ledge emerges from the dirt road and slants up under a remarkable stone wall. The granite slabs could have been stacked by a giant. Here, alerted by cairns and by the double blaze that indicates a turn on the Greenway, you find the trail leaving the road north and left, through a gap in the stone wall. The trail enters an overgrown clearing. You are about 1 mile from your car.

The trail leaves the clearing beyond the wall and winds gently up into spruces whose branches have been cut to open a tunnel toward the next clearing. The trees alternate with open spaces. Cairns are older than the white blazes. You walk between head-high blueberry bushes and tall junipers. More junipers will in time die as shade spreads over them from growing trees; junipers must have sunshine.

About 20 minutes from the old road and height-of-land, you come to a stone wall on your right. Watch for the white blazes. Rising more steeply, the trail slabs into a patch of lovely green New York ferns, then climbs left onto the south shoulder. Northward looms the 2473-foot summit.

Once more cairns mark the way, which now leads northwest through scattered small spruces and low blueberry bushes. A much larger cairn, 6 feet high, stops the trail's northwest direction. It now bears right to a cairn about 4 feet high. Here, turn right into a broad patch of meadowsweet, bracken, and spruce. Thereafter the trail curves northeast, again in the open, past another large cairn built of flat rocks.

Frequent small cairns guide you to the trail's final entry into the upper spruce woods and more white blazes. You climb steeply to a spur trail on your right. Take this a few yards for a lookoff above an intervale farm and East Washington. Back at the main trail a short climb brings you to a rock from which you can see the islands of Island Pond (behind you to the south). Beyond, Highland Pond is a long channel.

After this view the trail rises to a low rock face. You climb a short distance to the summit ledges surrounded by spruces. For a northern outlook keep to the right past the summit cairn. Across the upper valley of Woodward Brook there's a long ridge on the horizon. Below this, and as though struck into the woods with blue pencil, Ayers Pond appears as an irregular line. Directly north Mount Sunapee rises beyond its southern ridges.

For the return go back to the summit cairn, bear left across the ledge into the spruce woods, and pick up the trail you ascended.

Before you decide to return as you came up, consider a loop hike. For the sturdy and adventurous hiker, another route is possible. The Monadnock-Sunapee Greenway continues northerly by leaving the summit to the right of the cairn as you face south. The trail descends along the north ridge before dropping into the valley and crossing the extension of the road past Halfmoon Pond. Turn left at the road and follow it back to your car.

You will be walking on the route of the original Monadnock-Sunapee Trail, before the 1938 hurricane closed it. The present Greenway, 47 miles of it, was reopened and relocated by the Society for the Protection of New Hampshire Forests, aided by the AMC and other organizations. The Monadnock-Sunapee Greenway Trail Club was formed in 1994. For information and a trail guide, write MSGTC, PO Box 164, Marlow, NH 03456, or call (603) 357-2115 or (603) 225-7274.

Lovewell Mountain

15

Mount Kearsarge

Distance (round trip): 2 miles

Walking time: 1 ½ hours

Vertical rise: 1105 feet

Maps: USGS 7 ½' Andover; USGS 7 ½' New London

Atop this mountain—not to be confused with Mount Kearsarge North between Conway and Jackson—the bare rocks and stunted spruces represent a harsh and primitive world in contrast to the man-made tower, warden's cabin, airplane beacon, and relay cones. When the wind is right, hang gliders launch themselves from the cliff like gaudy birds and land at Winslow State Park picnic area (except when they land in trees). The trail for this hike starts at the picnic area.

How to Get There

To reach the mountain and park, take the Kearsarge Valley Road, which runs south from NH 11 between Elkins and Wilmot Flat. (Or from the south pick up the Kearsarge Valley Road via I-89, Exit 10, and Sutton.) The intersection with NH 11 is marked by signs. After 1.5 miles on the Kearsarge Valley Road, you are directed left onto the Kearsarge Mountain Road. From here it's 2.5 miles to the parking spot. Signs will keep you from taking any side roads. Mount Kearsarge looms ahead as this asphalt road winds up through farmland and woods.

There's a gate near the ranger's cottage and a booth for collecting the fee before you drive to the picnic area and the site of a hotel, the Old Winslow House. Grassy banks now surround the cellar hole. Birches shade some of the picnic tables and fireplaces. Wide views stretch away, but the 2937-foot mountain dominates the scenery.

The Trail

The Winslow Trail and the new Barlow Trail both start at the southeast corner of the

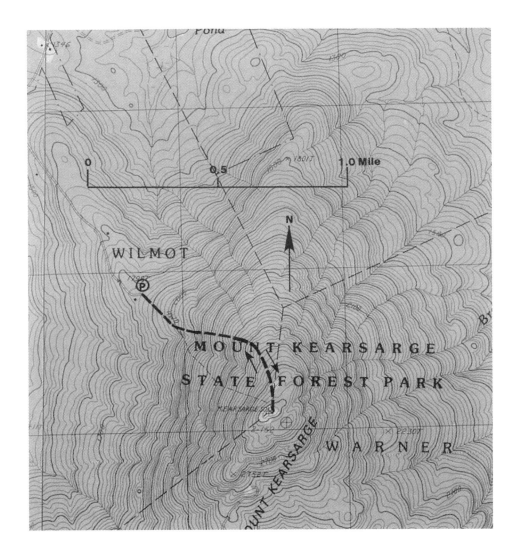

picnic area. Take the Winslow Trail, right. Through spruces it is wide and at first presents springy duff to walk on. Then it becomes eroded and steeper, making for rough climbing. Follow the red blazes. You swing into a more gradual eastward 0.25 mile. White birches mix with the spruces for a time. At a higher elevation the woods change almost entirely to spruce and fir.

The first set of smooth ledges is the halfway point. Here and at the next two sets of smooth ledges are recently constructed rock steps. Just above these ledges you come to a lookoff rock to the left, worth a visit for views and a breather. Trees get smaller through here.

The trail takes you into the open. Barren rocks, marked with red-paint arrows, lead you in a southerly curve through islands of scrub spruce. About 50 yards from the summit, the Barlow Trail comes in on the left. A final knoll of rock supports the tower. Another crest beyond a little hollow is a foundation for the beacon. The warden's cabin, north of the tower and lower than the summit, avoids the prevailing west winds. The ledges, through the years, have been profusely chiseled with names, initials, dates.

People wander about, climb the tower, study the views, or watch the hang-glider daredevils launch into space. Some of the pilots carry rope around their waists to lower themselves from accidental landings in tall trees.

You may also wonder about apparent tourists in nonhikers' clothing. They *are* tourists, having driven out of Warner to park 0.5 mile below the summit. This auto road through Rollins State Park is also the access route for the hang-glider people. The tourists seem to regard the trail from the road's end as a city walk. It's not. Mount Kearsarge can be suddenly cold and blustery or very wet.

The view is wide to all points of the compass. Pleasant Lake on the west reflects sunlight, and farther away parts of Lake Sunapee gleam near Georges Mills. Identified by their ski trails, King Ridge and Mount Sunapee are easy to locate. To the northwest you see the mountains along the Connecticut River above Hanover—Smarts and Cube, particularly. Nearer, Cardigan's rock dome topped by a tower drops off to the shoulder called Firescrew because the ho-

locaust that burned the forest to bedrock in 1855 twisted smoke and flame into an awesome spiral. In the distance, Moosilauke, the westernmost peak of the White Mountains, shows itself.

Swinging your gaze more to the northeast, you see the long Sandwich Range's varied peaks. Mount Washington stands out on the horizon. The Ossipee Range billows from ridge to ridge in a form of great solidity and breadth beyond the few visible patches of blue water in the Lakes Region. The Belknap Mountains are nearer, south of Lake Winnipesaukee.

Much closer, the valley only 4 miles northeast shelters the village of Andover, where white houses, brick school buildings, and a church steeple look like toys set among artificial green trees and fields. The town, like all the countryside, is watched over by the New Hampshire state warden ever alert for smoke. You may hear the warden talking to other wardens, exchanging compass bearings on strange smoke and speculating whether it's caused by an out-of-control grass fire, blueberry bushes being burned over, or a lightning strike in the forest.

Your descent to the picnic area will be quick. Make sure you take the Winslow Trail straight ahead, not the Barlow Trail to the right. You'll need only 30 minutes to return along the paint marks and down the wooded trail.

16

Red Hill

Distance (round trip): 3½ miles

Walking time: 2 hours

Vertical rise: 1370 feet

Maps: USGS 7½' Center Harbor; USGS 7½' Center Sandwich

I lived only 20 miles from Red Hill for 38 years before I climbed it. Now I wish I had long ago known enough to take my two daughters up it before having them tackle Mounts Washington, Moosilauke, and Lafayette. It would have been good experience and conditioning. What a view we'd have had: lakes all around and peaks arrayed to the north along the Sandwich Range—a fine reward for so easy a hike.

None of this implies that Red Hill is ignored by others. Many hikers enjoy it. You'll have lots of company. Its 2029-foot dome, topped by a fire tower, rises in flat country 1500 feet above Lake Winnipesaukee to the south and Squam Lake to the west. Heavily traveled NH 25 between Center Harbor and Moultonborough curves under Red Hill's eastern shoulder.

How to Get There

At the traffic lights in Center Harbor, take the Bean Road 1.5 miles to Sibley Road on your right, where there is a sign for the Red Hill Forest Fire Lookout Station. Drive 1.2 miles to parking areas on the right and left.

The Trail

At the trailhead, a locked gate keeps out vehicles, while a turnstile accommodates hikers. Walk up the service road 0.25 mile. The Red Hill Trail bears off to your right; there may be a wooden arrow on a post. This is the old service road, which follows the general route of an old farm wagon track and is prettier than the new road, which continues straight. These two roads later rejoin, so your final destination is the

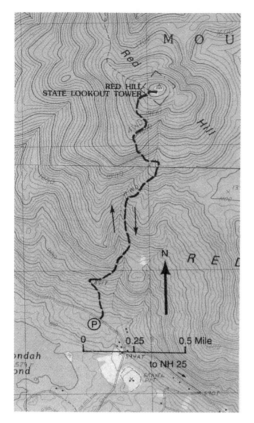

A turn of the trail to the left circles a barn foundation and cellar hole surrounded by shrinking, overgrown fields. Here the service road joins the trail. Turn left at the cellar hole. There may be a sign: RED HILL TOWER 1.4 MILES. And the way may be chained against all-terrain vehicles.

You enter a long, gradual rise. Hikers ambitious for steeper climbing avoid the easy route by turning right up a path that was the clearing for an old telephone line, but the road is more relaxing.

Beyond the straight section it leads upward in winding S-turns. A cut has eroded to glaciated ledge marked by the tire tracks of the fire warden's four-wheel-drive vehicle. The trail passes bracken ferns, blueberry bushes, and swamp cranberries, these last at the highest altitude I can recall. These are not mountain cranberry's creeping vines, but upstanding little plants that grow in bogs with leatherleaf and sphagnum moss. I ate some one fall and proved them to be cranberries, and properly puckery, to my own satisfaction.

In May you'll see mayflowers along the banking. Don't pick them, but bend down to enjoy their lovely scent. In all months you'll notice round nest holes and oblong feeding holes chiseled by pileated woodpeckers in dead trees, and if you're lucky you may hear or see a pileated woodpecker itself. You'll also notice that some trees have been charred and blackened by forest fires.

The trail levels for a few yards until, on the left, springwater gushes from a pipe. Some folks once called such a treat "Adam's Ale," especially if the pipe was absent and the water bubbled into a sidehill pool. Depending on the season, the pool here may be deeper than it looks, so be careful with children.

Winding on up past oaks and some pines, the trail lifts you higher. Near the top, it di-

same in either case.

If you take the new road, in a few minutes you'll come to a junction where a snowmobile trail goes forward. Turn right up a switchback.

The older route, the Red Hill Trail, climbs almost 0.4 mile, making a right turn up to a bridge across a brook, which starts as a spring halfway up the mountain. Red oaks grow over most of Red Hill. The forest floor seems to suit fringed polygalas with their evergreen leaves and flowers that flare like pink wings in May and June. In spring, oaks are late putting out leaves. Maples and beeches begin to close in the aisles of gray trunks long before the end of May, and hemlocks sprout new tips on darker green branches.

vides briefly, then rejoins in about 50 yards. The Eagle Cliff Trail comes in on the left.

Walk past the generator shed and old garage and the shingled warden's cabin, and climb the rock to the tower's steel girders. In the surrounding glade amid oaks, the blueberry bushes and grasses compete for the earth unoccupied by protruding ledges.

Vistas of lakes and mountains open to a 360-degree panorama as you climb up the fire tower and look over the treetops. There's no way to describe the view briefly. I must list it to get it all in. So here's the panorama starting southeast and turning full circle to south, west, north, east, and southeast again: Mount Major across Lake Winnipesaukee, Mount Belknap also across the lake, Mount Kearsarge (the southern one), Mount Cardigan across Squam Lake, and Smarts Mountain. There's Cube, Stinson, Carr, Kineo, Moosilauke, Kinsman, Cannon, Welch (nearer in front of Cannon), Black at the Sandwich Range's west end, then Sandwich hiding the Franconia Range. Next, and nearer, rises Israel. Away back is Carrigain to the left of Tripyramid. Sleepers, Whiteface, Passaconaway, Paugus, and Wonalancet are closer. Again far back come the Moats left of Chocorua's rock spire, and then Cranmore, Little Sugarloaf in Maine, the Ossipee Range (best view of it anywhere), more Winnipesaukee, and Copple Crown in Wolfeboro.

I've forgotten to mention the white and yellow and red sails of boats on Lake Winnipesaukee and Squam Lake. They look like kites in an upside-down blue sky.

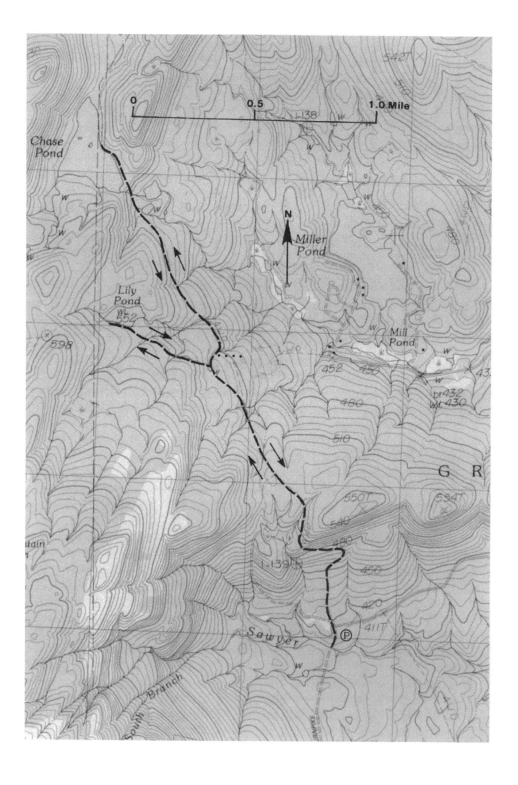

17

Old Croydon Turnpike

Distance (round trip): 6 miles

Walking time: 3½ hours

Vertical rise: 500 feet

Map: USGS 7½' x 15' Enfield Center

This woods walk follows a main highway of the 1850s. Antiquities remaining include stone walls, cellar holes, a mill site, and a road graded for horses and wagons that once rumbled over stone culverts. Fascination grips you as you walk through—as G.M. Trevelyan describes the poetry of history— "that land of mystery which we call the past." His country, England, goes back to far more remote and stirring times than those of the Old Croydon Turnpike, yet the aura of time lost haunts these forests that were once fields and pastures. Farmers, tradesmen, blacksmiths, carpenters, housewives, grandmothers, young lovers, and laughing or crying children lived and died here. Trevelyan points out: "Their place knows them no more and is ours today. Yet they were once as real as we, and we shall tomorrow be shadows like them. In men's first astonishment over that unchanging mystery lay the origins of poetry, philosophy, and religion."

What other thought-provoking wonders? You will see bridges for snowmobiles over streams and a wire fence high enough to keep in elk. The fence is evidence that the harsh, stony land was bought for a game preserve in the 1880s by a very wealthy man. You'll also see two watery gems, Chase Pond and Lily Pond, each completely different.

Located north of Newport, this turnpike traversed farmland. Some figures from an 1855 gazetteer, *New Hampshire as It Is,* by Edwin A. Charlton, published by Tracy and Sanford of Claremont, will give a surprising evaluation of Croydon's people and production for 1850.

Population: 861—Legal voters: 215
Bushels of potatoes: 14,285
Pounds of wool grown: 15,735
Pounds butter made: 50,970
Pounds cheese made: 1072
Pounds maple sugar made: 17,120

Now for the animals that roamed fields and pastures, where you'll walk through forest, and the more fertile land along the Sugar River.

Sheep: 3833

Neat stock (i.e., domestic bovine animals): 1297

Horses: 188

If the number of horses seems small, remember the oxen included under "neat stock." Every farm had a yoke or two of oxen. I should also mention the area of Croydon: 26,000 acres. The above figures are not unique to Croydon. Similar figures are quoted for adjacent towns, and while I cannot guarantee their accuracy, they do tell something of our country's rural past. Trees are the big crop now.

Despite the name of this hike, you aren't really in Croydon. The township begins south of this section of the turnpike. The name seems to have derived because it was put through from the south; a full-scale map shows it passing beyond Croydon Four Corners as an improved road. The turnpike was a link from the hill settlements to the lush Connecticut River valley when commerce plied the water.

How to Get There

To reach the Old Croydon Turnpike built for real horsepower (or oxpower), you'll drive your vehicle with its internal combustion engine on a modern turnpike: I-89 between Concord and Lebanon. Take Exit 13 for Grantham and NH 10.

Turn right, north, on NH 10, and drive about 1.7 miles toward North Grantham.

Watch on the left for stone posts and a street sign that says Olde Farms Road. Turn onto Olde Farms Road. You'll go beneath I-89 on a one-lane underpass. At 0.3 mile from NH 10, bear right on Olde Farms Road. At the next junction bear left, staying on Olde Farms Road. It turns to gravel. At a junction at 1.1 miles, go straight on Walker Road. (Olde Farms Road bears left.) Continue on Walker Road to the dead-end parking area, 2 miles fron NH 10.

The Trail

Start walking on the small road that leads off the parking area. It quickly connects to a woods road, the Old Croydon Turnpike, which runs right and left, roughly southeast—northwest. Turn right.

You'll see a fence on the left—and what a fence! Often paralleling the woods road, the heavy wire mesh 8½ feet high stretches between posts as stout as small telephone poles. The wire closes gullies and streambeds. Locked gates and signs appear occasionally.

In the late 1880s Austin Corbin, a New York banker and railroad man, bought 26,000 acres north of his birthplace, Newport. He enclosed the property with 36 miles of fence. The cost of the park and the wild animals he stocked it with came to over a million dollars. He bought elk, buffalo, moose, and wild boar. Today the park, without most of the exotic animals, is a private club owned by the Blue Mountain Forest Association. Through the fence you may still glimpse a boar.

The turnpike ascends. In about 1 mile, you reach a four corners. Ignore the short trail to the right; it goes past a cabin that belongs to a snowmobilers' club. To the left and at a higher elevation lies Lily Pond, which you'll visit. But Chase Pond to the north should be your first destination. Keep

An abandoned cellar hole along the Old Croydon Turnpike

straight along the Old Croydon Turnpike.

At once you find evidence of the old days, when the turnpike carried traffic from the surrounding farms. It's a stoned-up cellar hole, the first of several you'll pass during the hike. In most of them a central platform of rock supported the chimney. A family once lived here in a house of wood and doubtless made lively conversation about the passing wagons or sleds, the coaches or buggies, and certainly the yokes of oxen, perhaps four pairs drawing massive skids of logs.

Old Croydon Turnpike

The houses that rose over these cellar holes were often abandoned to the weather as families left for better lands in the West, or men never returned from the Civil War. Many survivors were attracted to jobs in mill towns. Young people sought better—and easier—lives, returning only to bury the old folks who stayed. Roofs began to leak, timbers rotted, and for some years the collapsed houses protruded from the cellars. Trees sprouted through the boards, which rotted away. Maybe someone came along with a horse and wagon to salvage the bricks from the great chimneys. Now big trees grow in the cellar holes, and nearby apple trees bloom in the spring and bear small fruit in the fall. In spring lilac bushes put out fragrant purple blossoms. In late summer the daylilies of the housewife still are a sturdy clump of narrow leaves below orange flowers that decorate the encroaching forest.

Your next landmark is a small brook, the outlet from Lily Pond. Freshets and the years have demolished the stone culvert. Snowmobilers replaced it with a bridge.

Now the turnpike takes you up into rougher land. You cross the outlet from Chase Pond on another snowmobile bridge. To the left a stone foundation identifies the site of a vanished sawmill or gristmill—maybe both.

Continuing uphill to more level walking, you come to a logging road that branches left. For the first view of Chase Pond, take this a short distance and almost immediately bear right on a path. It leads you to the lower end of the pond flooded by a beaver dam. Skeletal trees killed by the high water show the former border of woods. This is not all of the pond.

Walk back to the turnpike. Turn left along it, north again. Bear right on a bypass of a flooded stretch of trail. At about 1.5 miles from the four corners, you see on your left a grove of fine evergreens along the east shore. They are a plantation of Norway spruce. You have crossed the invisible town line between Grantham and Plainfield. Two-thirds of Chase Pond is in Plainfield.

From the shade of the Norway spruces you can observe the oval pond. Walk down a path to the shore and, if it's now time for lunch, have your picnic here. Enjoy this setting of middle New Hampshire with the leafy trees on the far shore where fields and pastures once stretched up toward hills impossible to farm.

Now after Chase Pond, for contrast, you start back to your second destination. Walk south to the four corners. Take the road on your right for Lily Pond. You'll see the great fence again as you climb uphill beside it.

At about 0.5 mile from the four corners, Lily Pond appears beyond the evergreens on the right. One-third the size of Chase Pond and at the same elevation, 1800 feet, the still water has a completely different setting. Pointed firs and spruces match reflections in the pond. Water lilies thrive. There's a northern atmosphere, helped along by the scent of balsam fir. Lily Pond could be farther north in the White Mountains.

The ecological contrast between the two ponds may hold you here for lunch, if you haven't already picnicked at Chase Pond. Then you return to the four corners and head south along it down the oak-grown hill. When you reach the road to the parking area, go past and continue on to Sawyer Brook.

After watching the minnows in the brook, face about and walk back, turning right for your car. You may even ponder the past you've walked through. I've forgotten who said *Sic transit gloria mundi*. Probably written, not spoken. I stopped Latin with Cicero—

but I know the phrase means: "So passes away the glory of the world."

The Old Croydon Turnpike was a small glory, and certainly in mud season a glorious mess, yet it can cause a certain pensiveness.

Note: This hike is a good route for learning elementary use of USGS topographical maps. You'll need the Enfield Center 7½' x 15' metric. The ponds and the various roads show plainly, and the contour lines may be used to form a picture of the elevations and valleys hidden in the forest.

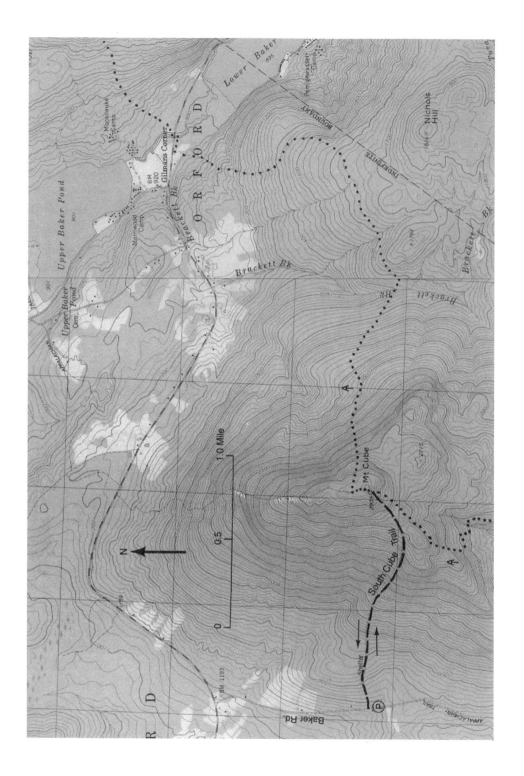

18

Mount Cube

Distance (round trip): 3 miles

Walking time: 3 hours

Vertical rise: 1200 feet

Map: USGS 7½' Piermont

This was the first mountain Dan climbed, at age 10. The 2909-foot summit—"quartzite-frosted," as he put it—was a landmark to him during his Orford boyhood and ever after.

The hike up the South Cube Trail is steep but short, suitable for young hikers such as Dan was, and of course for other hikers. If you'd like to make a longer hike out of it by continuing north over the summit and down to NH 25A 3.3 miles away, on the Mount Cube Trail, the hike will then be 4.8 miles, taking about 4 hours, and you will need two cars.

How to Get There

From the east, turn off in Wentworth onto NH 25A. If you are doing the long version of the hike, watch for the AT sign on the left in 5 miles and leave one car there. At 8.5 miles from Wentworth, turn left at an old schoolhouse corner onto Baker Road and drive 1 mile to the trailhead on the left, just before a culvert and a clearing with a small building on the right. There may be a sign: CUBE SHELTER.

If you are coming from the west, take NH 25A out of Orford and drive 6.5 miles to Baker Road on your right. The NH 25A trailhead for the Mount Cube Trail is 10 miles from Orford.

The Trail

Blazed blue, the South Cube Trail leads into old pastureland grown up in hardwoods and hemlocks. This area of abandoned farms inspired Dan's novel *Amos Jackman,* in which he gave Mount Cube and Smarts Mountain the names Quartz and Cobblestone.

The view of Smarts Mountain from Mount Cube

Donald K. MacDougall

As you walk along the trail listening to the birds, you may hear a hairy woodpecker and notice high in a birch a round hole from which on a July morning I heard the insistent mews of a noisy nest of babies.

A little farther on, at 0.2 mile, you come to the ramshackle Cube Shelter and a mortared fieldstone fireplace and chimney with some cabin remnants. Fifty yards up the trail you pass a moss-covered doorstep and a small foundation wall on the right.

Continue past old stone walls and maples. The trail gets narrow, stony. Old barbed wire has been absorbed by trees. At about 0.75 mile, the trail begins to steepen. You may hear the leaf scuffling of a chipmunk. The trail widens again.

At about 1 mile, the trail bears left. In the woods, spruce/fir become more evident and wood sorrel abundant, its cloverlike leaves and white flowers a fragile carpet. The trail

steepens up rocks. Turn and look back at the glimpses of views beginning to emerge through the trees. You enter a short fern glade and admire white birches, then climb rocks. It's a varied combination here, the lovely woods, the slanting and sometimes slippery rocks. Then the trees close in over a rougher trail. You scramble up ledges.

And now you are climbing up the broad expanse of the summit ledges, pausing to look behind you at the views dropping and widening across the upper Connecticut River valley into Vermont. You have arrived on South Peak.

The near mountain that dominates the view is Smarts Mountain. This is the second mountain Dan climbed in his boyhood and the scene of many of his youthful adventures. The trail he used, out of Quinttown, has been renamed by the Dartmouth Outing Club the Daniel Doan Trail. (See Hike 15 in

50 Hikes in the White Mountains.) A loop route out of Lyme he incorporated into a Smarts Mountain backpack. (See Hike 47 in this book.)

Looking south at Smarts, begin the sweep of the panorama. To the left of Smarts is Mount Kearsarge; farther left you see the rock dome and fire tower of Mount Cardigan. To the right of Smarts, southwest, there are the ski trails marking the Dartmouth Skiway near Holt's Ledge, then Mount Ascutney in Vermont, and other Vermont mountains including Stratton, Bromley, Killington Peak, and Pico Peak. To the northwest, across Orford's Sunday Mountain where Dan owned his first farm on Dame Hill in the 1930s, there are more Vermont mountains, including Mount Abraham, Lincoln Peak, Mount Ethan Allen, the distinctive Camel's Hump, and Mount Mansfield.

As you explore the summit, you'll discover a sign for the AT to Smarts and another sign for the AT north to NH 25A. The latter will be your descent via the Mount Cube Trail if you have decided to do the longer hike. If not, still take 15 minutes to follow this trail to the North Peak side trail for the North Peak view. You may prefer to have your lunch on North Peak, if you are early on South Peak.

Below the sign for the AT north, turn right, then left. In 2 minutes you'll reach the junction where the AT and the Mount Cube Trail turn right and the North Peak side trail (an old AT route) goes straight ahead. Follow the North Peak side trail's yellow blazes over ledges, past patches of sheep laurel. At about 0.3 mile you come to North Peak.

From the northeast outlook on these

It was an eastern-facing farm. Amos Jackman stood in the door of the barn while the sun came over the ridge between Quartz Mountain and the long hump of Cobblestone. The mountains lay on the eastern horizon with the mists of dawn still upon the budding forest which covered their slopes. It was a wide view, and lonely. No house or plume of smoke appeared. There were only the fading shadows of the valley and the mountains. The farm was at the end of the road.

—Daniel Doan, Amos Jackman

quartzite ledges you gaze down on NH 25A running beside Upper Baker Pond. Looking up, you see Mount Moosilauke dominating this view. In the distance to the left of Moosilauke are the Kinsmans. To the right you might be able to make out Mount Washington. Heading east, there are Mount Carrigain, Mount Osceola, Mount Kineo, Mount Tripyramid, Mount Passaconaway, Mount Whiteface, and Sandwich Mountain. From the northern outlook the view includes Jay Peak in Vermont and Black Mountain in East Haverhill.

Those who are returning by way of the South Cube Trail will go back to the South Peak summit. Others will descend the AT and the Mount Cube Trail, a pleasant path through spruce and fir down over roots and rocks into hardwoods and ferns, past a rock armchair, across brooks, on through overgrown pastures out to the car left beside the highway.

19

Lake Solitude/Mount Sunapee

Distance (round trip): 6½ miles

Walking time: 5 hours

Vertical rise: 1550 feet

Map: USGS 7½' x 15' Newport

Most people travel partway to Lake Solitude in chairlifts, riding to the top of Mount Sunapee. From the summit they walk the 1 mile to the lake. For hikers there is a better way: the Andrew Brook Trail.

Mount Sunapee State Park features a ski area on the north slopes of the 2726-foot mountain, with the standard assortment of park headquarters, summer picnic grounds, and lifts. There's also the state park beach on Lake Sunapee. An extensive forest insulates Lake Solitude from these attractions. Approached from the south by the Andrew Brook Trail, the little pond at 2500 feet seems far removed from the activity on the northern side of the mountain.

How to Get There

The road to the Andrew Brook Trail leaves NH 103 at 0.8 mile south of Newbury and the southern end of Lake Sunapee, partway down a hill. On the USGS map it has the engaging name of Between the Mountains Road. It's commonly called just the Mountain Road. A sign so designates it on the right side of NH 103. Turn right. The asphalt ribbon winds up the valley westward 1.2 miles to the start of the Andrew Brook Trail on the right. There's no sign, but you can identify the trail by an opening in the woods just before a bridge over the brook. A wide road shoulder accommodates several cars on the same side as the trail.

The Trail

Initially, the Andrew Brook Trail follows an old logging road. It keeps east of the brook and then crosses to the west bank. Soon it

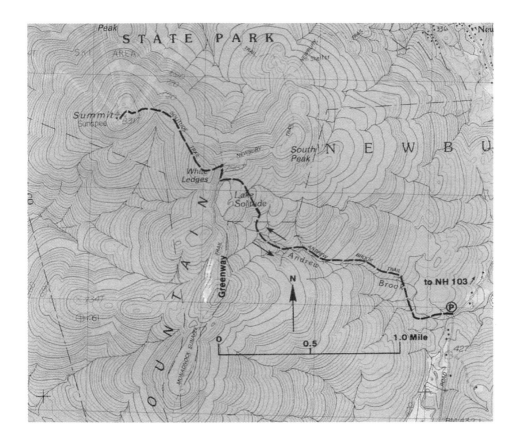

becomes a woods path paint blazed in blue rectangles, living up to its name with several crossings of the brook. The grade grows steep, and you have many stepping-stone lessons. You pass some extremely large, isolated yellow birches among the lesser leafy trees.

Approaching the lake, the trail leads through a boggy area of evergreens (mostly red spruce), levels for a short distance, and surmounts a geologic formation, in effect a dam that holds Lake Solitude on the mountainside. A wide and shallow ravine exposes layered metamorphic rock and glacial debris. Beyond this you climb among spruces to a little grassy flat bordering the lake. Directly opposite, White Ledge rises from the shore for 200 to 300 feet.

After this first outlook the trail turns right and skirts the eastern shore. At the north end of the lake and a little east of the cliffs, the Andrew Brook Trail ends at a junction about 2 miles from your car. You take the Lake Solitude Trail uphill on the right. Because it is now part of the almost 50-mile Monadnock-Sunapee Greenway, it's marked with rectangular white blazes similar to those on the Appalachian Trail. Signs direct you northward. (In a few hundred feet the Newbury Trail comes in on the right; this trail is blazed in orange.) The trail soon angles left steeply above the cliffs but still in the woods.

As you climb above the cliffs to the top of White Ledge, you step out on a great lookoff—and it *is* white! Far below, Lake

---

Solitude reflects blue sky. Looking out and away your eyes cannot take in the panorama all at once. It begins to the south at the Uncanoonucs near Manchester and sweeps east and north to the Franconia Range.

From White Ledge, which extends into the woods 50 yards north from the cliff, the trail makes a lengthy descent to a wooded col. The sinuous course of this path should be explored at a leisurely pace, for it traverses a varied mountain environment. The forest becomes mixed evergreen and deciduous. In June warblers flit in the trees that shade white starflowers, pink lady's slippers, and hobblebushes that display their large white blossoms. The trail rises over a slight knoll and levels again. The woods open up. Sunlight ahead turns out to be shining on the grass of a cleared slope east of the summit.

The trail swings across the ski slope and under the chairlift to another ski trail called the Skyway, which it crosses toward another chairlift's access path. Here you turn left and climb the last yards to the summit lodge.

Crossing green lawns you walk up steps to open sundecks around the lodge. You are level with leafy treetops and spires of evergreens and level, too, with blackpoll warblers, cedar waxwings, and perhaps a male redstart fluttering its black-and-flame-colored plumage. The sundeck also shows off the far northern mountains and nearby Lake Sunapee.

Inside the lodge, the snack bar is closed nowadays.

The return is by the same route. Descending across the ski slopes, don't become too absorbed with the scenery open before you. Watch for the signs at the entrance into the woods. Later at the junction near Lake Solitude, keep left onto the Andrew Brook Trail. Take a last look at the blue water below White Ledge. Then you're ready for the decent through the woods.

20

Mounts Morgan and Percival

Distance (round trip): 5 miles

Walking time: 4 hours

Vertical rise: 1452 feet

Maps: USDA/FS 7½' Squam Mountains; USGS 7½' Squam Mountains

This hike up two of the Squam Mountains starts from NH 113 north of Squam Lake. On a warm June day after a rain, the air here is heavy with the aroma that stirs my memory. The scent is from balm of Gilead trees growing near an old cellar hole beside the parking area. I think of summer days when I was a boy. These poplars or aspens give off a cloying but delightful odor. My past has nothing to do with Squam Lake, but homes in my boyhood were often shaded by balm of Gilead trees.

Here, the large granite foundation and tree-grown pit are all that remain of such a house. From among the scented trees it must have overlooked wide lawns and commanded a view across fields and pastures to Mount Morgan.

How to Get There

At Holderness just west of the bridge on NH 3, turn northward onto NH 113. Drive along the winding asphalt, which follows many of the irregularities of Squam Lake's shoreline. After 5 miles you pass a road to the right marked for Rockywold and Deephaven Camps as NH 113 bears uphill north of Rattlesnake Mountain. About 0.5 mile beyond the camp road along NH 113 you'll see a sign on the right for the Old Bridle Path up West Rattlesnake. Opposite it on the north side of NH 113 is the parking area for Rattlesnake and Morgan. If you're lucky, there'll be the aroma of balm of Gilead trees.

The Trail

The Mount Morgan Trail leaves northwest from the parking area. Keep to the left of an

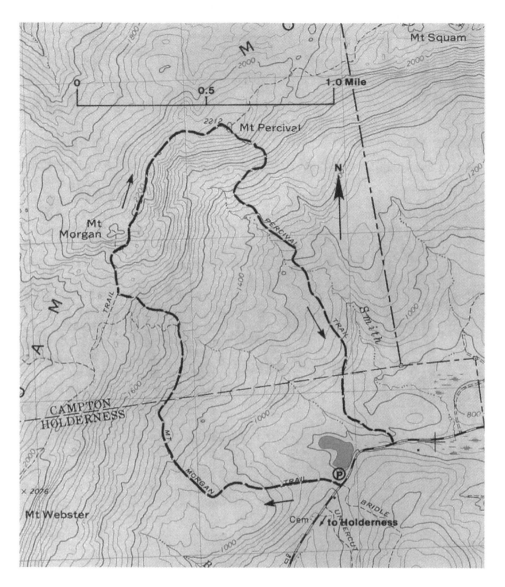

overgrown logging road. The trail, shown clearly on the current 7½' map, continues in a northwest direction following an old road. It heads more westerly, away from Mount Morgan, but don't worry, you're on the right trail. The good path is maintained by the Squam Lakes Association, whose yellow paint blazes mark it between neat signs at the junctions.

After a 20-minute warm-up with easy walking, you discover that the trail assumes its true character as a mountain path. You turn north, to the right, from the old road and begin the real climb.

The mountainside seems to have been cut over several times, and thus there's more reason for wonder at the survival of a huge, fallen hemlock you pass at about the 1-mile

Ruth Doan MacDougall

The view from Mount Morgan

mark. It's the biggest hemlock I ever saw.

At 1.7 miles the Mount Morgan Trail joins the Crawford-Ridgepole Trail, which extends the entire length of the Squam Mountains from the Sandwich Notch Road to Cotton Mountain near Holderness. Steps of rocks and logs help you climb. You begin to get glimpses ahead as the trees open toward the rocky summit, and a cliff appears on the left.

Ignore the wooden ladders and the cliff route. Straight ahead is safe, on the Crawford-Ridgepole and Mount Morgan Trails that curve below fallen rocks and the eastern precipice. You climb on stone stairways through thick spruces. Then you pass a junction where the Crawford-Ridgepole Trail bears right on its way to Mount Percival 0.8 mile away. You'll return here after climbing to Mount Morgan's lookoff and summit. Keep left up through the spruces.

After a few yards you see daylight to the left. A spur trail leads to a rounded ledge wide open to the south. In that direction the lookoff affords better views than the summit. Squam Lake extends east and west beyond Rattlesnake Mountain. Larger and farther away is Lake Winnipesaukee. The blue waters are intricately patterned with peninsulas and islands. Small ponds and lakes lie cupped in the forest. Ossipee Mountain, really a range of summits, looms in the east.

Returning to the summit trail, turn left and climb a few steps to a north view from the 2220-foot elevation. A rock cluster for a lookoff gives you wooded Sandwich Mountain and its west shoulder, craggy Black Mountain, above Sandwich Notch.

Now go back to the Crawford-Ridgepole Trail and turn left. Avoid an old trail branching right to a minor viewpoint. It may attract your feet despite the logs barring the way. Before the barrier, the main trail's yellow paint blazes and arrow lead up a ledge to the left.

The trail is then plain enough as it curves

toward Mount Percival over rocks and past oaks, with vistas on either side. You can see Mount Percival from some of the knolls. After almost a mile you climb finally over a rough section between evergreens and then step out on the open rock. Eastward you face a dropoff. The true summit is to your left, a rounded knob at 2212 feet.

Southward as on Morgan, the lakes absorb your attention. I wouldn't be surprised if Percival shows you more fresh water than can be seen anywhere in New Hampshire. The Belknap Mountains rise beyond Lake Winnipesaukee. Lake Kanasatka lies between Squam and Winnipesaukee. You see the northern tip of narrow Lake Winnisquam almost due south.

For mountains, turn east and north. Mount Chocorua's pinnacle identifies the eastern end of the Sandwich Range. Then nearer, Mount Paugus announces itself by its slides. Mount Passaconaway is a rounded triangle beyond Mount Whiteface. You recognize the long hump of Sandwich Mountain. With binoculars on a clear day you can see the tower on Mount Carrigain. It's to the left of Sandwich's west shoulder. You can also see Osceola and two ski trails on Tecumseh.

For the descent turn southeast and walk down the ledges to the woods where a sign marks the Mount Percival Trail. (The Crawford-Ridgepole Trail continues east along rocks with yellow blazes and cairns.) I'm never sure whether this first rough section of the Mount Percival Trail would be easier climbing down or up. A jumble of loose rocks and jagged chunks provides the most rugged terrain of the hike.

A path to the right from the summit descends and passes through the caves under the summit and joins the Mount Percival Trail on the other side.

Use caution picking your way down the Mount Percival Trail over the rocks, following the yellow blazes. Eventually the route becomes less precipitous. Part of the long descent has some stone steps. The the trail settles into a forest path.

Out of place in the woods, a stone wall appears, and the trail leads through it where there originally must have been a gate or barway. The land was once a hill farm. Farther along you pass a cellar hole on your left. Two great white birches grow on the chimney base. Stone walls continue under the trees.

TheThe trail follows the old farm road, crossing two overgrown clearings and becoming a truck road down to NH 113. At the asphalt you turn right, to the west, for the 0.5 mile to your car. You pass the site of a former beaver pond on your right, which Smith Brook flows through. The narrow winding road is in keeping with the balm of Gilead trees: They seem part of another era.

The White Mountains

The distances everywhere, and the wind, and clouds over the sun. I pulled on the big old heavy sweater and turned up the high collar as the rain came at us in sudden sheets.

The joy of resisting the elements, leaning into the wind, face and hair streaming water, but oh, the glory of it!

—*Daniel Doan,* Our Last Backpack

21

Mount Willard

Distance (round trip): 3 miles

Walking time: 2½ hours

Vertical rise: 950 feet

Maps: USDA/FS 7½' Crawford Notch; USGS 7½' Crawford Notch

The little railroad station at the north entrance to Crawford Notch is an information center operated by the Appalachian Mountain Club, which acquired the site of the vanished Crawford House. There at the station you might ask about the visibility before you climb Mount Willard; only a day of "ceiling and visibility unlimited" does justice to the breathtaking views from the 2865-foot summit cliff.

How to Get There

In Twin Mountain at the junction of US 3 and US 302, take US 302 east and drive 8.5 miles to the Crawford Notch Visitor Information Center, usually called the Crawford Depot. If you are coming from North Conway, the information center is 21 miles from the junction of US 302 and NH 16 in Glen.

For the Mount Willard Trail, hikers park their cars near the station or on the wide shoulders of US 302. Across the road, and despite the whizzing cars, Saco Lake manages to preserve its charm and typifies the romantic term "mountain tarn."

The Trail

From the station, you step over the Conway Scenic Railroad tracks and take up the Mount Willard Trail, which coincides with the Avalon Trail as you enter the woods and come to a junction. Turn left and follow the Mount Willard Trail through woods at the base of the slope. (The Mount Avalon Trail continues ahead to Mount Avalon and Mount Field.)

As you climb, at 0.5 mile you come to a short path right, from which you can look down at the golden rock slabs of Centennial Pool with its little waterfall.

Return to the trail. It has avoided a totally eroded section of the old carriage road, but now it rejoins this road that once served guests from the famous Crawford House, which burned in 1977. (The Crawford House property is now the site of an AMC hostel.) The grade was engineered for horses pulling surreys and passengers to the top.

At 1.5 miles, you'll see a sign for Hitchcock Flume to the left. Don't make this 20-minute side trip if you are hiking with children or if you have vertigo. The trail descends steeply over rocks and roots for 0.2 mile to reach a dangerous and dizzying gorge, 10 feet wide, 375 feet long, and 60 feet deep. Be extremely careful. The view swoops down to the highway and across the notch.

In 0.1 mile from the HITCHCOCK FLUME sign, the Mount Willard Trail brings you out on top of the cliff.

There before you spreads a vast and open sky. Mount Chocorua is the rocky peak. Nearer on the right looms Mount Willey, solid, bulky, and so steep its spruce forest is scarred by slides. Fortunately they have been less devastating than the slide that buried the Willey family in 1826. Nearer you toward the right, Mount Field rises to 4326 feet. That's 24 feet more than Mount Willey.

Opposite the notch and forming its eastern bastion, cliffs brace Mount Webster. Beyond Mount Webster, the southernmost of the Presidential Range's peaks, Mount Jackson, carries a tangle of spruce and fir to its topmost crags. Beyond those rocks, Mount Washington is a splendid sight against the sky. You may see above the western ridge a puff of smoke from the cog railway's engine.

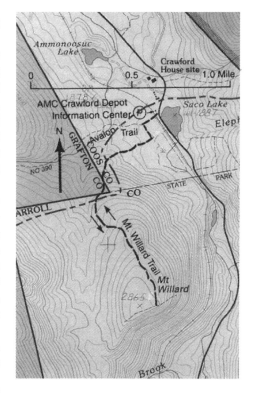

So far your eyes have been distracted out and aloft. If vertigo is no problem, you can gaze down into the impressive depth of the notch below the cliff. It's 1300 feet—and no protection—down to the highway and railroad tracks. The combination of Mount Willard and children tends to make parents nervous. A length of clothesline and a sturdy tree might be the best solution. Cliffs attract kids to the very edge.

People come and go. This is a popular hike. The universal reaction at the instant of stepping out on the rock is awe blended with delight (usually indicated by an involuntary gasp). The impact lingers in your memory. It's not the scenery alone; it's the power underlying our green and stone-ribbed world.

Descend by the same route.

22

The Sugarloaves

Distance (round-trip) : 3¼ miles

Walking time: 2¼ hours

Vertical rise: 1150 feet

Maps: USDA/FS 7½' Whitefield SE;
USGS 7½' x 15' Bethlehem

The two Sugarloaf summits, burned to the rock by a forest fire in the spring of 1903, handily satisfy the mountain-climbing urges of campers at nearby campgrounds. Families, couples, and loners run, walk, and saunter to the open ledges. The trail is easy and short. The summits are spectacular.

Except for some bushes and scrub spruces on Middle Sugarloaf, the views are totally exposed. North Sugarloaf lacks northern vistas because of screening spruces. Another peak in the series, South Sugarloaf, has no trail. It's not, therefore, part of this hike although it's the highest of the trio at 3024 feet. Middle Sugarloaf is 2539; North Sugarloaf 2310. The series forms a ridge that runs north and south, separating the Zealand River on the east from the Little River on the west.

The two Sugarloaves in this hike, rising only 10 miles west of Mount Washington, present one of the finest views of the peak as your reward for a climb that is only a slightly strenuous jaunt. Surely another reason why the Sugarloaves attract hikers is their challenging appearance, peculiar in their rounded, bare rocks. They resemble not today's sugar cubes, of course, but old-time conical loaves that housewives had to take a hammer to before pulverizing the pieces with mortar and pestle. The barren summits catch your eye while you drive past on US 302.

How to Get There

To reach the Sugarloaf Trail turn south off US 302 onto the forest service's Zealand Road, 2.5 miles east of Twin Mountain vil-

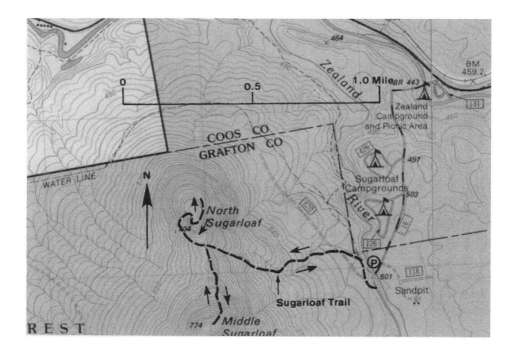

lage. If you are driving northwest on US 302, the turn is about 6 miles from the Crawford Notch Visitor Information Center. The paved road is the entrance to Zealand Recreation Area.

Here tents and campers have replaced sawmills, lumberjacks, teamsters, and railroad men. Zealand was a busy lumber settlement north of the present US 302 until 1897, when the sawmills and houses went up in smoke. This put an end to J.E. Henry's Zealand operations, but he went on with his other lands and became the lumber baron of Lincoln and the Pemigewasset River's East Branch country. The upper Zealand River valley, and incidentally Henry's logging railroad camps, suffered their most devastating fire in 1886. From Middle Sugarloaf you can look south and see how miraculously the forests have returned.

Follow the Zealand Road over the Ammonoosuc River and uphill. High on the flat above the river, you pass to the east of the Sugarloaf Campgrounds. You are approaching the tributary, Zealand River, and at a little less than 1 mile from US 302 you come to a bridge over it. There's plenty of parking to the right before the bridge. (The Zealand Road continues another 2.7 miles to a dead end and the start of the Zealand Trail up the river to Zealand Pond and the AMC's Zealand Falls Hut.)

The Trail

In June, watch for lady's slippers beside the trail and on Middle Sugarloaf summit.

The Sugarloaf Trail is blazed yellow. It begins on the far side of the bridge, and initially it coincides with the Trestle Trail beside the river. The path is level along the west bank. The stream flows transparently, showing each stone on the bottom.

After 0.25 mile, the Sugarloaf Trail leaves the river at a left fork. (The Trestle Trail continues ahead to complete its loop over the river on a bridge and back to the

On Middle Sugarloaf

road.) Turn left. The trail crosses a woods road. Soon you pass two monstrous rocks pried loose by the glacier and dropped here, along with smaller ones farther on. Both peaks show the rocky southeast faces typical of mountains filed down by the great ice sheet's rock teeth.

The trail leads up more steeply to switchbacks and rock steps. As you approach the col between Middle Sugarloaf on the left and North Sugarloaf on the right, trail signs direct you to routes for both summits. This hike chooses Middle Sugarloaf first. Bear left at the fork and cross a flat with spruce woods and bracken ferns. Look for wood sorrel and bunchberry. Perhaps you'll hear an ovenbird's *teacher, TEAcher, TEACHER!* The trail circles to its final approach in the upper spruces. The last steep angle on crumbly rock and gravel is by way of a set of ladder steps provided by the forest service for safety and assistance. You

emerge on the bare granite summit.

To the southwest you see North Twin Mountain rearing its sharp, wooded peak above a precipitous buttress. North Twin seems to join the ridge that extends left toward South Twin. (It doesn't.) Walking west toward the edge, you look down on Twin Mountain's long line of motels, stores, restaurants, and amusement enterprises. By moving south and over the low vines of three-toothed cinquefoil (white flowers in late June), you come to the cliff of rocky outcroppings I've previously mentioned as having been filed away by the glacier. Before you, Mount Hale appears 2 miles away as a truncated pyramid slightly notched on top.

But these views are pale in comparison to the great panorama—the Presidentials—eastward. Beyond the Rosebrook Range on the horizon, sometimes in haze or clouds, sometimes as sharp as its broadcasting towers, Mount Washington displays its treeless summit. Mount Monroe flanks it on the south. Mounts Clay, Jefferson, and Adams do the same on the north. Directly north and nearer stands isolated and shapely Cherry Mountain.

Middle Sugarloaf is more popular than North Sugarloaf. You are more likely to find privacy for lunch by heading back to the col between the peaks and keeping straight toward North Sugarloaf. Bearing left, the trail descends briefly. Then you circle west under a wooded cliff and loop back toward the summit on a gradual climb. Then abruptly you step out on the open ledge of North Sugarloaf.

Your more northern viewpoint here reveals another Presidential peak beyond the Rosebrook Range. It's Mount Eisenhower. "Peak" is a misnomer for this bald dome. (An easy way to identify Mount Eisenhower is to remember that Ike was bald.)

Here on the summit "rock hounds" have collected smoky quartz. A permit to remove specimens with hand tools is not required in the national forest. No explosives are allowed, and you should fill in any holes to restore a natural appearance.

For your return, retrace your steps to the col. Turn left, to the east. Now you have a relaxing walk back to the Zealand Road.

Arethusa Falls/Frankenstein Cliff

Distance (round trip): 4½ miles

Walking time: 3½ hours

Vertical rise: 1200 feet

Maps: USDA/FS 7½' Crawford Notch; USGS 7½' Crawford Notch; USDA/FS 7½' Stairs; USGS 7½' Stairs

Arethusa Falls and Frankenstein Cliff: such baroque names for a waterfall on Bemis Brook and a series of exposed rock strata above US 302 in Crawford Notch State Park—but they are special.

Plunging more than 200 feet, Arethusa Falls are the highest in New Hampshire. The orchid arethusa, with its magenta-crimson flowers, is said to have once bloomed at the falls. This orchid usually displays its three-pronged, tongued flowers in bogs. There is no bog at the falls. I wonder whether some poetic young lady of the horse-drawn-carriage-and-hotel era named the falls while reading Shelley. The nymph Arethusa appears in his poetry.

The magnificent geologic formation that drops Bemis Brook at the falls appears again northward as Frankenstein Cliff. Named not from Mary Shelley's novel but for an artist, Godfrey N. Frankenstein, who loved to paint the mountains, the cliff provides a lookoff to sweeping views of the notch.

A loop hike takes you to both of these natural wonders. The opportunity to study a man-made wonder—the steel railroad trestle—is a bonus. I suggest a visit to the falls in early summer or after a rainy spell, when the flow of water is more spectacular than during dry weather.

How to Get There

Three miles south of the Willey House site on US 302, or about 8.5 miles north of Bartlett, a large sign on the west side of the highway identifies the approach to Arethusa Falls. Leave your car either in the parking

Arethusa Falls

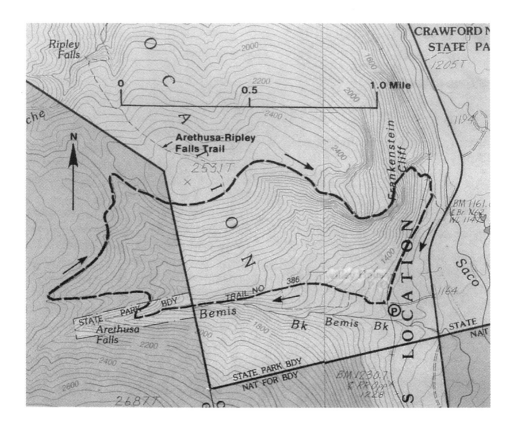

area immediately off the access road or in another area farther uphill.

The Trail

Beyond the railroad tracks there's a private house. The little white cottage—or Willey House Post Office, as it was known—is gone. You'll find the sign for the Arethusa Falls Trail on the left across the railroad tracks. Frankenstein Cliff dominates the northern view along the tracks.

The 1.5-mile trail to the falls is easy and popular. I've met tourists in city clothes and street shoes. More comfortable clothes and sturdy boots are necessary for a full hike around the cliffs.

The path leads up a slope with fine white birches. Soon the Bemis Brook Trail forks left at a sign. (It leads to pools and minor falls before returning to the main trail.) Now you begin to climb. You pass the upper junction of the Bemis Brook Trail and find yourself high above the brook, which is mostly hidden by trees on the precipitous bank. The trail, more level, clings to the valley wall.

Trail wear here has exposed spruce roots in an intricate pattern. They do a good job of stopping erosion. You can see how their intertwined tentacles hold the earth on mountainsides.

Gradually the trail slants down to the brook, which you cross on a bridge. The trail remains close to the brook and becomes rough. Then you see the falls through the branches of big spruces.

The water forms a long, narrow veil over

the cliff. During times of freshets the cascade becomes a clear drop. For the best view, and for the distance necessary to get the falls in a camera viewfinder, cross the brook as the trail sign indicates and observe the falls near the trail's entrance into the woods.

Continuing through the spruces, you are now on the Arethusa–Ripley Falls Trail. Don't assume that this graded path will continue for the remainder of your loop hike. Just enjoy it for about 0.5 mile. There is still rugged hiking ahead.

The Arethusa–Ripley Falls Trail leads you toward Frankenstein Cliff. You swing left over a ridge and up between trees that line a small stream on your right. The trail turns north again as you cross the brook at an abrupt right angle.

Climbing more steeply to a fork 1 mile from the falls, you leave the Arethusa-Ripley Falls Trail and keep right onto the Frankenstein Cliff Trail. It descends easterly, and you soon come out on a glacier-smoothed stone dome. The trail skirts the north side of this rounded ledge and enters a notable spruce forest where tree trunks are tall, straight, and without branches for 20 feet or more. The spruce needles are springy underfoot. The trail is 10 or 15 yards from the cliffs, so you pass various lookoffs.

After walking about 0.5 hour from the Arethusa–Ripley Falls Trail junction, you come to the best view. Over the treetops and across the valley, a broad, green slope rises toward the summit of Mount Bemis. The white line at the head of the valley is Arethusa Falls. Bemis Brook drains into the Saco River, which flows between wide sandbars on its way to meadows in Bartlett and Conway. Miniature cars speed along US 302. The highway is straighter than the railroad tracks curving along the grade above

it. The more you look down, the higher you seem, although the elevation is only about 2000 feet above sea level. The total drop to the parking area and your car is 800 feet.

Chocorua displays its distinctive spire in the far distance southeast, with the long ridge of Moat Mountain to the left. Mount Paugus is a hump to the right of Chocorua overshadowed by Mount Passaconaway. Eastward across the highway and up the ridges beyond the Saco River, you see Mount Crawford's squared crown at its northside cliff.

When you've enjoyed the scenery, follow the trail again on a gradual descent through the spruces that continue growing to the cliff's edge. Here you must watch for the woods to change from spruce and fir to leafy trees because the trail is obscure as it drops abruptly to the right down a break in the cliffs. You could be misled by the easier walking straight ahead in the leafy trees; I was.

Keep to the right climbing down among ledges and small maples and beeches. A big fallen oak lies beside the trail as the slope moderates. Watch for several switchbacks in the hardwood forest. You may notice old ax blazes along with newer paint. Your general direction is north under more cliffs. Steep descents alternate with slabbing. Soon you turn south (right), and you have to scramble over fallen rocks in the cool shade where water drops off a cliff. From here you enter beech woods once more.

Rotten stone grades the trail with gravel. It results from the natural weathering of certain granites. Rain and carbon dioxide form carbonic acid; this washes out the orthoclase, or potash feldspar, so the rock almost literally comes unglued. The effect is common in many areas of the White Mountains. On steep slopes the gravel can be treacherous underfoot.

During the final descent you'll be walking through the open woods. Looking ahead you'll see black lines gleaming through the oaks and beeches. You are approaching the great steel curve of the Frankenstein Trestle's girders.

The trail takes you under the massive, curving steel frame whose giant legs rest on foundations of squared rock, not on concrete. If you look up and study the girders you'll see, under layers of black paint, the name CARNEGIE.

Beyond the trestle the trail keeps to the contours below the railroad grade. To your left you look into the tops of beeches and yellow birches. A moderate slope up brings you back to the parking area.

By the way, don't walk on the tracks. That's trespassing, which, like investigating the trestle, is strictly forbidden.

24

Welch and Dickey Mountains

Distance (round trip): 4½ miles

Walking time: 4 hours

Vertical rise: 1860 feet

*Maps: USDA/FS 7½' Waterville Valley;
USGS 7½' Waterville Valley*

The sparsely wooded, rocky hump of Welch Mountain looms up from the north bank of Mad River at the entrance to Waterville Valley. Tourists on I-93 speculate about the strange and barren formation. Hikers at once want to climb it.

Welch, elevation 2605 feet, is a small yet varied peak. Exciting ledge scrambles lead to spectacular views and a rare evergreen: the little jack pine of the far north.

Dickey, 2734 feet, a short distance north of Welch and similarly composed of rounded rock faces and flat ledges, provides an unusual look at Franconia Notch and the mountains bordering that famous pass.

Welch and Dickey are fine for a spring hike because snow melts early on the open, southerly rocks. In autumn, these two give you a really special foliage hike. The treetops in the depths west of the summits are dazzling in sunlight. I have stared into the gigantic montage and thought I must be seeing every conceivable blend of red and yellow.

How to Get There

From Campton off I-93's Exit 28, NH 49, the route into Waterville Valley, leads east along the Mad River. At Goose Hollow, 2.7 miles from the traffic lights in Campton, it crosses the river. Stay on NH 49 another 1.7 miles; then turn left onto the Upper Mad River Road. At once you cross Six Mile Bridge, which despite its name is only 4.5 miles from Campton.

Beyond the bridge drive up a steep hill. Keep going past the Gateway Townhouses on the right and several other roads for the

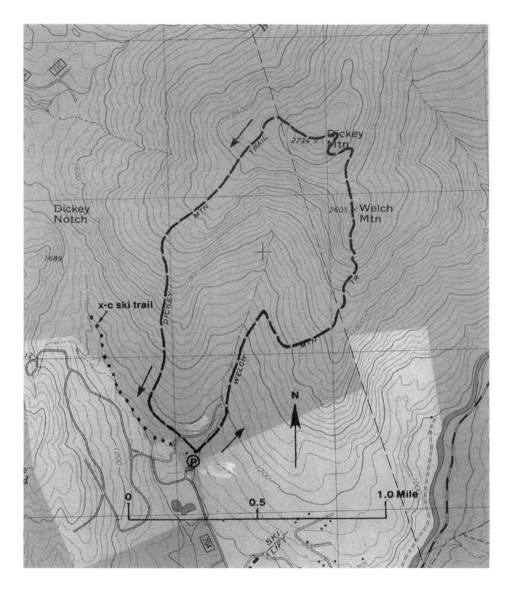

homes and condominiums nearby. At 0.7 mile from Six Mile Bridge, turn right onto Orris Road and drive another 0.7 mile. Just beyond Woodwinds Drive on the left, you come to the parking area on the right.

The Trail

This hike loops up and over both Welch and Dickey Mountains, descending Dickey's west shoulder to your car here at the parking area. The trails meet at a junction in the woods behind the bulletin board.

I must warn you against undertaking this climb in wet or icy weather, as it involves many steep, bare rock faces. But in good weather it's a joy.

At the junction mentioned above, take the fork to the right, the Welch Mountain

Tripyramid in the distance

Trail. It follows an old logging road, soon crosses a brook, and maintains a moderate grade up the east bank through fine hardwoods. On at least one of the beeches you may notice the claw marks left by a bear climbing after beechnuts. The view to the left, in seasons when the trees are leafless, reveals the cliffs of Dickey Mountain. You will descend along the tops of them.

As the Welch Mountain Trail becomes steeper, it also turns right. Well marked with yellow paint blazes, it climbs into spruces. Near the top of the ridge you step out onto sloping, bare bedrock, typical of the trails over these mountains. Not far above, and about 45 minutes from your car, you reach the barren ridge below Welch. Turn left (north) toward the crags leading to Welch's summit. Be careful not to step on the fragile soils; stay on the trail or ledges.

Here you walk along cliffs overlooking boulder-strewn Mad River, the ribbon of asphalt called NH 49, and the eastern valley. Across the river and highway, the great ridge is Sandwich Mountain. The gap to the

south is Sandwich Notch.

Beyond this lookoff, the cairns and yellow blazes lead you up among the ledges and sparse, windblown trees. The summit crown rises directly ahead. Trees grow below and above a huge stone sphere that seems to protrude from the mountain. The grade is easy but impressive because you're climbing the spherical face.

You walk through an entrance into the spruces; the trail curves high into jumbled rocks. Here you encounter a briefly demanding climb and passages through narrow clefts.

Angling up open ledges, you find yourself among jack pines. They occur in three other New Hampshire areas: near Mount Chocorua, Mount Webster, and at Lake Umbagog. Short, twin needles surround tight cones that cling for years to the wiry branches. Limbs protrude in twisted toughness along the length of the trunks. Some of the jack pines grow as high as 20 feet.

Beneath the sheltering boughs, snowshoe hares have scattered numerous pellets

Welch and Dickey Mountains

as they nibbled at undergrowth during the snowy season, to which they adapt by turning from summer brown to white. A more obvious scat than the pellets decorated a ledge when I was last there. It was a product of a bobcat, who is, as was demonstrated by the compacted white hair within the scat, higher on nature's food chain than the hare.

Climb on to the summit. The crags offer an almost entire round of distant mountains closed only to the north, where Dickey's stone knob and scrubby trees hide Franconia Notch.

To the east the slide on the southernmost of three peaks identifies Mount Tripyramid. In the opposite direction, to the west, Mount Moosilauke stands above adjacent mountains. The pool of water in the forest southwest of the rock ridge that braces Dickey is Cone Pond. To complete the panorama, continue the hike for a look north from Dickey, only another 0.5 mile on.

The descent north from Welch begins along yellow blazes on the summit rocks and continues down ledges that form natural, wide steps. Cross the open col and enter spruce woods. You climb to the broad, spherical rock face, similar to Welch.

Follow the yellow blazes to Dickey's summit, where bushes and evergreens surround areas of rock. Look to the east and you'll see an extensive bare rock surface beyond scrub spruces. For tremendous views up into Franconia Notch, you must go to that rock surface. You may follow a trail through the spruces, or you may descend the summit rocks and take a more direct route marked by random cairns and footpaths in sphagnum moss and scrub.

As you walk up the easy slope of the rock, you see glacial erratics scattered all about. On the long dome, if you can look down from the panorama, you'll see a distinctive vein of white quartzite in the bedrock as straight as a chalk line.

Far up the valley of the Pemigewasset River, silhouettes sharply outline the northern horizon. Mounts Lafayette, Lincoln, and Flume rise as triangular peaks east of deep Franconia Notch. For a contrast in mountain shapes, Cannon Mountain west of the notch appears as an inverted bowl. Looking south and west you see Moosilauke, Kineo, Stinson, and distant Cardigan.

For your descent, return to the summit of Dickey. Follow the trail into evergreens and thicker woods. There is another outlook toward Franconia Notch before the trail turns left and you start down. It soon emerges from the woods and crosses areas of rough but rounded rock, mostly slanting south toward the valley that separates you from Welch. You briefly enter woods again, only to cross more bedrock exposed to the sky. Watch for cairns and blazes. A blaze on a tree at the far side of each open rock slope shows you the entrance into the next patch of woods.

About 15 minutes from Dickey's summit the trail turns left up a rock knob, then descends along a rounded rock ridge bordered by trees on your right. You begin an interesting walk along the dropoff over the cliffs. Because of the rounded surface, there is no actual "edge" in the usual sense of the term. Keep close to the woods on the right.

Below the rock ridge you enter the woods and pass to the right of a vertical ledge 8 or 10 feet high and over 100 feet long. The trees change from evergreen to deciduous, with many large red oaks. In June you'll see lady's slippers. The trail keeps to the top of a narrow ridge that slopes gradually down to an ancient logging road. Stay on the trail; then after 5 minutes turn left at a junction with another woods road, now a bike trail. You soon reach the junction with the Welch Mountain Trail and step out of a little ravine into the parking area.

25

Mount Doublehead

Distance (round trip): 4 miles

Walking time: 3¼ hours

Vertical rise: 1770 feet

Maps: USDA/FS 7½' Jackson; USGS 7½' Jackson; USDA/FS 7½' Chatham; USGS 7½' Chatham

There's a Mount Doublehead near Jackson and another in the Squam Range. I'm talking here about the Doublehead northeast of Jackson. The rounded wooded summits have elevations as nearly identical as their contours: North Doublehead, 3053 feet; South Doublehead, 2939 feet.

I recommend this loop hike for the views and for the log cabin atop North Doublehead. The outlooks from the ledges are fine and sweeping. The Presidentials, the Carter-Wildcat Range, and the Saco valley are all seen from unusual angles. The cabin is so perfect it belongs in a museum. A US Forest Service project built long ago, and an adjunct to the old ski trail, the cabin is as delicate as the mountain environment. It has recently been renovated and can be rented. For details about reservations, call or visit the Saco Ranger Station on the Kancamagus Highway in Conway, (603) 447-5448.

How to Get There

The access road toward Doublehead leaves Jackson north of the stores. It's the east section of NH 16B. (Don't take NH 16B west of the stone bridge.) Drive up the hill, bearing right on NH 16B at a fork. From the hilltop you can look to your right across fields and woods to Doublehead. Drive down to the corner at Whitney's Inn and turn past onto the Dundee Road. (NH 16B forks left.) Keep past the Black Mountain Ski Area and the Black Mountain Road on your left. Less than 0.5 mile from the Black Mountain Road, you come to the start of this hike's climb: Doublehead Ski Trail, also on your left, 2.5 miles from Jackson.

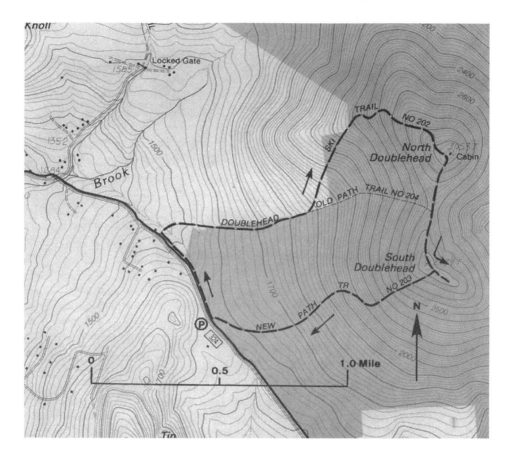

But don't get out of your car yet. Drive on another 0.5 mile and park off the road opposite the New Path, which will be your return route. Shoulder your rucksack and walk back down the road to the Doublehead Ski Trail. This warm-up for the hike leaves your car ready and waiting when you descend by the New Path.

The Trail

If confronted with the Doublehead Ski Trail, the modern skier probably wouldn't believe that this 12-foot corridor winding up through hardwoods was a ski trail at all (or if he did he'd chuckle over the quaintness of it). I shudder to think that we skied such corkscrews in the 1930s, not to mention first

climbing them. The forest service, anticipating disaster, housed a rescue toboggan and other emergency equipment in a small shed partway up the trail. It was built on posts to raise it above snow and lined with tin against squirrels and mice.

At about 0.5 mile, you pass the Old Path forking right from the ski trail. (The Old Path leads to the col between North and South Doublehead and meets the Doublehead Ski Trail at the summit of North Doublehead.) Continuing on the ski trail, you next pass the remains of the forest service shed.

As you climb on, following the curves from contour to contour, you may wonder where all the mountain came from; it didn't

The forest service cabin on Mount Doublehead

look so big as you drove toward it. The trail goes at the steep upper section without much regard for the angle. Evergreen woods are deep in forest duff, which supports thriving colonies of clintonia and bunchberry.

The cabin appears through the spruces just north of the trail junction with the col trail to South Doublehead, on the right. Evergreens nearly surround the cabin. An outlook has been cut to show Mount Washington, Lion Head above Tuckerman Ravine, and Huntington Ravine. In the opposite direction from the cabin, an opening in the woods reveals the eastern view to Mountain Pond and the Saco River's East Branch valley.

Sunlight and shadows pattern the cabin's peeled spruce logs. They have a special sheen that seems remarkably light despite the years of weathering. The walls are joined at the corners by rounded notches on the lower side of each log so no rain can accumulate to rot the wood—and they fit snugly. Asphalt shingles on the roof are more recent protection. The center room has essential furnishings: tables, benches, a woodstove. Off this communal room, four bunkrooms, two on each side, contain two bunks apiece.

Everywhere is evidence of skillful work by men using simple tools such as ax, crosscut saw, and adze. The rafters fit true to the plate logs so the roof is absolutely true. Walls inside dividing off the bunkrooms are made of smaller poles carefully trimmed and fitted. Door frames set nicely into the logs. A cabinetmaker might well approve of all the joints in the cabin—allowing for the tools and material used.

This is the cabin all of us dream about at one time or another when the real world becomes too much for us. It should be preserved and cared for not only by the forest service but also by those who use it.

Your route to South Doublehead begins with the Old Path at the junction south of the cabin. It descends through the evergreens to the col. Here the Old Path departs right to rejoin the Doublehead Ski Trail. Continue ahead on the New Path, climbing South Doublehead. Lookoff ledges appear on the right. When the New Path turns to descend to Dundee Road, stay on the spur trail to the various open outlooks on the east-west summit ridge. (You will return to this junction for your descent.) Cairns mark the two main viewing spots.

Explorations on these ledges reward you with views to Kearsarge North and Jackson village. Vistas east reveal Chatham, Baldface Mountain, Evans Notch, and Kezar Lake in Maine.

The west lookoff from South Doublehead shows you Mount Washington and a section of the auto road at the Horn. The Wildcat summits, Carter Notch, and Carter Dome appear from the unusual angles I mentioned. You can see the Dome's south-

east shoulder and eastward as far as the rocky eminence at the headwaters and beaver ponds (out of sight) on Red Brook, which drains into Wild River.

Northwest with binoculars you can pick out the summit cairn on Mount Eisenhower in the line of southern Presidential peaks. To the south Moat Mountain's craggy summits show clearly, and farther away, to the west, Mount Carrigain can be identified with binoculars by locating the lookout tower.

Return to the New Path to descend South Doublehead. The way is very steep. Soon you drop to a growth completely mixed with mountain trees: spruce, fir, mountain maple, moosewood, birch, and poplar. The trail, continuing steep, takes you into larger spruces. Here, in June, both pink and white lady's slippers grow in open shade. The forest becomes leafy with beech and yellow birch.

Following an old logging road, the trail completes its descent to the Dundee Road. You pass stone walls built when all this was pasture and cropland. Your car is nearby.

26

Black Mountain

Distance (round trip): 3¾ miles

Walking time: 3½ hours

Vertical rise: 1800 feet

Maps: USDA/FS 7½' East Haverhill; USGS 7½' East Haverhill

Two or three New Hampshire elevations named Black Mountain come to mind. I have often wondered if the adjective originated when early settlers looked up at the dark spruce forests in the days before logging and fires laid bare the summits. This one in Benton, with its 2830-foot elevation, exposes to the sun a long ledge that sparkles with quartzite. An open shoulder gives you a 0.5-hour climb among spruces and bare outlooks before you reach the summit. The ledge offers wide views. This western outpost of the White Mountains overlooks forested valleys to the east toward imposing Mount Moosilauke. To the west it shows you the Connecticut River valley and green farmland extending to the Vermont hills. Don't be misled into thinking that this is an easy hike by Black Mountain's relatively low elevation. The upper section of the Chippewa Trail is *steep.*

If you climb Black Mountain during the last week of May or early in June, you'll find splendid rose-purple masses of flowers among the upper rocks. The shrub rhodora blooms before its leaves unfold, so there is almost no green. On a sunny day when you climb over a creamy quartzite ledge and look down on a pocket of solid magenta, the color hits your eyes.

How to Get There

Although the mountain rises in Benton, your route to the Chippewa Trail lies through East Haverhill. The village is on NH 25 between Pike and Glencliff. In the center of town, turn right at a sign saying E. HAVERHILL. You are now on Lime Kiln Road, which soon turns to

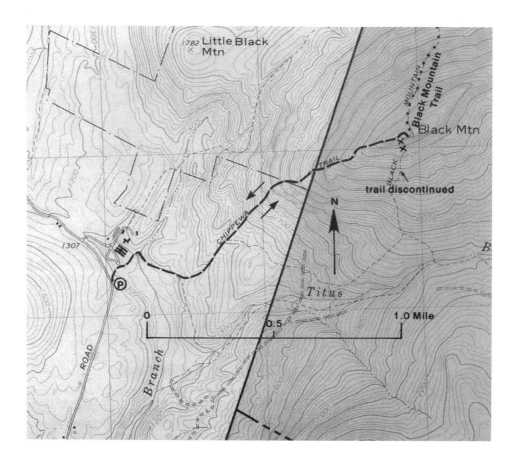

gravel. After 1.5 miles bear left at a fork. Drive 1.7 miles more to a small clearing on the right for parking. There may be no sign.

The Trail

Your way is marked by yellow blazes. The trail at once descends to a small brook, then maneuvers around some beaver activity and reaches a woods road.

Here is an opportunity for a fascinating detour to the Lime Kilns. (Depending on your schedule, you may want to postpone it until your descent.) The trail turns right, but to see the Lime Kilns you turn left and walk about 0.1 mile to a small brook. There may be a LIME KILNS sign. Turn right here and walk another 0.1 mile up to the kilns, where in the

1800s limestone was heated to release lime.

After marveling at these huge ovens, retrace your steps to the point at which you reached the woods road. About 50 yards farther, you come to a fork. Keep left as indicated by an arrow on a tree. The road leads uphill into spruces and overgrown fields. You're walking an old farm road. In the cellar of a vanished house white birches grow. Ahead you look up at Black Mountain rising steeply. To the right is a similar, quartzite-crowned mountain, Sugarloaf.

The trail goes directly upward among dense pines and then among juniper through more overgrown fields. The trail is dirt, like a cow path, but this one is not from

Trying to tip Tipping Rock

cows' hooves. It goes up too straight. Cows, no longer in evidence here, always graze along contours.

The skyward climb is quite serious for about 20 minutes. Then a turn to the right gives you a respite with level going. But a left turn takes you up steeply again, this time into a fine stand of spruces thriving on the mountainside as far up as you can see. Branchless for 20 feet or more, straight as plumb lines, they're just right for a log cabin.

You'll be seeing blue blazes that mark a property line. Ignore them. Many of the trees are now red pines. The yellow blazes lead you up until the trail begins to wind among looming stone outcrops. Smooth and rounded by the glacier, the ledges show striations etched by sharp rocks embedded in the ice sheet. Here rhodora and blueberry bushes grow in the openings, and from several ledges you can look west to North Haverhill and to the green meadows bordering the Connecticut River.

One lookoff ledge, about 100 feet to the right, shows you a vista south down the valley. The trail bears left. You climb toward the blue sky and are now and then briefly in spruces. You feel like a mountaineer as you scramble with both toeholds and handholds. You are exposed to white rock, cool shade, sun, and wind. Then you are clear of trees on a bright quartzite knob, and suddenly ahead, beyond a short col, a cliff rises to the topmost ledge.

At the base of the cliff the Chippewa Trail turns sharp left. Here once stood the cabin for the lookout who manned the vanished summit tower. Keep left around the cliff's base. There's a short grade through spruce woods; turn to the right. (Ahead the Black Mountain Trail descends 2.5 miles to a town road in Benton.) You leave the evergreens behind and step up on bare rock.

From the summit you face a sweep of

forest all the way to Moosilauke, massively occupying the horizon beyond Mount Clough. To the left of Mount Clough, almost hidden in trees, Long Pond's shoreline extends to a glimpse of blue water at the north end. Nearer on the right, Sugarloaf presents its rocks, now lower than you are by about 220 feet. From it a ridge called the Hogsback extends to Blueberry Mountain. Away to the left, to the northeast, bulky Mount Kinsman hides some of the Franconia Range.

For views to the south, walk along the ledge. I like to look south because I can see the hills of Orford, my boyhood summer home, and Mount Cube, my first mountain. Its shining quartzite stands out between wooded Piermont Mountain to the north and Smarts Mountain to the south.

One of the main attractions on Black Mountain is the bird-watching from the summit. Swallows always skim by; sometimes there are hawks and ravens; warblers and white-throated sparrows are often in the spruces.

Another attraction awaits you northward.

Keep to the crest of the ledges. You may find faded yellow arrows in places. Pick your way down to a narrow line of evergreens and into open space again. Tipping Rock is plainly visible to your right. Maybe once this glacial erratic, 7 or 8 feet through and equally high, actually tipped. Now it rests solidly above the cliff on rocks jammed under it.

When you are ready to descend from the summit, you'll be facing west toward the green valley. North Haverhill appears as a double row of toy houses along the main street. Beyond the Connecticut River in Vermont you can see Newbury's church spire above the treetops. The serene fields, farms, and villages contrast with the wild forest and mountains behind you.

The descent is the Chippewa Trail in reverse. Below the summit turn left, to the south. Below the cliff turn right. When you reach the woods road near the end of the hike, remember to visit the Lime Kilns, unless you made this side trip earlier.

If you've had the forethought to park your car in morning sunlight, it's probably shaded and cool now in the afternoon.

27

Mount Tecumseh

Distance (round trip): 4¼ miles

Walking time: 4 hours

Vertical rise: 2000 feet

*Maps: USDA/FS 7½' Waterville Valley;
USGS 7½' Waterville Valley*

A springtime mountain, Tecumseh overlooks sunny Waterville Valley from the west, and its slopes receive the warmth necessary for a new hiking season. Or course, you'll have to expect snow under the shading spruces as you approach the 4003-foot summit, as well as back across the ridge to the ski-lift terminal. But during your descent, the ski slopes will be bare turf and gloriously open to the mountains and the greening valley.

I've climbed Mount Tecumseh as early as May 3. I carried no snowshoes and relied on packed snow in the trail left by winter climbers. Snowshoes, however, if you plan to hike early in the season, would be good insurance.

How to Get There

Take Exit 28 off I-93. From Campton, NH 49 follows the Mad River to Waterville Valley's ski resort. Ten minutes from Campton a left turn puts you onto the Tripoli Road and across the river. Drive 1.2 miles to the access road for the Tecumseh Ski Area. Turn left onto the access road and continue to the beginning of a loop, where you go right. In a very short distance you'll see the trailhead for the Mount Tecumseh Trail on the right. Park in parking lot 1 or 2 on the left, opposite the trailhead.

The scarred mountain to the east is Tripyramid with its North Slide.

The Trail

In early May you'll notice the trees are still bare as you climb an easy grade along the south bank of Tecumseh Brook, which has

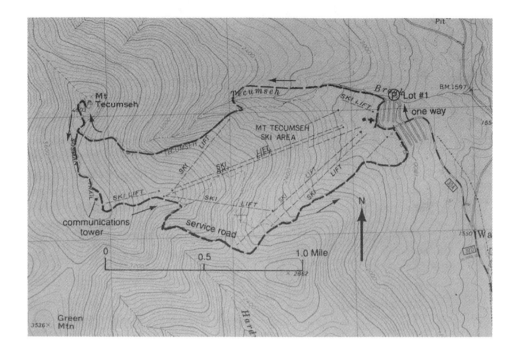

a seasonal flow. Yellow blazes direct you onto the 1-mile section of the trail that was relocated off the ski slope. You cross Tecumseh Brook on stepping-stones for a moderate steady climb along a small ridge. A log staircase descends to the brook, and after you cross it another log staircase ascends to where the new trail joins the old trail 50 feet from the ski slope. A signpost indicates the trail to the summit and the view from the slope.

The great advantage of spring climbing is the leafless forest. Yellow birches have green-tipped twigs, buds on beeches are lengthening, but the sudden bursting of foliage is a week or two away. No leaves hide the view north to Mount Osceola and its separate East Peak.

Below these wide views, tree trunks stand in scattered rows along aisles extending in all directions. The forest is spacious and lively with migrating birds. A myrtle warbler, yellow, white, and black among a shadbush's white-lace flowers, can make

you a lifelong birdwatcher.

When you turn from the view and continue up the trail, you glimpse a spruce-clad flattened dome, which is your destination on this hike.

The seasons reverse themselves as you climb. Early spring surrounded you at the start along Tecumseh Brook. There all kinds of plants were rushing to airy life after a winter protected by fallen leaves. Now at 3000 feet, late winter encloses you. Snow crunches beneath your boots, and the air is cold. If you step off the packed track, you plunge at once to your knees. The woods have changed to wintry evergreens.

The trail swings northerly up toward the summit. The Sosman Trail, on the left, joins and will be part of your descent route. After about 200 yards, it branches left up through the spruces; the Tecumseh Trail keeps on straight. Either will take you to the summit, but for spring walking on a packed snow track, Sosman probably offers more solid footing.

The view of the Waterville Valley from the summit of Tecumseh

So turn left onto the Sosman Trail. It circles west of the summit, opens to a good view toward Mount Moosilauke, then climbs steeply in an S-turn past wooded ledges to the partially open summit. (The Mount Tecumseh Trail, arriving at the summit from the east, descends north to the Tripoli Road 3.25 miles away.)

The northern horizon is the commanding sight from Mount Tecumseh. In May it centers on snowy Mount Washington, seen between Mount Osceola and East Peak. It is left of Mount Carrigain.

After lunch return by the Sosman Trail. Beyond the section where it coincides with the Tecumseh Trail, it branches right and descends before climbing to a 3740-foot nameless knoll with excellent views. You look northwest to Mount Liberty, Mount Lafayette, and Cannon Mountain's spectacular precipice south of the famous Old Man of the Mountain's profile ledges and above Franconia Notch.

Beyond this lookoff and lofty knoll, the trail's general direction is south-southeast through open spruce woods. As the trail approaches the top of the ski slope, you come to a new communications tower. Proceed past the tower and a building on your right on a gravel road. You soon reach the site of a former lift. Walk down the slope onto a little plateau and past the Bird's Nest Restaurant, which is a refreshment building for skiers. Take the service road, turning right on the road at the sign for No Grit.

The road provides good walking down the precipitous mountainside all the way to the base. You can relax and walk with minimum attention to your footing and maximum enjoyment of the surrounding mountains—mostly the Sandwich Range—and the deep valley with its evergreens and river, its chalet and condominium roofs, and its golf course. Looking out over it all, you may wish you could take flight as easily as the robins coasting ahead of you.

Turn left at the access road. You pass the lodge on your left as you return to your car.

Mount Tecumseh

28

Mount Israel

Distance (round trip): 8½ miles

Walking time: 5½ hours

Vertical rise: 1780 feet

Maps: USDA/FS 7½' Squam Mountains; USGS 7½' Squam Mountains; USDA/FS 7½' Center Sandwich; USGS 7½' Center Sandwich

This 2630-foot mountain north of Sandwich could be climbed in an afternoon. You'd get the striking views of Lake Winnipesaukee, Squam Lake, and the Sandwich Range, but you'd lose out on a memorable loop hike that includes part of the ancient Sandwich Notch Road.

How to Get There

In Center Sandwich, note your mileage at the overhead blinking light. You'll see a sign for Mead Base at the junction near the grocery store. Drive out Grove Street 0.4 mile to the junction of Diamond Ledge Road and Mount Israel Road. Take Diamond Ledge Road. After 2 more miles, the Sandwich Notch Road bears left. (It will be your return route afoot.) Keep right and drive across the intervale past a farm on your left. The road ends 2.8 miles from the Center Sandwich light, at the Mead Wilderness Base. Park in the field below the white house.

The Trail

The Wentworth Trail begins at the north edge of the clearing, passing to the left of the house. Rising steeply into the forest, it crosses a small stream and slabs to the right through a gap in a stone wall. A growth of maples on the nearly vertical slope suggests that this might have been a sugar orchard, although gathering the sap would be a feat in mountaineering.

The wide path narrows and zigzags to get you up the mountainside. Soon you enter spruce woods as the trail leads northeast across a shoulder. Then it swings northwest. You pass a lookoff that opens

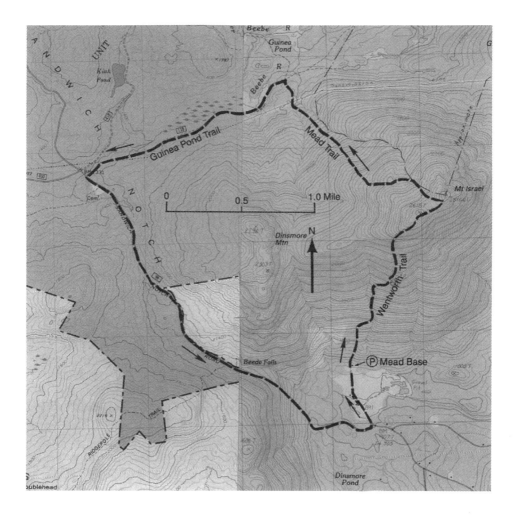

left to Squam Lake and Winnipesaukee.

Now a curve to the north takes you to another view from a wide ledge. The massive ridge is Sandwich Mountain. It's so bulky that the elevation appears less than the 3993 feet. Sometimes called Sandwich Dome, it forms the south wall of Waterville Valley. Its west end, called Black Mountain, terminates the Sandwich Range above Sandwich Notch.

Between Mount Israel and Sandwich Mountain lies the valley where Beebe River begins as a brook draining Black Mountain Pond and Guinea Pond. A former logging railroad grade traverses the valley.

From this viewpoint the Wentworth Trail dips down left into spruces and then curves right to the main, eastern summit. It passes the Mead Trail on the left, a few yards below the rocky crest. (The Mead Trail will be your route of descent.) The summit is a rectangular rock extending above the spruces and firs. The opening again reveals Sandwich Mountain and also the whole range to the east: Mount Whiteface, Tripyramid, Passaconaway, Paugus, and

Chocorua's rock-faced pinnacle framed by spruces. An unofficial side trail along the ledges leads to lake views.

For the descent and the next section of the loop, return the few yards west to the Mead Trail and turn right for a rapid downgrade through the spruce woods to a leafed forest. A spring on the left becomes first a trickle and then a little brook beneath hobblebushes and towering yellow birches. The trail follows an old logging road. There is a crossing of the brook to the west bank and another at a tributary. Bright sunshine ahead becomes, as you walk into it, the long opening under a power line. The trail crosses below the cables through bushes and tall grass. You are down from the mountain.

The Mead Trail ends at the Guinea Pond Trail running east and west through the valley. It mostly follows the old railroad grade you saw from above. (Opposite the Mead Trail at this junction, the Black Mountain Pond Trail leads to the pond and then up Black Mountain to the Algonquin Trail for Sandwich Mountain. See Hike 47 in *50 Hikes in the White Mountains*.) Turn left, to the west, onto the Guinea Pond Trail. (To the east it links with the Flat Mountain Pond Trail and the Bennett Street Trail from the area of Whiteface Intervale on NH 113A.)

The Guinea Pond Trail gives you flat walking for a change. It quickly bears left onto a detour path. Depending on the season and the beavers, there may be flooding. Bordering the trail, tall grass grows with joe-pye weed; in midsummer the weed's pinkish purple blossoms are as high as your head.

The trail slants down beside Beebe River on your right. You walk under the power line and join the Sandwich Notch Road within sight of the bridge over the river. This is the terminus of the Guinea Pond Trail.

Here you turn left, to the south. The dirt road ascends a long hill. Chopped from the forested notch about 1800, the road became a thoroughfare for the people of remote northern settlements. Those pioneers needed markets and products available only in towns settled earlier to the south and even as far as the coast and Portsmouth. By 1850 well-established families occupied the notch along the road's 8 miles. They logged and operated farms, sawmills, a tavern, a whiskey still, and schoolhouses. Now all that remains are a cemetery and cellar holes beside the road.

At the top of the hill you've been climbing there's a sandy excavation on your right. Walk across it to the cemetery. This primitive burying ground and its headstones are hidden in the trees and surrounded by a wall. The hill is called Mount Delight.

Back at the road you pass a cellar hole on the right in which poplars and raspberry bushes have made themselves at home. You enter the woods again. Branches interlace overhead. You may not realize you are walking across the height-of-land. It's about 1480 feet in elevation and almost imperceptible. You know you've passed the area when you come to an open ledge slanting to the right from the edge of the road. The shape of depressions on it resulted in an appropriate name: Devil's Footprints.

A little farther, but on the left, an early advertisement for a general store still announces its message to the traveler. Letters chiseled on an overhanging rock read: P WENTWORTH 6 MLS 1838.

Two more points of interest are worth investigation. First, the Pulpit, a pinnacle of rock on the left beyond the second of three bridges across the brook that grows into the Bearcamp River. The rock provided a stone rostrum from which a Quaker preacher, Joseph Meader, spoke on fair-weather Sundays to the assembled people of the notch.

The second, Beede Falls and Cow Cave

in the Sandwich town park and picnic area, may be reached from a parking area on the left, about halfway down the road's last slope. A path leads to the Bearcamp River—here still a brook—and Beede Falls. A wide, misty curtain of water slides down a rounded ledge into a pool surrounded by dark hemlocks. Cow Cave is downstream and farther east in the woods. Legend has it that a wandering cow was marooned there one winter. It's a long rock formation gouged out by the ice sheet's melting water 10,000 or 15,000 years ago.

Back on the Sandwich Notch Road it is only 0.75 mile to the junction with the road to Mead Base. You will have a final view of the mountain you achieved. Walk past the farm fields and up to your car.

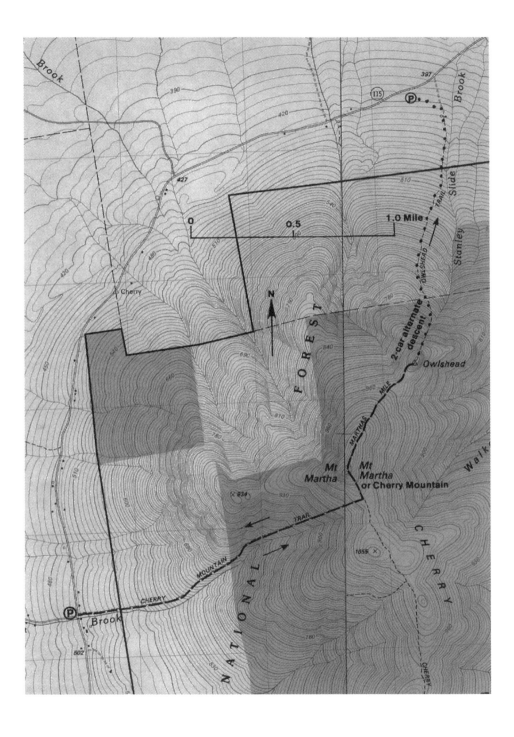

Cherry Mountain

Distance (round trip): 5¾ miles

Walking time: 4½ hours

Vertical rise: 2469 feet

Maps: USDA/FS 7½' Whitefield SE; USGS 7½' x 15' Bethlehem; USDA/FS 7½' Mt. Washington SW; USGS 7½' x 15' Mt. Washington

Perhaps in October when the leaves are yellow and red, you'll see from the ledges called Owl's Head those colors in sunlight carpeting the 10 miles to Mount Washington. I've never chosen the right autumn day. Once I was on the summit in an October snowstorm. One year I climbed too late, for the leaves had already fallen.

This hike includes Cherry Mountain's main peak (Mount Martha on the USGS map) and a pinnacle named Owl's Head. The spruces around the summit's clearing have been trimmed away in two places for views of Mount Washington and the Presidential Range, or Mount Lafayette and the Franconia Range. Owl's Head, 0.75 mile northeast of the main peak, offers open ledges and a more impressive panorama. This to me is the real destination, but if you want to shorten the hike you need not continue to Owl's Head.

How to Get There

The Cherry Mountain Trail leaves the east side of NH 115 at parking and a forest service bulletin board 1.9 miles from US 3 north of Twin Mountain. Watch for a blacktop road (Lennon Road) opposite the trailhead and a sign that says TRAILS PARKING.

The Trail

The trail begins as an old farm road recently used for logging. You'll notice a few yards into the road a glistening tank on the right and a hose suspended from trees. Their purpose is the storage of maple sap from a grove up on the mountainside. These woods were once cultivated fields and pastures, as you'll realize when you see an overgrown stone wall and a strand of barbed wire. Keep straight ahead at a right fork. The trail leads more uphill. Water bars drain melting snow and rain into the woods, so the old road is not eroded. Climbing more steeply, you enter spruce woods and then emerge into an open forest of beech, maple, and birch. The woods road becomes a mountain trail along the angular slope. A stream on the right flows through a ravine below another ridge.

One of the sources of this Carter Brook trickles across the trail about halfway up the steep climb. A few yards higher a 50-foot spur trail on the left ends at a spring. Moosewood and mountain maple grow in thickets under large yellow birches and other hardwoods, which blend into the upper evergreen forest.

Above the spring the Cherry Mountain Trail continues straight despite the steepening angle. This is the style of old trails before switchbacks came into common use.

The trail becomes rocky, then levels somewhat toward the junction with a service road for the former tower. Turn left toward the summit. (The Cherry Mountain Trail follows the service road to the right and descends about 3 miles to the forest service's Cherry Mountain Road between NH 115 and Fabyan.)

For 0.25 mile you're on easy grades and switchbacks. You enter the grassy clearing at the site of the tower, which was removed in 1982. Like other forest service lookout towers, its usefulness in fire protection was over. Plane patrols now spot fires in the White Mountain National Forest.

After you enter the flat clearing on this 3573-foot summit, turn left for the cutaway outlook to Mount Washington and the Presidential Range. The second opening through the spruce and fir that surround the summit is beyond the overgrown remains of the tower. Mount Lafayette dominates the Franconia Range to the southwest. Here you see nearer and to the east at a definitive angle Mount Garfield, North Twin, and South Twin.

Now for the great view from Owl's Head. You will find the trail, Martha's Mile, at the northeast edge of the clearing. You pass an outlook ledge among spruces on the right. Don't linger; there's a far better vista in store for you. The trail descends along the ridge in an evergreen forest deep in moss, fallen trees, and shade. Maintaining elevation along the 3140-foot col, the trail approaches big rocks that loom ahead and provide a short climb to the left. A log ladder assists at one ledge.

The trail swings to the right. All at once the spruces part around barren stone, and you're looking back west across the green slope toward the site of the tower and over to the Lancaster-Whitefield area, the Connecticut River valley, and Vermont. Then ahead a few yards there are the Presidentials: Mount Monroe south of Mount Washington, its unspoiled rocks contrasting with the buildings and towers on Washington. Looking north and east, you see three more peaks: Jefferson, Adams, and Madison.

Between the Presidentials and the mass of Mount Willey on the west, a gap—Crawford Notch—opens all the way to Mount Chocorua. The nearer ridge between you and Mount Washington includes Mount Dartmouth and Mount Deception. In the valley, squares of lighter green have been logged by clear-cutting. Away to the distant east and north, seen past spruce branches, stretches the Mahoosuc Range with Mount Success, Goose Eye, and Old Speck. Your hike plan should include an hour here for lunch or for just looking. It's one of the great sights in the mountains.

To make sure you can say you've surmounted Owl's Head, climb the knoll above the rock lookoff. Through the branches of spruces you catch glimpses northwest to Whitefield Airport and Cherry Pond in Pondicherry Refuge, a preserve of the Audubon Society of New Hampshire.

From this knoll the Owl's Head Trail to NH 115 has been relocated by the Randolph Mountain Club (and is now part of the Cohos Trail that runs the length of Coos County). Until recently it descended precipitously along the upper section of the disastrous slide of July 1885, when, after a cloudburst, tons of boulders, trees, and mud destroyed a farm on the lower slopes. Now the trail heads due north, following the crest of an open, hardwood ridge, then turns east, slabbing slowly but steadily downhill, passing the White Mountain National Forest boundary and entering Mead Paper Company land. It rejoins the old Owl's Head Trail about 0.5 mile from the knoll. Nearing NH 115, the trail goes through a logged area and makes a few turns to accommodate requests of private landowners. At about 2.5 miles from Owl's Head, it meets NH 115, and there a New Hampshire historical marker commemorates the slide. Hiking parties with two cars may choose this descent.

Most hikers return from Owl's Head by way of Martha's Mile and the summit. Watch for the right turn off the service road onto the Cherry Mountain Trail. You can easily keep swinging down past it.

30

Carter Notch

Distance (round trip): 8¾ miles

Walking time: 5½ hours

Vertical rise: 1600 feet

Maps: USDA/FS 7½' Carter Dome; USGS 7½' Carter Dome; USDA/FS 7½' Jackson; USGS 7½' Jackson

The remote and craggy gap between Wildcat Mountain and Carter Dome has two approaches through long, forested corridors. I think of them as the front-door trail and the back-door trail. The popular front door opens from NH 16 north of Pinkham Notch as the Nineteen Mile Brook Trail. This is the usual way to the notch, the two ponds, the ice caves, the AMC hut, and the bunkhouses. I prefer the less traveled way from the south—the Wildcat River Trail out of Jackson. This back-door trail is more private and more in keeping with the primitive character of the notch and its wild mountain scenery.

How to Get There

To reach the village of Jackson driving north toward Pinkham Notch, turn off NH 16 onto NH 16A over the much-photographed covered bridge. Passing the village stores, keep left across a stone bridge spanning the Wildcat River and at once turn to your right onto NH 16B. You pass a hotel on the left and drive up a steep hill beside the cascades of the river on your right. Then the valley opens up toward Carter Dome, Carter Notch, and Wildcat Mountain. After about 2 miles NH 16B branches right across a bridge. Keep straight ahead on the Carter Notch Road. It follows the river to the valley's steep upper end. Asphalt changes to gravel.

From the end of the asphalt, drive slowly for 0.7 mile to a small parking area on the right. There you'll find a forest service sign for the Bog Brook Trail and an AMC sign for the Wildcat River Trail, which here coincides with the Bog Brook Trail.

Note: In spring or early summer or after heavy rains, the crossing of the Wildcat River may be dangerous. To avoid it, continue driving on the Carter Notch Road less than 0.25 mile to a dead-end gate straight ahead and a gate for a forest service road (FR 233) on your right. Park here and walk the forest service road about 1 mile to a bridge across the Wildcat River. Turn left onto the Wildcat River Trail.

The Trail

Beyond the signs, the trail—here a former logging road—enters the woods. From the right or southeast arc of an overgrown turnaround, the trail descends slightly, and you soon cross a tributary of the Wildcat River. The trail then levels along the contour.

You cross another tributary in a little ravine and swing left, again following the slope's contour. Wildcat River appears as a sparkling clear stream in a bed of smooth stones. At low water you step across on the plentiful rocks. I've also waded it. But don't try it during high water. Go back and use the forest service road (see *Note* above).

Up the east bank, the trail takes you a few yards to a former logging road and a sharp left turn. This ancient grade will be your footpath north for most of the next 3 miles until the final climb to the notch. Almost at once it takes you to the sign for the Bog Brook Trail branching right. (The Bog Brook Trail links to the Wild River Trail 2 miles east.) Another sign directs you straight ahead on the Wildcat River Trail.

Ten minutes from this junction you come to the forest service road (FR 233). On your left is the bridge over the Wildcat River. Keep straight across the road and up a bank where the trail continues along the grade you've been following.

There's fine walking, with a few steep pitches at times, on the east bank of the

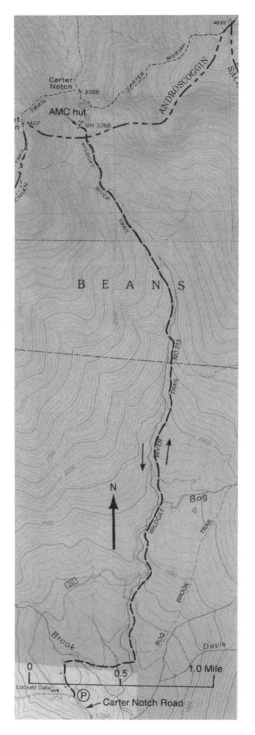

The AMC cabin at Carter Notch

river, which becomes smaller as it divides toward its sources. In season, white lady's slippers are seen here.

About an hour from your car you come to Bog Brook. It falls into Wildcat River where a ledge forms a chute for its last splash. Cross it to a narrow embankment grown to alders. After a few yards the trail resumes the steady but gradual rise in open woods.

This walk is most spectacular around Memorial Day weekend when acres of trout lilies bloom yellow above their mottled leaves, overspread by birches and beeches. Along some sections of the trail, hobble—bushes hold up their flat, white clusters of flowers, which can be seen for long distances through the aisles of the forest.

The junction with the Wild River Trail, 1 mile beyond Bog Brook, marks the approach to real climbing. (The Wild River Trail forks right to Perkins Notch and eventually reaches the Wild River Campground 9 miles east.) The Wildcat River Trail bears left at

the junction and soon makes the final crossing of Wildcat River. It has dwindled, so here the term *river* would be applied only by an elf running the rapids on a beech leaf.

The trail follows the uphill grade of another wide old sled road. It curves around a shoulder and leaves the brook. You walk up this loggers' "dugway" excavated from the ridge. It's an easy climb, but you're about to leave it for the heights. There's 1000 feet of vertical gain in the next mile.

Extemporized campsites down in the spruce and fir woods show that backpackers often lack either cash or reservations for the AMC bunkhouses at the notch. Carter Notch is a Forest Protection Area in the White Mountain National Forest, which means no camping.

The trail winds upward, rough and rugged over boulders and spruce roots or around ledges. Vistas to Carter Dome's south ridge begin to open through the evergreens. Boreal chickadees may flit nearby

The White Mountains

as you look past treetops. Great rocks and other debris from cliffs block the entrance to the notch itself. You make your way to the top of this 3388-foot elevation. Look to your right and see the massive jumble of rocks known as the Rampart. The geologic term for the rocks is *talus*. Your imagination must conjure up the great ice sheet thousands of feet thick that wrested the rocks from Carter Dome and Wildcat while it scoured out the notch.

Keep past a spur trail to the Rampart. You pass the first of two bunkhouses in the evergreen woods. They are long, low frame barracks enclosing porches. The trail descends a short distance to the old stone hut built in 1914 and now converted to a dining room, kitchen, and crew's quarters. Carter Dome's crags dominate the scene.

Continue down from the earthen platform in front of the hut. You come to the elongated pool into which the larger pond drains. Beavers, eager to build a dam across any running water, once plugged the pool's outlet and raised the water level. Scarcity of food trees (beavers require leafy species), and perhaps sore paws from the rocks, caused them to abandon the dubious project. The neglected dam opened up and lowered the water to its former level.

The larger pond, a circular acre of perfect blue water, fills the notch and reflects the pointed spruces and cliffs. At the south shore a huge boulder offers a scramble for a wider view and a look down into the sunny

> *"The woods ain't really dark except on a cloudy night. Not like a house, that is."*
>
> –*Daniel Doan,* Amos Jackman

shallows where little trout lie motionless. The pond is never over 15 feet deep and is always ice cold. It was stocked years ago by Fish and Game Department conservation officer Paul Doherty and others.

Wildcat Mountain just west of the pond rises almost straight for 1000 feet. Carter Dome's summit on the east side is as rounded as the name implies; yet the mountainside is so steep that slides have gashed down it.

Save time for the Rampart. Beyond the last bunkhouse turn left onto the spur trail. Leaving the spruces behind, you walk or crawl among the giant boulders. You feel the refrigerator chill of the air in the ice caves—it lingers long into the summer. Higher climbs to boulder crests open wide views south to the valley floor, Jackson, and away to the Saco River. The scene is pastoral in contrast to the jagged cliffs and overpowering dome behind you.

I always leave Carter Notch with reluctance and consequently sometimes reach the road at twilight. The fast downhill walk along the logging road, after you descend the upper, rough section of the trail, can take you out in 2.5 hours.

31

Nancy and Norcross Ponds

Distance (round trip): 8½ miles

Walking time: 6 hours

Vertical rise: 2100 feet

Maps: USDA/FS 7½' Mt. Carrigain; USGS 7½' Mt. Carrigain; USDA/FS 7½' Bartlett; USGS 7½' Bartlett

Four related attractions combine to make this a hike worthy of an annual excursion. As with Shakespeare's Cleopatra, "age cannot wither" the enticements because the surrounding 460 acres have been set aside by the US Forest Service as a scenic area preserved within the White Mountain National Forest. The four major rewards of the hike are, in order of their appearance: Nancy Cascades, virgin spruce woods, remote ponds, and an outlook into the federally created (1984) Pemigewasset Wilderness.

Extensive damage during the hurricane of September 1938 closed the Nancy Pond Trail, which had been opened for the first time that year. It wasn't reopened until 1960.

How to Get There

Two landmarks help locate the Nancy Pond Trail on the west side of US 302 between Bartlett and Crawford Notch. A mile north of the trail and east of the highway is a large asphalt parking area for the Davis Path to Mount Washington, about 15 miles away. Just beyond this but west stands the Notchland Inn, whose granite walls rest solidly above a grade crossing for a side road that once was US 302.

Approaching the Nancy Pond Trail from the south, it is 1.2 miles from the Sawyer River Road, which branches west from US 302 just north of the Sawyer River Bridge.

By driving US 302 slowly toward the Nancy Pond Trail from either north or south, you'll see the trail sign to the west of the highway.

The Trail

The Nancy Pond Trail first follows an easy woods road, so for the moment you may trust your hiker's subconscious to select places for your boots while you think about Nancy. In the fall of 1778 after an absence from her work for Colonel Whipple's family in Jefferson, she returned to find that she apparently had been deserted by the man she was to marry. He had left the settlement that day without explanation but with her two years' wages, which she had given him for safekeeping. Believing he had started for Portsmouth by Crawford Notch, she followed him. A fierce snowstorm and darkness overtook her. She froze to death on the south bank of Nancy Brook. Colonel Whipple's men found her body the next day. She had walked 30 miles through the forest following blazes on trees, fording streams, and making her way among the rocks of the wild notch.

The Nancy Pond Trail turns left off the woods road after 0.25 mile and winds among trees to a crossing of Halfway Brook. About 100 yards beyond the brook, you come to a logging road. Turn left, uphill. Houses are visible ahead through the trees. Stop and look back at the trail junction. This old woodsman's trick will give you a picture to watch for coming back. There may be no sign.

You enter the White Mountain National Forest at a pile of stones painted red and walk up the south bank of Nancy Brook through a forest of large beeches and yellow birches. Then the logging road heads for the brook and the first crossing. Step or leap your way to the north bank on rocks. (High water? Best avoid it.) Bear left along the old logging road. To the right there remains evidence of the tractor road for the former fire tower on Mount Bemis.

Along here you'll see the ruins of a brick furnace and other vestiges of the Lucy mill,

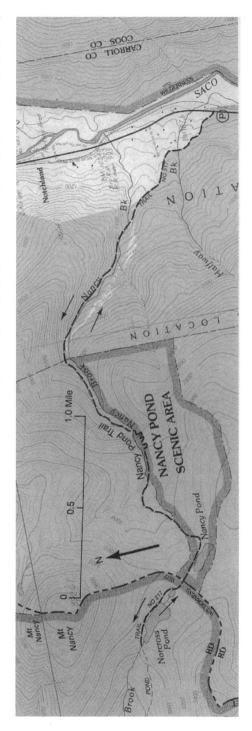

where the Lucy family of Conway salvaged trees downed by the 1938 hurricane.

The trail gets steeper and is overlaid by rubble from a landslide. You traverse the gravelly base of another slide, negotiate small rocks, and step from a massive spruce trunk half buried in sand.

At the brook once more, the crossing is plain enough, but on the south bank the way is a bit confusing (at least on returning). An unmarked branch trail on the left leads to a small overgrown clearing. The inclination is to press on to the falls, which appear as a shining whiteness through the spruce branches. But pause and look back so you'll fix this section in your mind for the return trip. Heedless hikers, having lingered overly long at the falls, have been known to hurry inadvertently into the little clearing and then take a false trail leading only to the bosky wilderness.

The falls are as lovely as any in the mountains. A circular pool to the right of the trail catches white water pouring down 60 feet or more over a ledge closed in by spruces. Your eyes follow the cascades upward. The glinting water, 300 feet up, contrasts with the dark evergreens.

The trail turns left and surmounts the valley's headwall. Switchbacks take you up to lookoffs across the Saco River valley to Mount Crawford and Giant Stairs. As the trail angles to the cascades, you can look down over the falling water. The last switchback takes you to more level ground beside the stream sliding quietly to the dropoff.

You find yourself walking through a virgin forest of red spruce and balsam fir. The trees were too remote and the terrain too difficult for profitable logging. They grow on gradually ascending slopes that extend across the 3000-foot contour to Nancy Pond. Because it's a climax forest, as seen by the first explorers of the mountains, you can observe complete cycles from seedlings through mature trees to fallen and decaying logs. Notice the dead stubs from which the bark has fallen. Sometimes weathering exposes the fibers in spiral array. Ever wonder at the strength of trees? You're looking at it—the power of continuous arches.

Split-log walkways here keep you above the boggy sections. Shade-loving plants abound: clintonia, goldthread, and wood sorrel.

You step across the main branch of Nancy Brook draining from the pond. The trail swings over a knoll with silent footing on a cushion of spruce needles. Now you begin to see through the trees to the 4-acre pond. The trail follows the north shore. The water's edge supports varieties of wet-root species known generally as "water brush." In this bog environment grow leatherleaf, sheep laurel, blueberries, and viburnums. White spruce, rare in the mountains, grows beside the common red spruce. You can easily compare the distinguishing characteristics. Tamaracks thrive in the wetland.

Beyond Nancy Pond an almost imperceptible ascent takes you over a height-of-land into the Pemigewasset-Merrimack Rivers' watershed. Little Norcross Pond and Norcross Pond drain that way. You may see a moose feeding here, dipping its antlered head deep into the water.

Norcross Pond's 7 acres are studded with rocks, and skeletal spruces bear stark witness to the beaver dam at the outlet that once raised the water and drowned the trees.

For the final reward of the hike, circle the north shore. The trail turns left at the west end and crosses the outlet. Here, to your left and above you, a bedrock plug holds Norcross Pond against the base of Nancy Mountain. Climb to the top of the plug and face about. Before you stretches the vast Pemigewasset Wilderness. The smooth rock on which you stand is your destination. (The Nancy Pond Trail continues to the Carrigain Notch Trail 3 miles farther on.)

Facing northwest, you are looking to Mount Bond, the dominant mountain of the East Branch valley. To the north, on the right, the rounded, connected summit is Mount Guyot. Between them, 7 miles away, Guyot Shelter's backpackers awaken in the morning to see the rising sun gleaming on the water behind you. All of the country before you was logged and much of it burned. Protection by the national forest allowed natural regrowth to heal the land.

Upon starting the return trip by the same trail, be sure to keep right along Norcross Pond's north shore. An old logging road on the left toward Mount Nancy could mislead you. Below the falls keep left past the little clearing I mentioned. And on the lower logging road near the houses, watch for the turn to the right among the beech trees as the trail heads for the crossing of Halfway Brook and soon to your car.

32

Webster Cliff/Mount Webster

Distance (round trip): 5½ miles

Walking time: 5½ hours

Vertical rise: 2633 feet

Maps: USDA/FS 7½' Crawford Notch; USGS 7½' Crawford Notch; USDA/FS 7½' Stairs; USGS 7½' Stairs

Webster Cliff is an awesome series of precipices opposite the Willey House site in Crawford Notch State Park.

How to Get There

The Webster Cliff Trail begins 1 mile south of the Willey House site, where the Appalachian Trail crosses US 302 to follow this spectacular route. Park off the highway.

The Trail

You cross the Saco River on a footbridge and discover that the trail heads northeast through the woods. It's taking you around the cliffs that would demand expert rock-climbing technique if approached head-on.

After 0.5 mile the Webster Cliff Trail curves northward to your left. You climb the steep slope on carefully built steps of logs and stones. Because it approaches the perpendicular and negotiates the mountainside by switchbacks, the trail leads you toward the sky. You can be confident that you'll reach a lookoff—and you do, about 1.5 hours from your car.

Thereafter the trail continues above the Saco River valley to many viewpoints atop the cliffs. You are treated to bird's-eye views of rugged Crawford Notch. You look down on the ribbon highway and its miniature cars. The other line curving parallel to US 302 has steel tracks—the Conway Scenic Railroad. Everything down there appears as if seen through the wrong end of a telescope. Toy roofs protect the buildings at Crawford Notch State Park. There, Samuel Willey Jr. and his family died in the terrible landslide of August 28, 1826.

Mount Willey, from its preeminent position across the notch, presents you with a gauge for your progress, although you'll not quite equal its 4302-foot elevation on Mount Webster. Slides scar the solid pyramid, which rises all at once from the highway and railroad.

On the night of violent storms and cloudbursts during which the Willey family perished, the Saco River rose 24 feet. Samuel Willey, his wife, five children, and two hired men fled from the house. They were all crushed or drowned in the avalanche of debris and water that poured down into the flooding river. The landslide, ironically, spared the house.

In 1832, when Nathaniel Hawthorne visited the mountains, he heard the story of the Willey family from Ethan Allen Crawford. Hawthorne wrote a tale based on his conversation. He called it "The Ambitious Guest."

From the Webster Cliff Trail, Mount Willey appears backed on the north by Mount Field and Mount Tom; it shows its foundation at the head of the notch in the cliffs of Mount Willard. As you climb from lookoff to outlook, you gaze down on Mount Willard's summit (2865 feet). The clearing there was for generations a viewing point for guests at the Crawford House, which burned in 1977. Hikers now arrive at the same spot by way of the carriage road; earlier, Crawford House guests rode up in style behind teams of horses.

But the notch is the great recurring interest. You draw nearer to, and higher above, the rocky cleft where it narrows to the few yards that admit only the highway and the railroad between the ledges. Originally a footpath, the first road (1803) occupied all the space in the cleft. Blasting opened the way for the railroad.

The railroad trestle over Willey Brook, which drops out of the valley between

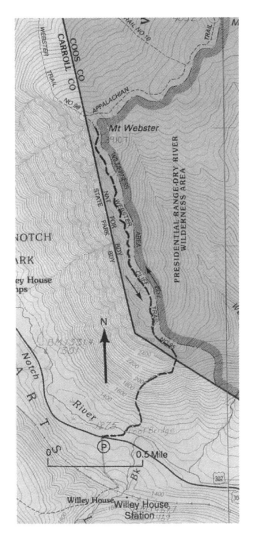

Mount Field and Mount Willey, lacks the impressiveness of an engineering feat when seen from atop Webster Cliff; yet below in the notch and seen from the highway, it's imposing enough. The nearby onetime boardinghouse for trainmen and track crews has burned, leaving only the foundation for you to pick out.

When you reach the pinnacle near the north end of the cliffs, you see ahead a spruce-grown knob beyond the final vertical

---

rocks. It's Mount Webster's wooded summit. Then you descend a few yards and climb again to the uppermost viewpoint, where you look down 2400 feet to the highway.

After this your rugged climb to the true summit at 3910 feet takes you into the shade of spruce and fir, which is welcome indeed on a hot, bright day. (The Webster Cliff Trail keeps on for 4 miles to Mount Jackson, the AMC's Mizpah Spring Hut, Mount Pierce [Mount Clinton], and the Crawford Path.)

For a lunch spot, descend a few steps beyond the summit rocks and turn right. Spruce woods are level to a vista, left, which opens away and away. You see north to Mount Washington, east across the Presidential–Dry River Wilderness Area to Montalban Ridge, and all the way to the southern Presidentials. Mount Jackson is the nearer craggy summit, and beyond it are the Mizpah Spring Hut and Mount Pierce. For this view alone you should save Mount Webster for a clear day.

Return is by the same route you climbed. The afternoon light will change the scenery and reveal unnoticed valleys and peaks.

Storms in the mountains overtake you quickly. I'll describe an escape hatch in the woods beyond Mount Webster in the event that you need to protect yourself from lightning and a sudden downpour: Instead of venturing onto the exposed trail you climbed, follow the Webster Cliff Trail 200 yards beyond the summit to a left fork. This is the west branch of the Webster-Jackson Trail. It leads down through the woods 2.5 miles to the highway between the notch's northern end and Saco Lake, not far from the Crawford House site. You'll have to hitch a ride south about 4 miles on US 302 through the notch to your car. But that's better than dodging thunderbolts on Webster Cliff.

Imp Profile/Middle Carter Mountain

Imp Trail only:

Distance (round trip): 6 miles

Walking time: 4¾ hours

Vertical rise: 2265 feet

For round-trip climb to Middle Carter add: *3½ miles, 3¼ hours, 1164 feet*

Maps: USDA/FS 7½' Carter Dome; USGS 7½' Carter Dome

The Imp Trail reveals not only a vast panorama across Pinkham Notch to Mount Washington, the Great Gulf, and the northern Presidentials but also connects with the North Carter Trail, which leads you, via the Carter-Moriah Trail, to the summit of Middle Carter Mountain. Yet you need not climb the extra distance to Middle Carter: The Imp Trail alone makes a fine day hike, especially at the beginning of a season before your legs and lungs are in the best condition.

The Imp Trail loops from NH 16 up the western slopes of North Carter and returns to within 0.25 mile of its start. I like to begin at the northern end. The trail leads to the top of the cliff whose lower ledges form Imp Profile at 3165 feet. Then it swings across the rim of Imp Brook's ravine, passes the North Carter Trail, and makes a leisurely descent by old logging roads to the highway.

The addition of Middle Carter (4610 feet) provides the hike with a peak that's included in the AMC Four Thousand Footer Club's list. Mount Washington and its neighboring summits appear in a new perspective. There are vistas across the Wild River valley to the mountains along Evans Notch as you pass just below the summit of Mount Lethe.

How to Get There

On the east side of NH 16, about 2.2 miles north of the Mount Washington auto road and the Glen House site, a US Forest Service sign marks Imp Trail's south end. The other end, which I think of as the beginning, is 0.2 mile north. I leave the car off the highway at the south end and walk the gravel shoulder to start at the north end.

The Trail

My northern beginning is almost opposite the Dolly Copp Picnic Area, from which you can look up at Imp Profile. The best view is from the Dolly Copp Campground, whose access road is about 1 mile farther north. There, a monument marks the site of the homestead that Hayes Dodifer Copp cleared from the forest. His wife, Dolly, named the profile, which she could see from the dooryard of their house.

Between 1832 and 1884 the Copps lived on their farm. Each year Hayes chopped out more open land until he cultivated or pastured 70 acres. The Copps sold produce and

put up travelers. Dolly charged 75 cents for a night's lodging—bed, board, and care of horse. Her blue-wool homespun cloth and her maple sugar became prized by vacationers who began coming to the mountains in the 1850s and 1860s. On the golden jubilee celebration of her marriage to Hayes, Dolly made the comment still quoted in the mountains: "Hayes is well enough, but fifty years is long enough for a woman to live with any man." They sold the farm to their son, Nathaniel E. Copp, and Dolly went to live with a daughter in Auburn, Maine.

But to return to the Imp Trail, blazed yellow all the way, the 2.25 miles to the cliff atop Imp Profile take you through big woods of mixed spruce, beech, and birch. Occasional towering hemlocks spread over the trail, which stays on the south bank of Imp Brook for the first 0.5 mile. Then it crosses to the north bank. There are two crossings, really, as the brook forks.

Leaving the brook valley you climb a ridge to the north. The trail levels in beech woods. On some of the trees the smooth gray bark shows initials and dates carved in the 1940s. Now you begin a moderate grade during a swing east over another ridge. Then the trail becomes steep and approaches a ravine. It turns abruptly right, to the south, avoiding the ravine, and you climb a rough section of mountainside. Spruce and fir begin to take over the forest cover.

All at once you step out onto open rock. You are standing on the Imp's "forehead." It's like a balcony 600 feet high. Mount Washington and its ravines, on a clear day, look to be just across NH 16, yet the cars on the auto road, around the great bend known as the Horn, are bugs. Their windshields and tiny mirrors sparkle in the sun. Off to the right of the auto road the Great Gulf's glacier-hollowed bowl drops away and rises again to Mounts Jefferson, Adams, and Madison.

From your eagle's aerie look left toward Pinkham Notch's east rim. Beginning at the south you can see Wildcat Ridge and Wildcat Ski Area, Carter Dome, South Carter, Middle Carter, Lethe, and the spruce-grown skyline leading toward North Carter, which is hidden by a nearby knoll.

The Imp Trail leaves the clifftop for the spruces on that nearby knoll. You climb briefly in the trees before turning down, to the right, to a minor lookoff into Imp Brook's ravine, where the sound of falling water rises from cascades far below.

The trail continues southeast and then gradually swings south around the head of the ravine. It's rough in places but pleasant under the spruces that shade the green wood sorrel and ferns. Beyond the trickling sources of Imp Brook, the trail begins to turn west. It descends a short distance to the junction with the North Carter Trail on your left. You are almost 1 mile from Imp Profile's forehead.

Here you may choose the 3.5-mile round trip to Middle Carter, to the left, or you may bear right on the Imp Trail and walk down 3 miles to NH 16.

If favorable skies and your own fitness tell you that this is the day for Middle Carter, turn left onto the North Carter Trail, blazed blue.

A moderate climb becomes steeper, but you should be able to keep at it steadily. After about 1 hour from the Imp Trail and 1.25 miles, you reach the junction with the Carter-Moriah Trail. Turn right, south. (The Carter-Moriah Trail along here is part of the Appalachian Trail.) Keep going 0.5 mile over wooden walkways across boggy ground, then over rocky knolls to the bare summit of Middle Carter.

From this angle, higher than from the Imp lookoff, Mount Washington and the northern Presidentials appear more remote. To the east you look into the broad valley through which flow Wild River and its many tributaries. The range of summits between you and Evans Notch includes North and South Baldface, Eagle Crag, Mount Meader, West Royce, and East Royce.

You return to the Imp Trail the way you came. Make sure you turn left off the Carter-Moriah Trail and onto the North Carter Trail.

At the junction with the Imp Trail, go straight down the south half of the loop. Soon you are walking on an old logging road above Imp Brook ravine.

The good path changes to washouts among rocks like a dry brook bed. Then you

Daniel Doan on Imp's "forehead"

leave erosion behind and follow a steady downward slant on the old logging road. The trail makes a sharp right turn away from Cowboy Brook. The remaining mile of trail parallels the highway as you walk north. Car noises penetrate the forest. The everyday world is off there through the trees. Make the most of the forest.

34

Mount Hale

Distance (round trip): 8½ miles

Walking time: 6 hours

Vertical rise: 2320 feet

Maps: USDA/FS 7½' South Twin Mountain; USGS 7½' South Twin Mountain; USDA/FS 7½' Crawford Notch; USGS 7½' Crawford Notch

On Mount Hale's 4054-foot summit you use your compass for fun. Holding it in hand beside the big cairn, which marks the site of a former tower, you can watch the needle swing toward the rocks. Move around the cairn, and the compass continues to point at the magnetic rocks instead of at magnetic north. Compasses can lie. Ask any deer hunter who once forgot that the steel of a rifle will attract the needle.

How to Get There

To reach Mount Hale, drive along US 302 between Twin Mountain and Fabyan. East of Twin Mountain village 2.5 miles, turn south at Zealand Campgrounds. Follow the US Forest Service's Zealand Road 2.5 miles to the hiker symbol and parking on the right for Hale Brook Trail.

The Trail

The Hale Brook Trail is the first section of this loop hike, which, from Mount Hale, descends the Lend-a-Hand Trail to the AMC Zealand Falls Hut. From there, your return follows the Zealand Trail and the Zealand Road.

The lower forest along the Hale Brook Trail consists of the familiar leafy trees common to 1700-foot elevations in the White Mountains. The pleasant path, mostly graded along its 2.2 miles, rises into evergreens.

Early in the hiking season the leafy forest is open, but the leaves spread out and close the aisles by June. When the last snow melts into rivulets and mud, reviving plants appear as green points emerging from

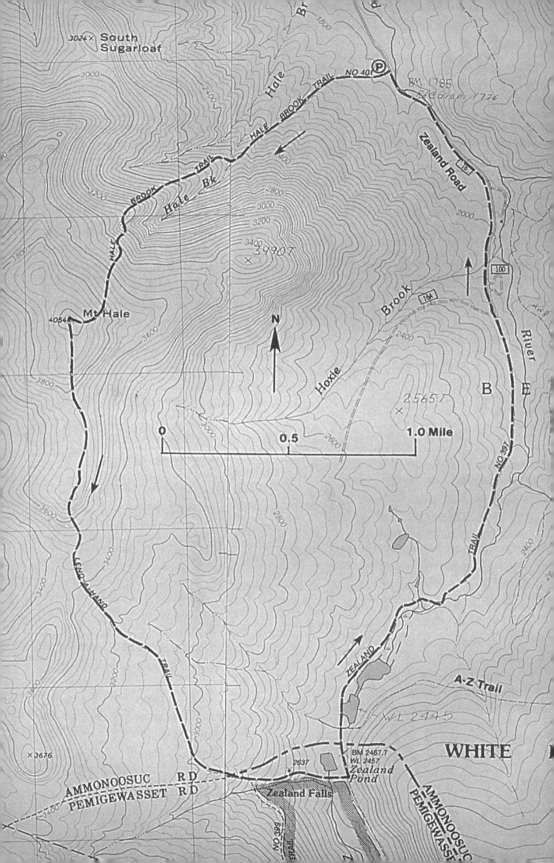

fallen leaves. Heavy snow has so flattened and packed these brown leaves that the new points, spearing upward, often lift them inches off the ground. Clintonia does this before the tuliplike leaves unfold. (The pale yellow flowers mature into clusters of blue berries giving the plant its alternate name, blue bead lily.) The green sprouts also turn into lady's slippers, purple trilliums, and painted trilliums. Up among the barren trees, shadbushes bloom earliest and decorate the woods with white lace.

Snow lingers in the upper spruces as late as the last week in May. Its melting turns Hale Brook into a lovely torrent. Approaching the first crossing 0.5 mile from the car, you see the brook ahead in cascades like white surf. Above this gushing, the brook runs quieter, and you cross on big rocks.

The trail goes up more steeply into spruces bordering a gully. It enters a white-birch forest along a gradual traverse of the valley's steep north bank. The brook is far below. At the head of the valley the trail turns sharply left. You step across the diminished stream and climb to another branch. Your way is eased by switchbacks into evergreens. As you proceed, the trees become smaller and form dense thickets.

The summit opens wide across green turf and stony earth that once surrounded a fire tower. Views are becoming overgrown. You're facing South Twin Mountain and its connecting ridge to North Twin. You look south to Mount Carrigain, from here a solid pyramid. Turn around northeast, and there's Mount Washington. If necessary, climb up on the cairn to see.

The panorama between Carrigain and Washington, starting at the narrow pass east of Carrigain (which is Carrigain Notch), includes Mounts Lowell, Anderson, Nancy, and Bemis. Blue distance follows, and then come Mounts Willey, Field, and Tom. Over

beyond those summits are Mount Jackson and the top of Webster Cliff forming the east wall of Crawford Notch.

Toward Mount Carrigain you look across Zealand Notch to Whitewall Mountain. It was burned to bedrock by a forest fire in July 1886, along with 12,000 acres and much of J.E. Henry's logging railroad, camps, logs, and equipment. In 1903 flames extended the devastation by sweeping over 10,000 acres in the Zealand River valley. The new forest is, quite simply, a natural miracle.

As for your compass pointing to the rocks in the cairn, the explanation, as you've probably guessed, has to do with iron. The rocks are of volcanic origin and contain iron.

This loop hike's next section, the 2.5-mile Lend-a-Hand Trail, begins in thick spruce and fir growth south of the summit. On the southwest North Twin Mountain, seen across the deep valley of Little River, vanishes behind evergreen branches. But the trail becomes scenic after you dip down among and over the big rocks on Mount Hale's shoulder. You enter open woods, and the sun beats down. White birches, often stunted and twisted, rise only 10 or 15 feet above bracken ferns. The spruces and firs, shapely in their pointed outlines, might be growing in a neglected park. Ruby-crowned kinglets flit among the trees, and white-throated sparrows call from the branch tips.

Dropping down the lower half of the Lend-a-Hand Trail, you come to spruce and fir woods again and small bogs. The trail spans the muck on split-log walkways.

The Lend-a-Hand joins the Twinway within sound of Zealand Falls. Turn left onto Twinway. (Twinway extends 7 rugged miles over South Twin Mountain and other peaks to the AMC Galehead Hut.) You'll also hear voices from the Zealand Falls Hut and the shrieks of grownups and kids splashing out of the icy pools along the cascades.

Views to Zealand Notch (near) and Carrigain Notch (far)

From the hut's porch and its gunsight aim through Zealand Notch to Mounts Carrigain and Lowell, the Zealand Trail descends a steep 200 yards to the level of Zealand Pond. Soon you cross the pond's southern outlet. Turn left (north) for the return section of your loop hike, 2.75 miles of the Zealand Trail and 1 mile along the Zealand Road. At this corner the Ethan Pond Trail branches right (south) in brushy flatland, where you may see a vireo or a veery. The former usually prefer tree branches; the latter stay near the ground.

The Zealand Trail keeps mainly to the grade of a former logging railroad. More than 100 years old, its gravel fill overlooks the east shore of Zealand Pond to your left. A bridge takes you over the northern outlet. You pass the A-Z Trail branching right from the wide path.

The stream, hardly yet worthy of the name Zealand River, flows into low ground on the right. Beavers have diverted the water into broad pools. These bogs are noted for the magenta flowers of rhodora that bloom here in June. The trail crosses low ground of poplars, willows, virburnums, and alders. Along the water's edge the insectivorous sundew plants show their little clusters of sticky-haired leaves all ready to trap bugs. You must look closely to locate them.

The Zealand River becomes a mountain brook flowing faster over smooth rocks in evergreen woods. Briefly leaving the railroad grade to wind among spruces, the trail regains the level. Suddenly you come to a forest service gate and a parking area for the end of the Zealand Road. You may be surprised at the number of cars. Keep walking, or stop to talk to other hikers, birders, and tourists.

The Zealand Road is the last mile back to your car at the Hale Brook Trail.

The White Mountains

35

Mount Tremont

Distance (round trip): 6 miles

Walking time: 5 hours

Vertical rise: 2600 feet

Maps: USDA/FS 7½' Crawford Notch; USGS 7½' Crawford Notch

Tremont's deficiencies are also its charms. It's removed from any popular trails between important peaks; it's only 3384 feet above sea level; and it's wooded to the crest.

The spruce forest is part of the charm. On the steep northeast slope the big trees have never been cut off. This is one of the few places in the mountains where you're not seeing second- or third-growth timber.

On the summit ledges, smaller evergreens are taking over after fire or hurricane, but the views are wide and impressive. The Swift River flows through the Passaconaway valley. One or two sections of the Kancamagus Highway could be the curves of a black river. The northern ridges of the Sandwich Range's many summits appear spread out east and west. Beyond the irregular oval of Sawyer Pond in its green setting, a smaller blue gem, Little Sawyer Pond, suggests a chip of lapis lazuli. Mount Carrigain, 5 miles to the west, is the eye-catcher until you turn southeast and see Mount Chocorua 8 miles away, viewed bright and clear through a frame of green boughs.

Stepping out on the ledges, you may not at first notice Mount Washington behind you. It seems distant in the composition of spruces and blue sky, and it *is* distant: 15 miles.

This is another hike off US 302 near Crawford Notch. The Mount Tremont Trail ascends the most southerly and highest of the three summits that form a ridge west of Bartlett and south of the highway. There are no trails on the other two.

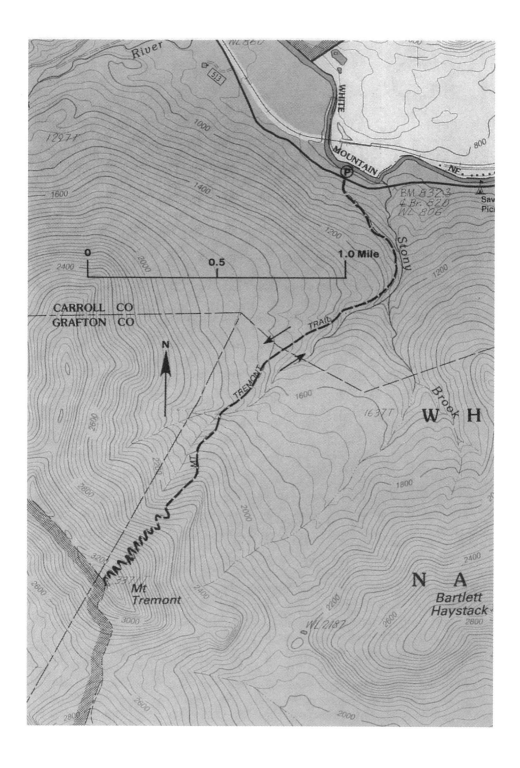

How to Get There

Three miles west of Bartlett, the Saco River and US 302 begin their curves north. The Mount Tremont Trail leads into the woods here. Parking is on the highway's wide north shoulder a few yards from the trail sign on the south side.

The Trail

Following an old logging road up a gradual slope in beech and birch woods, you soon come to Stony Brook on the left. The stream forms dark pools below cascades that sparkle in the morning sun. Hemlocks are several shades of green, from the deepest—almost blue—to the delicate tones of new growth. In the valley of Stony Brook, light and shade are the theme.

After about 1 hour, there's a short, steep climb, and the trail swings up in an S-turn. The brook is now far below. You walk into a clearing, once a logging site. The trail continues on along the high bank above the brook.

You enter a growth of white birches; shortly after, the trail slants down to cross the west branch of Stony Brook. The trail heads upstream but climbs steeply above the brook and eventually leaves it behind by a series of switchbacks through woods composed almost entirely of white birch.

Spruce and fir gradually take over, first as low-growth seeding in from higher on the mountain and then as young trees 6 feet or more tall.

Now several dead spruce stubs of unusual diameter appear, suggesting fire (as did the white birches that often reforest burned land). A little farther on, living trees seem to tower into the clouds as you look up. They are red spruces. I suspect there may be two possible explanations of why this virgin forest was saved: (1) It was too remote and steep to be profitably logged; (2) a fortunate change of wind or a sudden rainfall stopped the forest fire before the trees went up in smoke.

This is virgin forest complete in itself from the seeds in its cones to the decay that replenishes the earth. Trunks having coarse, ancient bark seem ageless and the upper branches forever vernal. But they live out their time; eventually the thriving undergrowth engulfs the fallen trees.

Through this forest, the trail—narrow, rocky, leading over roots and logs as your shoulders brush the big trees—winds upward between thickets of hobblebush and colonies of trillium, goldthread, and wood sorrel.

Here on the mountainside you can occasionally look off to Crawford Notch and to Mount Washington beyond its long southern ridges and valley. The trail zigzags up at a knee-bending angle toward light above. The evergreens become smaller and younger. You've left the virgin forest. (My guess is that the summit burned over once.)

An opening between trees leads to a lookoff ledge on the right atop a cliff that falls away to green treetops. Sawyer Pond shines blue 1447 feet below and a mile away. Mount Carrigain rears up between Carrigain Notch on the northeast and its southwest neighbor Mount Hancock.

About 100 feet farther, the Mount Tremont Trail ends at the summit. (The Brunel Trail descends south 3 miles to a forest service road at Rob Brook, 2.5 miles from the Bear Notch Road.) A little brushy gap in the ledges surrounded by evergreens may be called the top, although the line of rock to the southwest is a few steps higher. The 30-foot, slanting rock face offers a precarious seat and footholds for studying the mountains and valleys. To the southwest, 2915-foot Green's Cliff rises beyond Sawyer Pond (100 feet deep and 47 acres). South of Sawyer Pond another small lake is Church Pond.

Ruth Doan MacDougall

On Mount Tremont

The entire Passaconaway valley—also called Albany Intervale—extends clear to a bend in the Kancamagus Highway over toward Mount Osceola.

You can see all the way to the mountains around Waterville Valley. Besides Osceola (minus its fire tower), there's Tecumseh and its ski slopes and Tripyramid, whose slides are hidden from this vantage. Swinging east from Tripyramid, the next peaks you see are Whiteface, Passaconaway, Paugus, and Chocorua.

A cooling breeze blows across the rock face from the western mountains. There's plenty of time to enjoy the view. The descent back down the Mount Tremont Trail is much faster than the climb up, or so it seems on the steep places. Two hours, however, should allow for another leisurely traverse of that majestic spruce forest.

36

Mount Paugus

Distance (round trip): 9 miles

Walking time: 6½ hours

Vertical rise: 2382 feet

Maps: USDA/FS 7½' Mt. Chocorua;
USGS 7½' Mt. Chocorua

Paugus is a remote little mountain with a low profile in the Sandwich Range. However, this loop will force you to revise any prehike expectations you may have had about its being mediocre or easy to climb. Sharing a characteristic with humans of this type, Mount Paugus conceals more surprises than at first seem probable.

The 3210-foot summit is tucked away between dramatic Mount Chocorua and bulky Mount Passaconaway.

How to Get There

Take NH 113A from the four corners in Tamworth and drive toward Wonalancet. Three miles from Tamworth, NH 113A crosses a bridge over the Swift River.

A road forks right. It is known as the Fowler's Mill Road, and it extends between NH 113A and NH 16 at Chocorua Lake. Follow it about 1.25 miles to a forest service sign (for Liberty and Brook Trails) and a side road on the left beyond a bridge over Paugus Brook. This is the Paugus Mill Road. Turn onto it and drive 0.75 mile to a parking area and a forest service gate.

The Trail

The Liberty Trail leaves on the right for Mount Chocorua. Your route north lies ahead along the Brook Trail, here a gravel logging road.

Walk the Brook Trail for 5 minutes until it also forks right to Mount Chocorua along the gravel road. Your way, the Bolles Trail, bears left to a stony crossing of Paugus Brook. Avoid this hike in times of high water. Beyond here, the Bolles Trail keeps northwest away

from the stream. In 0.5 mile you come to the next link in this loop hike: The Old Paugus Trail begins on the left for the mountain's ascent. (The Bolles Trail leads due north 5 miles to the Kancamagus Highway.)

Turn left onto the Old Paugus Trail. Almost at once you are crossing Whitin Brook on rocks. The Old Paugus Trail follows an ancient logging road. Just beyond Whitin Brook you pass the Bickford Trail. (The Bickford Trail surmounts the west ridge 2 miles to Wonalancet.) You are entering the Sandwich Range Wilderness.

Along the wide curve of the logging road, you circle the wooded flat that once was flooded by water behind a dam. The pond stored logs before they were hauled into Paugus Mill, whose by-product, sawdust, still forms a heap among the trees east of the stream.

The Old Paugus Trail here provides grand walking as it swings gradually up the valley beside Whitin Brook through a fine leafy forest. You cross to the north bank of Whitin Brook. The graded sled road of lumbering days and the trail coincide so pleasantly for 1 mile that you must watch for the junction where the Whitin Brook Trail takes over the road. Close to Whitin Brook on the left, the Old Paugus Trail turns north at a right angle up the ridge. The Whitin Brook Trail starts straight ahead. (The Whitin Brook Trail will be a section of your return loop.)

Now begins the real climb as the Old Paugus Trail ascends a steep slope to a relatively level breathing place past the left-branching Big Rock Cave Trail. (The Big Rock Cave Trail aims southwest over Mount Mexico to Wonalancet.) Beyond graceful white birches you scramble up a gully to the first cliffs. The trail skirts the base between the smooth rock face and spruces towering on the right. Then you climb steadily around the cliff's east end.

On springy brown spruce needles the trail leads along the mountainside and plunges into a green tunnel. You clamber over roots and old logs where trail crews sawed clear the spruces flattened by the 1954 hurricane. In open woods again, the Bee Line Trail joins from the right. (The Bee Line Trail links the Old Paugus Trail and Mount Chocorua.) Beyond it you ascend—hands helping boots and legs—a jumble of rocks to a ledge, on the right, overlooking the forest toward the Ossipee Mountains. Ossipee Lake shimmers in sunlight.

From the ledge you continue into spruce and fir woods that shade you above several smooth slopes of New Hampshire bedrock. The trail levels and then descends to a junction from which a spur trail used to lead to Old Shag Camp and a spring 0.25 mile beyond it.

Sagging Old Shag Camp, gone but not forgotten! One evening my companion Doc Sharps whistled up a flock of migrating white-throated sparrows to entertain us with their clear, descending notes—and blackflies and mosquitoes devoured us till we built a smudge. The log walls dated from 1933 and replaced an even earlier structure.

From the junction with the abandoned path, the Old Paugus Trail turns south a few yards and then bears sharply right across a trickle of water dark from the swamp that was once a beaver pond. At almost 3000 feet it was perhaps the highest of such ponds in the mountains.

The last short climb up rocks and over tree roots surprises you when you look back. Mount Chocorua's bare peak rises only 2.75 miles away. Another summit, to the west about the same distance, greets you beyond sparse evergreens as you step out on open ledges. It is the triangular silhouette of Mount Passaconaway.

Here the Old Paugus Trail ends. Beyond

The summit of Chocorua from Mount Paugus

open rock, to the west, a sign on a tree marks the Lawrence Trail, which is the first section of your return loop.

But there's time for lunch and enjoyment of the sunny, glacier-smoothed ledges, which fall away into fragments rimming the valley of Whitin Brook. Although the true summit is about 100 feet higher and 0.3 mile north in woods without a trail, this lookoff is summit enough, as the view manifests the more you study it. Attached to Mount Passaconaway by a long ridge, Mount Whiteface drops to the wide lake country. Away to the south the ski trails you see are on Mount Gunstock in the Belknap Mountains.

The Lawrence Trail, identified by blue blazes, winds briefly among spruces before it precipitates you down over log staircases into two ravines and the sources of Whitin Brook. Beyond them you are facing the climb to the Overhang.

This unsung delight consists of a fascinating array of fallen rock, precipices, tangled spruce, and mountain maple over which the trail keeps to a seemingly impossible route. The steepest part is the descent down a gully under the Overhang and into a forest of beech and maple.

Spruces begin once more at the junction with the Cabin Trail. Turn left onto the Cabin Trail, a short link (less than 0.5 mile long) to the Whitin Brook Trail. Turn left onto the Whitin Brook Trail. (The Cabin Trail continues 2.5 miles south to Wonalancet.)

The Whitin Brook Trail here is a narrow corridor down through a thick stand of spruce and fir. It is studded left and right with the sawed butts of old blowdowns.

The spruce forest ends abruptly in the valley's beeches and yellow birches. Make a sharp right turn. Watch out for rotten bridges. After crossings of tributaries forming Whitin Brook, however, you can stride down the good footing of the old logging grade beside the main brook, on the right. Pass through a junction with the Big Rock Cave Trail. A few steps farther you meet the Old Paugus Trail descending from the left to take over the road. This is the end of the Whitin Brook Trail.

The route is familiar now, but in reverse. Make the final crossing of Whitin Brook, turn right onto the Bolles Trail, walk to Paugus Brook, and cross it. Then the gravel road is open, bringing in the Brook Trail on the left, and leading you back to your car.

Probably the time is late afternoon and that delicious weariness of complete relaxation cradles you. Mount Paugus is just right.

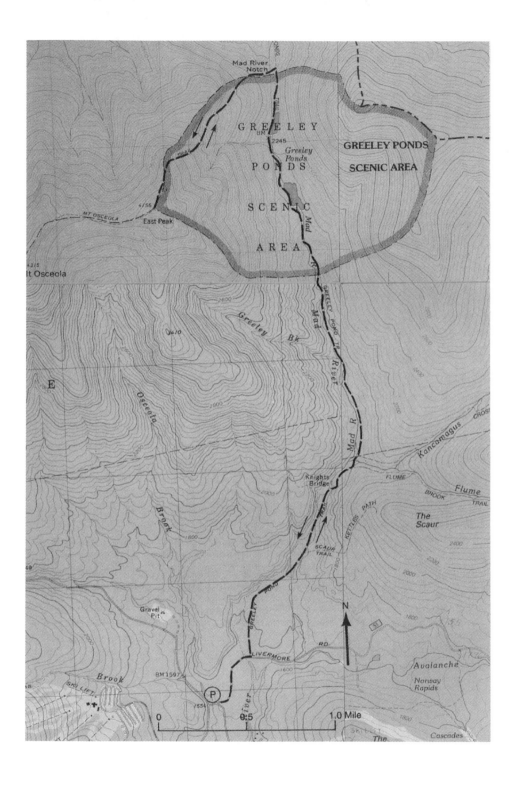

37

Mount Osceola: East Peak

Distance (round trip): 8½ miles

Walking time: 6½ hours

Vertical rise: 2605 feet

Maps: USDA/FS 7½' Mt. Osceola; USGS 7½' Mt. Osceola: USDA/FS 7½' Waterville Valley; USGS 7½' Waterville Valley

Thrusting above the precipices west of Greeley Pond, East Peak's 4156-foot wooded spike presents a climb of 1876 feet in somewhat over a mile—steep enough for most of us. Greeley Pond is a perennial joy, so I like to climb East Peak by the trail north of the pond, rather than from the main summit of Mount Osceola, as peak-baggers do (thus collecting two 4000-footers in one hike). But that's not for me.

How to Get There

Ten miles east into Waterville Valley from Campton, the Tripoli Road branches left off NH 49 across the Mad River before you reach the golf course and buildings of this mountain resort. Drive on the Tripoli Road past the Tecumseh Ski Area road on your left and continue along the Tripoli Road for 1.75 miles from NH 49. Turn right onto a road and bridge over the Mad River's West Branch. (The Tripoli Road climbs north and west through Thornton Gap between Mount Tecumseh and Mount Osceola, descending to I-93 near Woodstock.) Just beyond the bridge, turn sharp left at the gate into the parking area. The road to the right continues on to Waterville village.

The Trail

The hike begins at the kiosk at the east end of the parking area. Turn onto the Livermore Road, which is also the Livermore Trail. At 0.25 mile you come to a clearing known from early logging days as Depot Camp. Continue past the clearing. You quickly reach the GREELEY PONDS TRAIL sign on your left. Turn left onto this former logging road.

The Greeley Ponds Trail stays on the logging road for 1 mile up the west bank of the Mad River. You leave the road at a fork and keep right across a footbridge. The trail stays near the stream for 1.25 miles. The old forest mostly survived the gale of December 3, 1980, which devastated Waterville Valley; its striking specimens of spruce and fir rise between spreading hardwoods.

Lower Greeley Pond is the elongated, boggy stretch of water on your right. Soon the trail passes a cold spring on the left and approaches Upper Greeley Pond. The lovely deep, dark mountain lake appears through the spruces under towering west cliffs and is cupped on the east by massive Mount Kancamagus.

Greeley Ponds are preserved by the forest service as the Greeley Ponds Scenic Area. No camping or fires are allowed within the 810 acres, just enjoyment of the green, craggy setting. Perhaps with this protection, and with nationwide reduction of deadly pesticides—particularly DDT—the cliffs will again become a nesting site of peregrine falcons.

After you have enjoyed the views of the stupendous cliffs from the little beach at the east shore beyond the outlet, return to the Greeley Ponds Trail. Walk on northward into the spruce-fir woods above the west shore. The trail crosses the inlet and climbs 0.25 mile to Mad River Notch and the Mount Osceola Trail on the left. You are 1.25 miles from East Peak. In the dense hardwood forest the notch appears more like a height-of-land, but you'll discover notch steepness. (The Greeley Ponds Trail continues down 1.25 miles to the Kancamagus Highway. See Hike 7 in *50 Hikes in the White Mountains*.)

Turn left onto the Mount Osceola Trail. It rises sharply at once and bears off southwest at a vigor-testing slant. You are heading back toward the almost vertical wall above the pond. On the far side of the notch rises trailless Mount Kancamagus. Among evergreens the trail's pitch eases. You climb under a 200-foot cliff, which drops off a shoulder of East Peak on your right. Soon the trail joins the old route and bears right at a serious grade. You achieve a sharp ridge upward at a steep angle in smaller spruces. The ridge leads to a false summit from which you glimpse the true summit. It's nearer than you think, and the trail takes you abruptly up to the top of East Peak's wooded cone. (From here the trail dips downward into the col between East Peak and Mount Osceola and beyond down to the Tripoli Road 4.25 miles away.)

Despite spreading branches, East Peak intrigues the hiker with views glimpsed through windblown branches. They give a sense of overlooking unexplored terrain such as an 18th-century trapper might have seen. That impression is sharpest looking north into the Pemigewasset Wilderness.

Of course, you must disregard the Kancamagus Highway and forget that the Pemi Wilderness is alive with backpackers. The trapper would have been intrigued not by the views but by the beaver pond down on Cheney Brook. Beavers have returned since they were trapped out and loggers cut the first forests and wasted the streams.

The descent from East Peak should be leisurely. Concern for sure footing and for those downhill leg muscles dictates a cautious pace. There'll be occasional views you didn't notice climbing up. At the junction with the Greeley Ponds Trail, turn right for the easy walk past the ponds and along the brook to Depot Camp and the parking area.

38

North Moat Mountain

Distance (round trip): 9½ miles

Walking time: 6½ hours

Vertical rise: 2740 feet

Maps: USDA/FS 7½' North Conway West; USGS 15' North Conway

Moat Mountain, an elongated, craggy ridge, establishes the horizon west of Conway. It is clearly seen along the much-used highway, NH 16. There are three summits: North, Middle, and South. North Moat, rising to 3201 feet beyond Cathedral Ledge and White Horse Ledge, is the highest. The colloquial name for the mountain is "the Moats." The term goes back to the time when settlers applied it to beaver ponds along streams flowing from the mountain. On this loop hike over North Moat, you'll follow a branch of Moat Brook for part of the descent.

The unnatural tree line at 2700 feet resulted from a fire in September 1854, when flames consumed the trees on this once-forested landmark above the Saco River. The Moats stand alone between major mountain ranges, and you can see in all directions. I know a man who was hooked on mountaineering for life by the exhilaration that comes from a hike on the Moats.

How to Get There

The trail up North Moat begins west of North Conway at the road leading to the potholes called Diana's Baths on Lucy Brook. From the north section of North Conway's long main street turn west onto the River Road, which links to the West Side Road. (This turn is just north of the Eastern Slope Inn.) You drive under the old railroad trestle and across the Saco River. Keep straight past the left turn onto the southern section of the West Side Road. Head northwest on the West Side Road for a clear 0.5 mile and pass the left-branching road to Cathedral

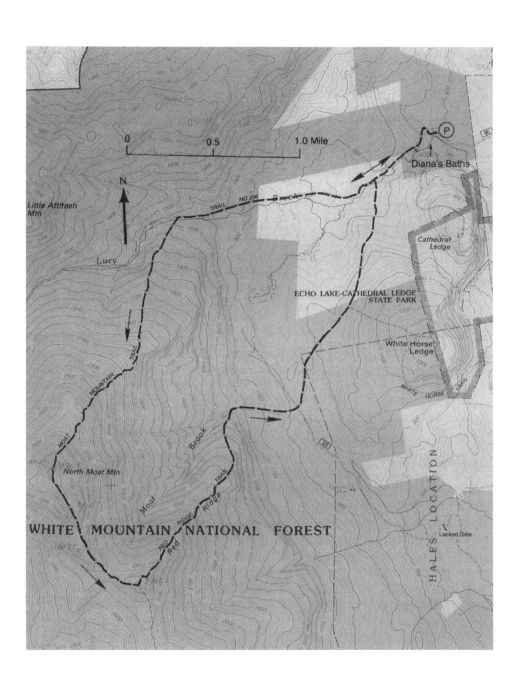

Ledge. Drive through a series of curves and across Lucy Brook.

At 2.4 miles from North Conway's main street, you'll see on the left a forest service sign for Diana's Baths. Drive into the parking area. There is a sign for the Moat Mountain Trail.

To avoid the traffic in North Conway, get on the West Side Road in downtown Conway by turning left onto Washington Street at the junction of NH 16 and NH 153. Drive north, keeping left on the West Side Road at the River Road intersection. Continue as described above, to the left turn to Diana's Baths and trailhead parking.

The Trail

Walk the road for 0.25 mile among the tall red pines. Lucy Brook flows by on your left, and you pass an old mill foundation. Diana's Baths in the rocks above and to your left are basinlike potholes, much wider and shallower than usually found. Lucy Brook drops over ledges squared into steps of a few feet.

The Moat Mountain Trail passes the base of the rocks where an old logging road enters the woods. A curve left soon has you climbing the slope among hemlocks and pines. The road levels along Lucy Brook. About 0.5 mile from Diana's Baths, the Red Ridge Trail forks left across the brook. Keep straight ahead on the wide Moat Mountain Trail. (The Red Ridge Trail will be your return route.)

The only interruption to this excellent walking comes at a layer of cobblestones and low ground through which Lucy Brook seeps across the trail. After that the logging road continues on the south bank of the brook to the base of North Moat, 1.75 miles from Diana's Baths.

Here at a trail junction, turn left up the mountainside. (Straight up the brook the Attitash Trail leads to West Moat and Bear Notch Road 7 miles away.) The ascent at once becomes steep as you climb this northwest shoulder of North Moat. The grade moderates somewhat at 2000 feet, and then you go up again steeply into smaller spruces and over occasional ledges. Moat Mountain is of volcanic origin. Like Mount Hale and a few others it's a recent formation—geologically speaking. Can you imagine magma and molten lava flowing where evergreens now grow?

From the tree-line spruce and fir you follow cairns and yellow blazes up the final ledges. Then you're facing off the peak toward the length of the Moats. The ridge is above tree line for most of its 3 miles. To the left you look east across the Saco River valley at North Conway's ski area on Mount Cranmore. You are also looking at nearby ridges whose eastern, hidden cliffs are Cathedral Ledge and White Horse Ledge. The conical peak with the tower is Kearsarge North, or Mount Pequawket, another volcanic mountain formation.

To the west the Kancamagus Highway traverses the valley of the Swift River. You can see Bear Mountain, Mount Carrigain, Mount Willey, and Crawford Notch.

But the grand view is to the north. Perhaps Mount Washington hides under a white cloud penetrated by broadcasting towers. Washington often makes its own vapors. They are a trademark and distinctive notice that this is *the* peak in the White Mountains. But you see all of the Southern Peaks—Monroe, Franklin, Eisenhower, Pierce (Clinton), Jackson—clear to Crawford Notch. East of Washington, Carter Notch is a slot between Wildcat and Carter Dome. Still more easterly there's a bare summit, which I take to be one of the two Baldfaces in Chatham.

After lingering and lunching, follow the yellow blazes of Moat Mountain Trail south beyond the summit's crags. You descend into spruces and cross an open shoulder with views to the west. The trail swings left and down steeply over ledges. You go down 640 feet. From this col you climb briefly. Emerging from the woods, you come to the junction with the Red Ridge Trail on your left. Two smooth rocks slope up on your right. The Moat Mountain Trail turns 90 degrees to the right and west of them. (The Moat Mountain Trail stays on the ridge and then descends from South Moat to the Dugway Road 4 miles away.)

Now you begin the spectacular Red Ridge Trail. Leaving the junction through spruce woods, the trail soon takes you out on a series of open shoulders. These are Red Ridge. You walk down ledges split into steps seemingly for your use. The trail is well marked with cairns and yellow blazes. I should warn you about the lichens on the rocks. Although innocent looking, they are slippery when wet, especially the map lichens.

Among these ledges you pass colonies of sheep laurel and blueberries. Smaller plants protect themselves from exposure by growing close to the ground: three-toothed cinquefoil, mountain cranberry, and crowberry. The small trees are red spruce, red pine, and white birch.

Entering taller woods, the trail swings left toward a branch of Moat Brook out of sight in a deep ravine. Care is required as you cross smooth ledges where scattered gravel along the top edge of the ravine slides down to the brook. Then you descend steeply among evergreens.

At the brook you cross on stones to a short bank and climb several yards into spruce/fir woods. The trail turns to your right. Watch for blazes and small arrow signs as you descend a slight grade through the woods and away from the brook. At a gravel logging road you'll need to pause and make sure of signs and blazes on the far side. Cross to the opening in the woods.

Proceed north through a formerly logged area. A discerning eye may notice skid roads that cross the trail occasionally. At two forks, arrow signs on trees point your way left. A slight rise in the forest floor lifts you to a junction with the Red Ridge Link Trail on your right. Continue along the Red Ridge Trail. (The Red Ridge Link Trail leads to the White Horse Trail from Echo Lake State Park.)

You are only about 1.25 miles from Diana's Baths. The trail passes through notable growths of ground hemlock. Also called American yew, this low evergreen is often scraggly and sparse. Here it grows luxuriantly under hemlocks, pines, oaks, and other leafy trees.

Lucy Brook appears to your left, and you make the shallow crossing on stones. Turn right at the junction with the Moat Mountain Trail. You're walking the last 0.5 mile back to Diana's Baths. On a hot summer's day those "baths" can cool your feet—or more of you.

King Ravine

Distance (round trip): 7 miles

Walking time: 6 hours

Vertical rise: 3400 feet

Maps: USDA/FS 7½' Mt. Washington SE; USGS 7½' x 15' Mt. Washington

Exploration of this mighty glacial cirque includes scrambling through the jumble of stupendous rocks, touching perpetual ice in caves, and sensing the doomsday weight of boulders above you. Then after a climb up the east wall, with rockbound Mount Adams looming beyond your perch on barren Durand Ridge, you gaze back into the depths and see the rocks reduced by distance to what looks like crushed stone for a road. This hike does not include Mount Adams's summit. King Ravine deserves a whole day.

How to Get There

From US 2 in Randolph, trails to the northern peaks of the Presidential Range lead south from a parking area known as Appalachia, which was its flagstop name on the Boston and Maine Railroad. It's 5.5 miles west of Gorham.

The Trail

Your trail at the beginning and end of this loop hike is Air Line. Facing the mountains, take the path from the right-hand corner of the parking area. Cross the railroad tracks. The path forks, with Valley Way bearing left and Air Line going right. Keep to the right under the power line. At the edge on a tree is a sign for Air Line, which leads ahead into maple woods.

You pass several of the many trails that crisscross these northern slopes. First, the Link and the Amphibrach diverge to the right; then you cross Sylvan Way and, after a few minutes, Beechwood Way. Now you are approaching Short Line 0.75 mile from Ap-

King Ravine

Robert J. Kozlow

The White Mountains

palachia. Turn right onto Short Line. (You will return here in the afternoon, descending Air Line.)

This fine trail provides easy, fast walking southwesterly up through the forest. At a gradual angle in big woods, Short Line joins the Randolph Path, and they coincide for almost 0.5 mile. (The Randolph Path continues 4 miles to Edmands Col between Mount Adams and Mount Jefferson.)

Short Line branches left, and you climb steeply to sparkling Cold Brook on your right. The stream is well named. Its source is the perpetual ice under the ravine's headwall and the destination of this hike. The environment itself becomes cooler as you approach 3000 feet of elevation; the woods change to spruce and fir interspersed with white birch and mountain ash. The terrain becomes rough and rocky but levels somewhat along the brook.

In 1857 Thomas Starr King, author of *The White Hills,* and his companion climbed this way into the ravine that now bears his name. Those early mountaineers followed Cold Brook from the valley and camped beside it.

Short Line ends at its junction with the King Ravine Trail, which comes in from the right. Turn left along the King Ravine Trail. Almost at once you face exquisite little Mossy Fall. Here Cold Brook pours from a ledge between two huge boulders covered with emerald green moss. Beyond and far above, the ravine's precipitous sides rise before you.

Here you should make sure that the rocks are dry and will continue so. They and their lichens give you only treacherous footing when wet.

The trail beyond Mossy Fall disappears among the first gigantic rocks. They engulf you for a short distance until the trail swings left. You climb for a steep 0.25 mile among

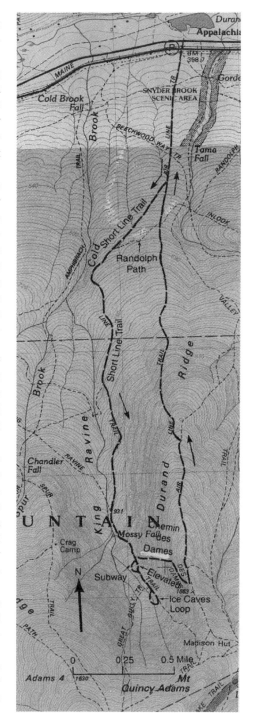

---

spruce, fir, and twisted birch, which somehow cling to the rocks and survive the fierce north winds. A final S-turn upward takes you into the open on the floor of the ravine. You're at 3500 feet and have climbed into a vast amphitheater—the typical bowl shape of a glacial cirque.

Immobile rivers of rock extend ahead to the base of the headwall and also to your left and right. The boulders were torn from bedrock during the glacial scouring of the ravine. The headwall rises above the rocks in a curve of cliffs and gullies. Its jagged rim is 1600 feet above you and 0.5 mile distant. To the left atop the east wall, hikers on Air Line are moving specks. An about-face will show you northern skies, distant clouds, and far mountains.

Here the King Ravine Trail meets a branch trail, on the left, from the east wall. Named Chemin des Dames, it connects with Air Line up on Durand Ridge above tree line. (It will be your exit from the ravine when you return from the ice caves.)

Just beyond Chemin des Dames, the King Ravine Trail divides into easy and difficult routes. To the right the Subway's orange blazes on the rocks lead through a tortuous passage of about 200 yards among rocks as large as summer cottages. To the left the Elevated stays on higher open ground east of the rocks.

Turn right if you want to discover what it's like to scramble and crawl between and beneath untold tons of rocks. At the end of the Subway you climb out into stunted woods, where the Elevated comes in from your left.

If you've taken the Subway, turn right up the reunited King Ravine Trail. It soon passes the Great Gully Trail forking right up the southwest wall. Keep left as the King Ravine Trail winds among more tremendous boulders. Soon the trail forks. You are at the lower

junction of a bypass trail to the ice caves on your right. Keep to the left along the King Ravine Trail. After about 15 minutes you meet the bypass trail joining from the right. (The King Ravine Trail continues ahead to tree line and ascends the steep, difficult headwall.) Now turn onto the bypass trail to your right. Follow the blazes down to three or four different ice caves formed by the tumbled boulders. A flashlight helps locate the ice in the darker caves. Some of it is clearly visible by simple daylight.

Chill air is a good clue to the ice. Look carefully down into caves because the ice has melted into the deepest recesses. It's gray and speckled with dirt and spruce needles. Lower yourself down to an irregular patch and stand on it. You are surrounded by the pervading cold. As you emerge from the cave you feel a rush of warm air.

After the last cave, continue on the bypass trail to the King Ravine Trail. Turn left. At the fork of Subway and Elevated, keep right and enjoy the openness of the Elevated. A few steps beyond the junction where the Subway rejoins from the left, you come to your exit route, Chemin des Dames.

Turn right and begin the climb up the east wall. Orange blazes lead you over the massed blocks of rock. Then you climb among the dwarf spruces and birches, which help you pull yourself up. Boulders form a narrow passage that opens to a gully and a high rock face on your left. The trail angles steeply toward an upper crag outlined against the sky. You leave the trees, climb on, and step out beside the crag to a sudden view of Mount Madison's distant summit. You're atop Durand Ridge on the Knife-edge at 4400 feet. Chemin des Dames ends here as it meets Air Line far above the ravine.

To your right Mount Adams—second highest of the Presidentials, a solid peak stacked with fractured gray slabs—backs up the deep gouge of the ravine. Northward the view is down to Israel River, flowing west, and across its valley to Mounts Starr King, Waumbek, and Cabot. To your right you can see as far as Berlin, Gorham, the Androscoggin River, and the Mahoosuc Range.

Northern views stay with you as you start down Air Line. Soon you enter a corridor between spruces. The evergreens grow taller and taller along the rapidly descending trail. They give way to leafy forest on the lower slopes. You pass Short Line on your left for the completion of the loop and proceed to Appalachia, your car, and the highway's traffic.

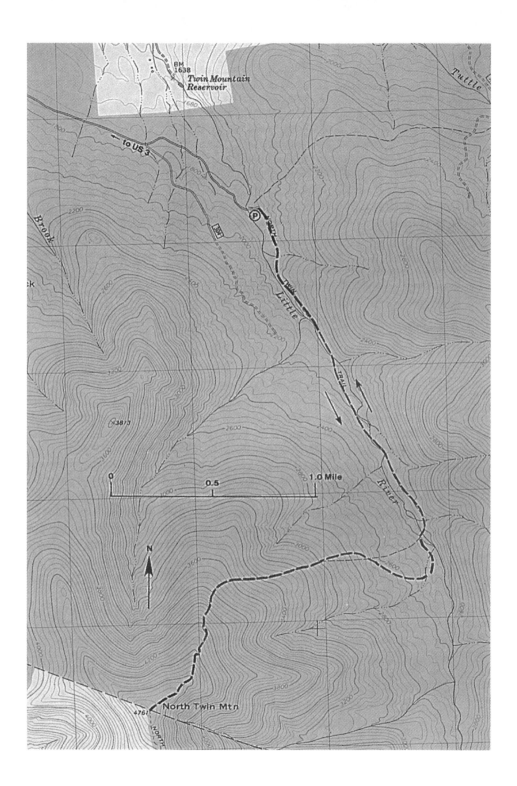

40

North Twin Mountain

Distance (round trip): 8¾ miles

Walking time: 7 hours

Vertical rise: 2910 feet

Maps: USDA/FS 7½' South Twin Mountain; USGS 7½' South Twin Mountain; USDA/FS 7½' Whitefield SE; USGS 7½' x 15' Bethlehem

The controlling natural element in this hike is Little River. The North Twin Trail crosses it three times. During spring runoff or after prolonged rainfall, this trail can be impossible. But I like it because its approach to the mountain is along a forested valley. The stream adds motion and sound. Then the steep climb to the 4761-foot summit (1000 feet per mile for the upper 2.33 miles) establishes North Twin in your mind as an individual mountain in its own right, which it is. Many hikers treat it as a shoulder of South Twin. They combine North and South Twin, usually climbing South Twin first from the AMC's Galehead Hut, continuing on to the North Twin Spur, and returning to South Twin. That's peak-bagging, and I'm against it. North Twin is its own mountain and deserves special attention.

How to Get There

For this respectful treatment you must first find a US Forest Service road branching southward from US 3, west of Twin Mountain village.

Starting at the junction of US 3 and US 302, drive west 2.5 miles on US 3. You pass motels, restaurants, and amusements. You cross Little River. Watch for a big sign, on the right, announcing that you are about to enter the White Mountain National Forest. A few yards beyond, turn left off US 3 onto the forest service road (Haystack Road, FR 304).

This narrow gravel strip, one car wide with turnouts, ends at a parking space 2.5 miles from US 3 on the east bank of Little River. Now you should walk back to the bridge and assess the depth and force of the stream. Remember, there are three trail crossings above and no more bridges. If you're sure you can cross here, get your pack and take the trail beyond the sign east of your car.

The Trail

The North Twin Trail follows an old logging railroad grade of the Little River Railroad, built by George Van Dyke before he became the famous lumber baron of the upper Connecticut River. Of course the standard-gauge tracks are gone, and the depressions from the rotted ties are hardly noticeable. This good walking takes you through a leafy forest grown up since 1900, when the virgin timber had been leveled and hauled out to sawmills.

Beside the North Twin Trail the river dwindles to a brook as you ascend the valley, leaving behind various tributaries. The water alternates between wide pools and miniature rapids, and the charm of fluid motion and sound are with you constantly. At the crossings both are all around you. If balancing on damp rocks bothers you, try using a staff.

The last crossing begins at a little clearing on the east bank and angles upstream to the west bank where the trail continues on the railroad grade. For the last few hundred yards that the trail follows the grade, the 2400-foot elevation becomes apparent in the change to birch trees mingled with spruce and fir. The valley's precipitous slopes have closed in. A sign on a tree marks the right turn off the grade. The summit is 2⅓ miles ahead.

It's uphill in earnest. Two hours will get you to the top, but patience is the watchword. Climbing is like sawing a log with an old-fashioned bucksaw. If you think ahead to the sawed pieces, the job becomes sweating drudgery. Don't think of the top.

Enjoy the climb.

A small branch of Little River borders the trail on your left. You step across, move away from it, and climb parallel to it up the first steep pitch for about 0.5 mile.

The trail here was once a logging road that must have given more than one teamster a wild icy ride on his sled behind leaping horses. The instant horses slipped coming down ahead of a ton of logs, their one thought was to escape. The teamster might jump, but if he valued his horses and took pride in his skill, he'd try to guide them down the mountainside. Many a team went off into the woods with the logs and sled on top of them—"sluiced," the loggers called it. Particularly steep descents, such as this you're climbing, were covered with brush and hay. The sleds were eased down by a heavy rope. Still, accidents happened.

Now you cross the little brook again as the trail swings right. This is the last water. It doubtless supplied lumberjacks once, but now beware of it, unfortunately. The trail passes through the site of a vanished logging camp. Investigation under the leaves reveals junk iron from the inevitable blacksmith shop—sled runners, peavey ferrules, hooks, and chain links.

After a wide swing northward, climbing steadily, you begin to appreciate North Twin as its own mountain. The trail becomes rougher and curves southwest over a sharp rise. You negotiate a short section of muck and ledge that requires a handhold or two. Tree-line spruce scrub begins; then you surmount bare ledges to a lookoff.

Here a striking view opens toward Mount Hale to the east, with Mount Washington stark and clear beyond. You look down into the Little River valley and realize you have indeed been coming up in the world.

A 5-minute walk along the ridge takes you to the wooded summit and the junction with the North Twin Spur from South Twin. Keep right at this fork, and you emerge after a few yards on the west outlook toward South Twin and down on the roof of the AMC's Galehead Hut. Beyond that rises Mount Garfield's rock cone, Garfield Ridge leading to Mount Lafayette, and the Franconia Range. The stretch of valley to the north beyond Twin Mountain village centers along the Ammonoosuc River, which flows west to Littleton and south to join the Connecticut River at Woodsville. Its source is in Ammonoosuc Ravine, 5000 feet up on Mount Washington. North Twin, rising above this wide valley, opens unequaled views across into Vermont.

The return is by the same route you came up, the North Twin Trail. Turn left at the junction with the North Twin Spur, proceed across to the east lookoff, and then hike down and down to Little River. On a long summer afternoon, if you had an early-morning start, the clearing beyond this upper crossing is a good supper spot.

But don't linger too long. Save an hour of daylight for the walk down the old railroad grade while you listen to the evening songs of thrushes and the sound of running water.

41

Mount Moriah

Distance (round trip): 9¾ miles

Walking time: 6½ hours

Vertical rise: 3100 feet

Maps: USDA/FS 7½' Carter Dome; USGS 7½' Carter Dome

A 19th-century writer, with the charming and verbose anthropomorphism of the time, might describe Mount Moriah's summit rock as "the lonely sentinel guarding steadfastly the northeastern ramparts of grim Pinkham Notch."

Mount Moriah does stand out there. From an open crag you look across the notch to Mount Washington. Its Great Gulf is open for your inspection but hedged in by spectacular peaks to the north: Jefferson, Adams, and Madison. To the northeast you see the rugged summits terminating the Carter-Moriah Range. Then, beyond the Androscoggin River, the Mahoosuc Range extends all the way into Maine. North up the river, which makes a right-angle turn at Gorham, you can see Berlin and the paper mills. Turning around to nearer views at the southeastern base of the mountain, you'll be attracted by the forested sweep of the Wild River valley. It stretches to North and South Baldface in Chatham and to the summits forming Evans Notch on the Maine border. To the south you get a skyline view of the Carter-Moriah Range.

Although the mountain may be climbed from Gorham by the Carter-Moriah Trail, I favor the approach up Stony Brook, which is not to be confused with the Stony Brook near Mount Tremont. This way you avoid first climbing Mount Surprise and several tough little knolls.

How to Get There

Drive south from Gorham on NH 16 for 2 miles. You cross the Peabody River just before the Stony Brook Trail on your left. The

The White Mountains

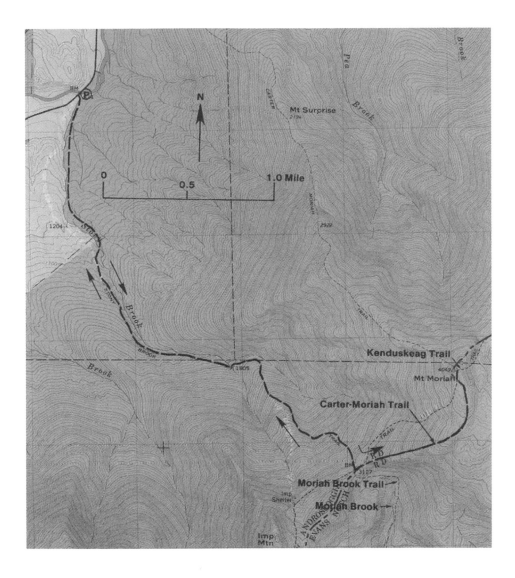

large parking area and the trail's start were new in 1990. The former start, along a development road, is bypassed with this relocation.

The Trail

The Stony Brook Trail begins outside the parking area 100 feet from the entrance. Cross the footbridge over Stony Brook, and you are on national forest land.

The trail parallels the brook on your right up a gentle grade at a good slope for stretching legs that have been confined in a car. Then you can use those muscles to climb more steeply and relax again on some level going. About 1 mile from your car, another footbridge takes you to the south side of Stony Brook, where you join the old trail.

This section leads up through woods logged in the 1970s with skidders that dis-

---

Mount Moriah

rupted the path by hauling logs from the cutting area. These high-wheeled tractors with front blades and rear hoists have replaced forever the woods horses and their less destructive hooves. Here the logging damage has mostly recovered. Watch for the blazes and the main trail.

Beyond this area, the trail follows the route of an ancient sled road. It has seen no lumberjacks since the days of crosscut saws and double-bitted axes. Leading steadily up the mountainside above Stony Brook, it is reinforced by numerous water bars of logs that divert eroding water into adjacent forest duff.

About 2 miles from NH 16, walking in this hardwood forest, you enter an overgrown clearing, the site of a former logging camp. Bottle collectors have dug over the dump, leaving broken glass, tin cans, and scattered leaf mold. On the opposite side of the trail, to the north, you can find the customary remains of the blacksmith shop: sled runners, horseshoes, and soft coal. The worn runners, broken shoes, and few chunks of coal weren't worth hauling out when the camp was dismantled.

Now the trail goes up a steep slope. It crosses a branch of Stony Brook. You are about 1.5 miles from the Carter-Moriah Trail on top of the ridge. You'll need an hour to get there.

The Stony Brook Trail climbs steeply. It bears left and then curves right into upper spruce woods and across another source of Stony Brook. Here in wet weather the little cascade over the mossy ledge can be slippery. The spruces change to white birches, probably grown into an old burn. The trail becomes steeper for the final climb to the Carter-Moriah Trail, which is part of the Appalachian Trail.

This junction in a little col has several plank walkways across the sphagnum bog.

To your left and right the Carter-Moriah Trail leads north to Mount Moriah and south to North Carter Mountain. (The Carter-Moriah Trail, to the south, ends at the AMC's Carter Notch Hut, 8 miles and several summits away.)

Turn left onto the Carter-Moriah Trail. Beside the plank walkway, Indian poke grows tall and green. Also named false hellebore, the plant yields a toxic alkaloid and has a long history as a poison and drug. It appears early, just after snow melts, beginning with pointed, green cones. On lowland meadows, if cattle are turned out before other pasturage tempts them with greenery, they sometimes eat the Indian poke and die. It's deadly for humans, too, of course.

You'll see a sign for the Moriah Brook Trail, which starts down the eastern side of the Carter-Moriah Range. (The Moriah Brook Trail descends 5.5 miles to the Wild River Trail 0.5 mile from the Wild River Campground.) Continue on the Carter-Moriah Trail.

It is a magnificent walk along the ridge crest between the Stony Brook Trail and the summit. The first 0.5 mile climbs steeply along the edge of Moriah's south cliffs, alternately in the woods and on open ledges offering sweeping views of the Moriah Brook valley, the Carter Range, and the Presidentials. Higher up the grade moderates, and the trail meanders through mossy fir forest and across scrub-fringed ledges.

In a little notch you approach the summit ledges on your left. The trail surmounts them by a slot in the rocks, after which you scramble up hand and foot. Scrub spruces line the trail. Turn left onto a short path to the summit rock above you. (The Carter-Moriah Trail continues ahead for its descent of 4.5 miles to a street in Gorham.)

The summit's flat, rectangular ledge—about 10 by 15 feet—contains three brass plugs recording government surveys. Elevation is 4049 feet.

Your arrival at the summit puts you facing Carter Dome, 5 miles south. Perhaps the precipitous rise of North Carter first catches your eyes. The mountain in between you and North Carter is Imp; the one beyond North Carter is Middle Carter. To the east Mount Hight (sic) shows as a jagged crest of rocks. Certainly, however, you'll turn to the Presidential Range before studying the Carter summits for long.

Mount Washington to the southwest seems far away, ethereal and inaccessible, although it's only 10 miles distant. Clouds and glowing sun above the peak create the illusion. Sometimes haze on Mounts Jefferson, Adams, and Madison softens the harsh slabs of rock overlying the peaks.

If you have hiked the Mahoosucs—or even if you haven't, for that matter—turn about and look north and east for memories or with anticipation. Look for Mount Hayes at the west end above Gorham, Cascade Mountain, and the silvery glimmer of Page Pond. Farther away, beyond Mount Success and Goose Eye Mountain, the summits blend toward a far silhouette: a pyramid with western shoulder, which is Old Speck Mountain in Maine. It is 18 miles away.

To the southeast, barren twin summits, North and South Baldface, still display the glaciated bedrock opened to the sky after the 1903 fire and subsequent erosion. That's the Wild River valley you're looking across.

The return down the ascent begins with the decision whether to face the rocks and lower yourself, or whether to gain some adherence from the seat of your pants, thus helping your hands and boots. Below the rocks turn right, to the south, along the Carter-Moriah Trail. (Avoid the Kenduskeag Trail to the left, which has the white blazes for the AT. It links to the Rattle River Trail and US 2 east of Gorham.)

Proceed down to the Stony Brook Trail for the right turn, to the west, from the boggy col. Your descent of the Stony Brook Trail can be one of the most pleasant, woodsy experiences in the mountains. Turn right at the upper footbridge over the brook and enjoy a wholly modern path to your car.

42

Champney Falls/Mount Chocorua

Distance (round trip): 9¾ miles

Walking time: 7½ hours

Vertical rise: 3250 feet

Maps: USDA/FS 7½' Mt. Chocorua; USGS 7½' Mt. Chocorua

If you mark the passing of days, as I do, on one of those scenic New England calendars that arrive in the mail each year, courtesy of your friendly bank or insurance company, you will on the first of some month find yourself gazing at the image of Mount Chocorua. It is one of the most photographed mountains in the East because it combines a spectacular rock pinnacle with a foreground of blue lakes framed by white birches.

In real life the scene has a predictable effect on hikers. As they drive down the hill north of Chocorua village on NH 16 and see the peak, their immediate reaction is to start for the summit on the nearest trail. This they discover 3 miles farther north. It's the Piper Trail and many hikers use it because it's available.

I prefer a northern trail from the Kancamagus Highway. This route gives you Champney Falls along with the interesting upper ledges of the Piper Trail. Mount Chocorua rewards you with rocky challenges that make up for its deficiency in elevation, which is only 3475 feet.

How to Get There

On NH 31 in the center of Washington, turn onto gravel Halfmoon Pond Road, passing the cluster of church, school, and town hall on your left. After 0.5 mile, turn left to Halfmoon Pond. Continue past the pond for a total of 1.9 miles from NH 31. The Lovewell Mountain Road branches off to the right. Here you should select a parking place off on a shoulder. Or if the road is passable a few yards for low-slung cars, there's a smooth, broad ledge a little ways in. Use cautious judgement. If necessary, drive back 0.5 mile to the pond's boat launch and park there.

The Trail

The Champney Falls Trail, a graded path, at once crosses a bridge over Twin Brook. You walk through a hardwood forest for 10 minutes to Champney Brook. This is a pleasant little stream named for the 19th-century White Mountain artist Benjamin Champney. The wide trail stays on the west bank. You gain altitude gradually until you climb more steeply above the brook. At 1.25 miles from your car you reach the Champney Falls bypass trail on your left. The main trail rises straight ahead, and you will return to it after passing the cascades.

Turn left and descend the bypass into the valley, which is a US Forest Service Scenic Area—no camping or fires. At the brook turn upstream to your right. About 0.25 mile from the main trail you come to the base of the cascades. You can step across the brook, on the left, to the short canyon where Pitcher Falls, a tributary, pours from a giant spout (if rain has been plentiful). Returning to the bypass, you mount stone steps to the right of the cascades. The clear water slides and splashes down smooth chutes. (Stay away from them. The slippery ledges could become a watery ski jump leading to a smashup on the rocks below.) The bypass, a woods trail again, rises to the right and takes you back to the main trail.

A steeper grade now continues up through the forest until you're on a rocky trail high above the brook. Switchbacks take you up the steep mountainside and across slanting bedrock. On the left in spruces a cutoff trail branches to the Middle Sister Trail, which you soon reach, also on your left. (The Middle Sister Trail crosses over the central summit of a ridge called the Three Sisters and descends to White Ledge Campground on NH 16.)

The Champney Falls Trail swings to the right across a broad ledge well marked with yellow blazes. Ahead over the treetops rises craggy Chocorua. You enter the spruce and fir woods again. The Champney Falls Trail ends 3 miles from your car. (To the left the Piper Trail drops past a shelter and out to NH 16.)

Turn right onto the Piper Trail. After passing through a little hollow, you climb again and immediately come to a junction. Straight ahead is the West Side Trail, sometimes called the Liberty Trail, which in 0.4 mile joins the Brook Trail. (This route to the summit avoids the ledges on the Piper Trail and is a safer alternative, at the cost of the spectacular views from the ledges.)

Turn left onto the Piper Trail, where spruces open to bare ledges and cliffs that extend the remaining 0.5 mile to the summit. If a storm threatens, this is the place to turn back. Also, in spring and fall Chocorua can be sheathed in dangerous ice and snow.

The yellow blazes and arrows lead you up to the east rocks and to the right until you're on the west side of the peak. Shrubs and plants grow in the scanty soil: Labrador tea, three-toothed cinquefoil, mountain cranberry, rhodora, and crowberry.

Climbing below the summit's west rock face, you come to a trail sign at a broken ledge. Here coinciding trails from the south and west join the Piper Trail. (Returning from the summit, you'll pick up this route for the next section of your loop hike.)

Turn left up the rock. Steep but simple in dry weather, the final climb is 50 yards up to the crags south of the summit. Turn left for this rock platform, where a steel pedestal once supported a steel table remaining from a vanished lookout. The summit is a sky-high perch 10 feet square with a lower ledge extending east another 12 feet or so. You are on a natural rock tower.

Directly ahead to the north, the great view centers on Mount Washington and the Presidential Range. Mount Carrigain's outline shows the tiny block of its lookout tower. To the west, across the treetops far below, the Sandwich Range extends over Mounts Paugus, Passaconaway, and Whiteface. Farther west Tripyramid and Osceola surround the hidden Waterville Valley. Far to the northwest the Franconia Range cuts the horizon.

Turning southwest you look down to the green meadow at Wonalancet and beyond to Squam Lake and parts of Lake Winnipesaukee. You can face east toward Pleasant Mountain in Maine (it looks like a whale) and then northeast for Carter Dome, Carter Notch, and Mount Wildcat.

According to legend these views were the last to be seen by the Native American Chocorua before he met his death at the hands of a onetime friend, Cornelius Campbell. The Pequawket chief's son had died while staying at Campbell's cabin. Retaliating, Chocorua massacred Campbell's wife and children. Campbell pursued Chocorua to this summit. Before he died the chief is said to have proclaimed a curse on the white men, beginning doubtless with Campbell. The sickness and death of many cattle followed. Not until shortly before the Civil War was the ailment traced to muriate of lime occurring naturally in the water the cattle drank.

The return hike begins as you retrace your steps down to the junction sign at the broken ledge. For this return to your car allow 4 hours. It's 6 miles away and includes 900 feet of vertical rise to the pass on the Bolles Trail. (Again, do not use this loop route if you are hiking with children or if you don't feel ready for it. Return the way you came.)

Your trail descends to the left. Don't worry that your route into the valley, Bee Line, doesn't show on the sign, which lists the Weetamoo Trail and others. Bee Line is down there 25 minutes away.

So turn left at the sign and make your way down into a corridor through scrub spruce. It takes you to a smooth, open ledge and yellow blazes. Near the bottom, joining from the woods on the right, the Liberty Trail coincides with your descent for about 100 feet to Bee Line on the right. The Liberty Trail bears left across open rock clearly marked with yellow blazes.

Turn right onto Bee Line. You again enter the spruce and fir woods but soon descend to open rock once more. Arrows there show the right turn above the dropoff, which is dangerous when wet. Keep right and descend where ledges separate and provide holds for feet and hands. You reach the top of a slide that also requires caution. There's gravel on smooth rock, as well as slabs to climb over. Then you are down to woods again.

Evergreens surround you as you head down steeply over roots and stones. About 0.5 hour from the start of Bee Line, the trail becomes more level and you're walking in leafy woods. Hobblebush thrives in the valley of the brook on your right. You cross to the west bank and take up an old logging road. After another crossing of the brook, you come to the Bolles Trail and Paugus Brook. (Bee Line continues west toward Mount Paugus and a junction with the Old Paugus Trail.)

Turn right, to the north, on the Bolles Trail. At once you cross the tributary you were following along Bee Line. The Bolles Trail, a wide old logging road, has an easy upward grade. It briefly takes to the woods on your right before crossing Paugus Brook and rejoining the logging road. You enter the clearing of a former camp, walk through the grass and bushes, and enter the forest again. Bearing left away from Paugus Brook past a seasonal, sandy tributary on your left, the trail traverses a fine growth of white birches that have grown into an old burn. Beyond a rock-strewn gully you begin the steep climb to the pass. This is a constant, 30-minute test of your legs late in the day.

At the height-of-land in the pass, rocks among the beech woods are burned black, and an occasional stub or stump black with charcoal still stands. After about 250 yards' walking beside a rugged, wooded knoll on your left, you begin the descent of the north slope. There a mucky area is the source of Twin Brook. Keep to the left as the trail leads along the accumulating water and down the west bank. The Bolles Trail follows with many crossings (ten, I think) until the ravine opens to the valley. Twin Brook swings away toward the parking area on your right, and at the highway you also turn right for your car.

43

South Twin Mountain

Distance (round trip): 11 miles

Walking time: 8 hours

Vertical rise: 3330 feet

Maps: USDA/FS 7½' South Twin Mountain; USGS 7½' South Twin Mountain; USDA/FS 7½' Franconia; USGS 7½' Franconia

Which way to look first? That's the problem on this open, 4902-foot summit. South Twin Mountain, located between the two major ranges of the White Mountains, exposes a great view of both. Actually, South Twin is much closer to the Franconias than to the Presidentials. Mount Lafayette is 5 miles away to the southwest; Mount Washington, 14 miles to the northeast.

I think South Twin is best saved for the clear days and blue skies of early October. From the summit rocks you look south over the forested East Branch watershed. The Pemigewasset Wilderness flames no more with the lumberman's forest fires but annually burns symbolically with the red leaves of swamp maples in the lowlands. The mountainsides display the yellow of birches, the tan of beeches, the orange of sugar maples, and the lemon of poplars.

How to Get There

To reach the Gale River Trail, drive north through Franconia Notch on the parkway. As this scenic route again becomes I-93, turn right onto US 3 and follow it for 5 miles toward Twin Mountain. Turn right onto the Gale River Road (FR 25). At 0.6 mile bear left. Continue another 1.3 miles and turn right onto FR 92 for 0.3 mile to the parking area on the left.

The Trail

On an October day, having arrived early, you'll face into the low sun. It shines through branches dropping yellow leaves, which rustle underfoot. The trail winds to an old logging road, crosses a small brook, and

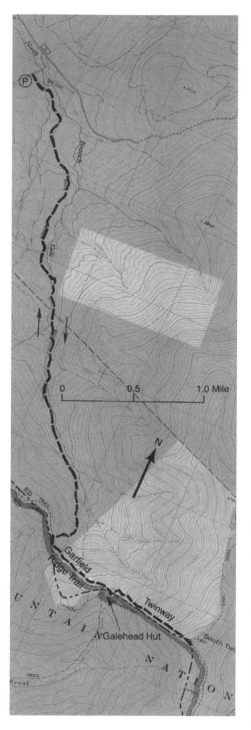

then heads into a steady, gradual approach to the North Branch. Meeting this water supply for Littleton, the trail stays on the west bank to a crossing on a footbridge.

The way becomes steeper along the east bank, past clear pools and little cascades. The water is so clear, I once took a picture of a trout on a gravel bar. The trail is rough in places to the next stream crossing (over stones this time). Then, once again on the west bank, it climbs to another logging road. You follow this easy route to the rocks and earth at the base of two slides. The second and longer slide gouged a deep path down the ridge and dumped rocks into the North Branch.

Beyond the big slide the trail soon turns right and begins the steep ascent of the valley's west wall. This 0.25 mile may suggest the stamina required of the Galehead hutmen and women who pack in supplies to the AMC's Galehead Hut (which is open from mid-May to mid-October, caretaker basis in May). You can rest in thick evergreens at the end of the Gale River Trail, where it joins the Garfield Ridge Trail.

Then turn left on the Garfield Ridge Trail. (To the right the Garfield Ridge Trail extends 6 miles over Mount Garfield to Mount Lafayette.) You continue in the spruce and fir woods as the trail slabs toward the head of the last valley, descends slightly, and climbs sharply for the last of this 0.5 mile on the Garfield Ridge Trail.

You pass a flat rock tipped at an angle in the middle of the trail. It's about the area of a kitchen table and knee-high. The gullied trail did not always divide around the rock. Dr. Claud Sharps, D.V.M., a hutman for five summers in the 1930s, told me he used to climb across the rock's surface knowing, he said, that he would soon make the hut and unload his packboard. (You can see one of those packboards hanging on the wall of

The summit of South Twin

AMC's Pinkham Notch Visitor Center. They were made by Roddy Woodward of North Conway. Hutmen are now called "hutboys" and women are "hutgirls." Both carry pack frames of wood and canvas.)

The Garfield Ridge Trail ends just east of the hut at a junction with the Twinway, which will be your hike's final section, on the left, to the summit of South Twin. But first turn right and walk the few yards to the hut.

Built of logs in 1932, remodeled and shingled over the years, it perches on a small wooded plateau, elevation 3800 feet. Its two porches give you views up 1000 feet of South Twin's spruce-grown dome. The west porch opens to a vista extending 12 miles southward across the Pemigewasset Wilderness to Mount Osceola and Scar Ridge. From the helicopter pad west of the hut you look at nearby Galehead Mountain. On your right, north of Galehead Mountain, Mount Garfield shows its summit rock. To the left and also against the sky the Franconias form a jagged horizon.

In season, the hut is a busy place. Two bunkrooms, dining room, kitchen, and the summertime crew—usually college students—can accommodate up to 38 guests. Reservations must be made through the AMC's Pinkham Notch Visitor Center. Thousands of other hikers pass by, including those trekking the Appalachian Trail, which follows the Garfield Ridge Trail and the Twinway.

The final climb to South Twin begins from the junction of the Garfield Ridge Trail and the Twinway. Keep straight through onto the Twinway. You pass a spur trail, on your left, to a lookoff ledge among spruces. The Twinway descends into a little hollow with a pool on your right.

Then upward for those 1000 final feet of vertical rise. Although the scant mile is not devastating to your legs, you may be glad for a brief pause at an opening in the woods halfway along; you can admire Mounts Lafayette, Lincoln, Liberty, and Flume. Climbing on, you notice the spruces getting smaller. When they are only head high, you emerge on the summit rocks.

Two hundred feet of glacier-scoured ledges and rocks give you the panorama I spoke of earlier. In addition, off to the west on this clear October day you can see into Vermont as far as Mount Mansfield and Jay Peak.

South and east from the summit curves the ridge connecting to Mount Guyot. South of bare and rounded Guyot, the horizon is dominated by its neighbor Mount Bond and the pinnacle of West Bond. But looking again eastward along the ridge followed by the Twinway, you can see the scarred hump of Whitewall Mountain forming the cliffs above Zealand Notch. Evergreens are slowly coming back after the searing forest fire of 1886.

Continuing around to your left, you see the horizon outlined by Mounts Willey, Field, and Tom, all connected, and in the distance Mounts Washington, Jefferson, and more, far more.

Let's not forget North Twin. It lives up to its name by being directly north only a mile away, as ravens fly. (Actually they don't fly

He felt a strange wild careless happy sensation, as when he was stepping out of the barn on a fall night as the moon came up over Cobblestone, orange as the hardwoods, with the wild smell of fall on the frosty air.
—*Daniel Doan,* Amos Jackman

that straight. They're always looping and sailing in fancy curves.)

If you are on South Twin during a busy weekend such as Columbus Day, you'll have the company of at least 40 or 50 people. The summit presents a gala scene in the bright sun as hikers come and go in groups, in couples, in marching files.

Turning to the descent, you find it steep. Now facing into treetops you catch glimpses of boreal chickadees.

From the Galehead Hut take the Garfield Ridge Trail back the way you came; turn right onto the Gale River Trail and so back to your car.

44

The Presidentials: Southern Peaks

Distance (one way): 12 miles

Walking time: 10½ hours

Vertical rise: 3600 feet

Maps: USDA/FS 7½' Mt. Washington SE; USGS 7½' x 15' Mt. Washington; USDA/ FS 7½' Crawford Notch; USGS 7½' Crawford Notch; USDA/FS 7½' Stairs; USGS 7½' Stairs

This hike traverses one of the most spectacular routes in the White Mountains. It starts on the western side of Mount Washington and soon encounters the pools and waterfalls in rugged Ammonoosuc Ravine. It goes up to the AMC Lakes of the Clouds Hut (5050-foot elevation) under Mount Washington's peak, turns south for 4 miles above tree line, and passes over Mounts Monroe, Franklin, Eisenhower, and Pierce (Clinton). Then from the AMC Mizpah Spring Hut it concludes the Southern Peaks with Mount Jackson and provides a great lookoff back the way you've come. Finally it descends to Crawford Notch by the Webster-Jackson Trail.

Perfect weather is an absolute necessity for this hike. Dangerous exposure in sudden storms above tree line on the Crawford Path can overcome unwary, overconfident, or unfit hikers.

Every hiker in your party should have sturdy clothing, including boots, wool socks, shirt, pants, warm caps, gloves, and parkas. In your rucksack carry lunch, extra food, water, and survival gear to preserve life in a subarctic environment. That's what you'll be climbing to.

How to Get There

Two cars are required. Park one either at the parking area for the Crawford Path on the Mount Clinton Road near the junction with US 302 or west of Saco Lake near the AMC Crawford Notch Visitor Information Center on US 302. You should be there by 6:30 AM or earlier.

In the second car drive 4 miles on the

Mount Clinton Road to the Base Road. Turn right and drive 1 mile to hiker parking for the Ammonoosuc Ravine Trail on the right.

The Trail

This new parking in the woods restricts views that formerly, at the base station and trailhead, made you take stock of your fitness and equipment. Those rocky heights are still in place although you start without their enticement—or warning.

Double-check your gear.

From the east side of the parking, take the Ammonoosuc Ravine Trail. It leads up an easy slope into a forest of spruce, fir, and hardwoods. You cross Franklin Brook after 0.25 mile. The trail leads southeast away from the noises of engines and descends to the former route from the base station. Here, 0.75 mile from your car, keep right and begin this worn old path along the Ammonoosuc River.

The Ammonoosuc Ravine Trail is a popular approach to Mount Washington; yet it gives the effect of lifting you into a lonely, forested, mountain fastness. An hour's hiking steadily upward through spruce and fir woods along the brook brings you to the first waterfall and pool. The trail crosses the stream.

Log steps hold the path on the mountainside. After 10 or 15 minutes of serious climbing, watch for a side trail on the right and a GORGE sign on a tree. Here you will find a lookoff up the ravine toward two rock sluices shooting white cascades at you.

Returning to your climb, you find other spectacular falls and views as the trail emerges into smaller evergreens. The brook divides. In rock crevices an alpine plant, mountain avens, blooms during July like an exotic buttercup. You are climbing into a gloriously barren world of sky and rock bathed in either mist or bright sunlight. Cairns lead up-

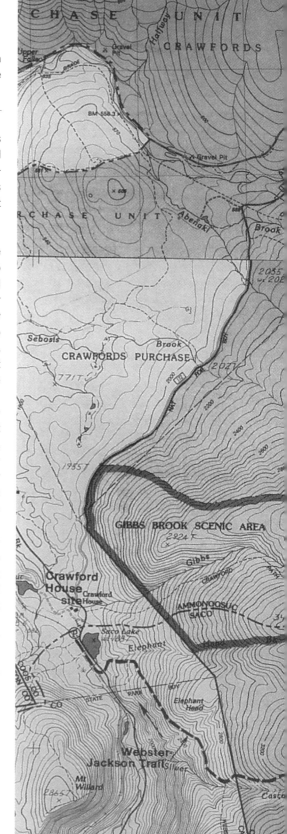

PRESIDENTIAL RANGE-DRY RIVER WILDERNESS

ward. The gray cone on your left is Mount Washington and, beyond it, Mount Jefferson. The ravine falls away behind you, clear to the diminutive base station.

Three hours and 3 miles from the parking, at the col between Mount Washington and Mount Monroe, the AMC Lakes of the Clouds Hut is a shingled haven and, for you, the point of no return. Examine the peaks for signs of storm. Go inside and check the weather report posted on the bulletin board.

Unless clear weather blesses you, go back down the Ammonoosuc Ravine Trail and try again another day. Aside from the exposure dangers of chilling rain, blinding clouds, sleet, or snow, the scenic values and joys are wasted during a slogging trek above tree line.

If the skies are fair and the forecast stable, take the Crawford Path south. You are on the AT with its white blazes, which leads toward craggy Mount Monroe. *Please stay on the path.* The alpine mosses, lichens, and plants such as diapensia, mountain cranberry, sandwort, three-toothed cinquefoil, crowberry, bilberry, and Labrador tea are rare and delicately balanced in their survival arrangements. Boots damage them easily and irreparably. Follow the trail's cairns. Stay within the rock guide walls that define the trail.

Approaching Mount Monroe, the Crawford Path bears left around the base. To reach the summit turn right onto the Mount Monroe Loop. The vertical rise from the hut to Mount Monroe is only 334 feet. You'll be rewarded by a tremendous view of the Lakes of the Clouds, the upper Crawford Path, tiny hikers, and Mount Washington's buildings and broadcasting towers.

The Mount Monroe Loop continues to the western summit, from which it descends to rejoin the Crawford Path.

The crossing of Mount Franklin, 5004 feet, is a nearly level section above the cliffs that drop into Oakes Gulf and the misnamed Dry River. Beyond the gulf, extending south from the minor peak called Boott Spur, a long ridge includes Mount Isolation and Mount Davis.

Along the Crawford Path here are relics of the past. Two pairs of iron rods, embedded in a ledge and bent to hold oak timbers years ago, gave hoofholds to horses scrambling up and down the rock. In the mid-1800s visitors rode horses up the Crawford Path. Winslow Homer painted and sketched along here.

Not far beyond these rods, as you descend rapidly and before approaching Mount Eisenhower's barren dome, you arrive at a ledge for lunching and sunning. A spring trickles across the path. Sandwiches and a brief rest prepare you for the Mount Eisenhower Loop over the summit, 0.25 mile farther on.

As at Mount Monroe, the Crawford Path swings east around the base of Mount Eisenhower from a junction near a little pool named Red Pond. (Here also is an escape route in bad weather: the Edmands Path, which runs 3 miles down through sheltering woods to the Mount Clinton Road.) The Mount Eisenhower Loop, to the right, takes you up to another exhilarating summit of 4761 feet. A giant cairn protects you from the steady west wind while you appreciate the miraculous adaptation of alpine plants around you.

The Mount Eisenhower Loop returns via cairns south to the Crawford Path in scrub spruce. This is your last mile on the famous old trail. Mount Pierce is ahead. At its northern base turn left onto the Webster Cliff Trail. (The less hardy members of the party may continue on the Crawford Path the easy 3 miles to US 302 just north of Saco Lake and your car.)

Mount Pierce was named in 1913 in honor of New Hampshire's only United States president, but is still sometimes called by its former name, Mount Clinton. It is a flattened, spruce-grown 4310-foot knob 150 yards beyond the Crawford Path junction. Your route drops away steeply for the 0.75 mile along the Webster Cliff Trail to the AMC Mizpah Spring Hut, the club's newest (1965). Situated in a clearing at 3800 feet, it's near the unfailing spring, now boxed in with concrete and a cover but still pouring from a pipe its cold water.

Keep to the right of the hut; don't linger, for the afternoon is waning. From Mizpah Cutoff's beginning, turn left. Take up again the Webster Cliff Trail. Climb through spruce woods and walk along sawed half logs laid on stringers resting on the boggy ground. You come out of the woods into a mountain meadow before the trail rises to the open ledges and Mount Jackson's summit at 4052 feet.

There's a magnificent exposure of the valleys and ridges extending north to Mount Washington. The Southern Peaks are all displayed.

Continuing from the summit to the southwest past scrub spruce, you come to a junction with the Mount Jackson section of the Webster-Jackson Trail. This is your return to Crawford Notch. (The Webster Cliff Trail, the AT, descends southeast.) On a northerly bearing, from which you may look across Crawford Notch to Mount Willey, keep to the cairns and paint marks until the trail descends the rocks to your left and dips into spruce woods. Then the way is clear, past Tisdale Spring on your right.

Forested for the remainder of the 2.75 miles to US 302, the Webster-Jackson Trail crosses several streams and passes a junction where a south fork leads to Mount Webster. Keep to the right. Bugle Cliff, reached by a short spur trail on the left, is a worthwhile lookoff into the notch from the thick forest.

The same cannot be said of the next spur trail on the left, to Elephant Head. The view is anticlimactic. Walk on down to a woods road. Turn left to busy US 302, then turn right past Saco Lake to your car.

The highway is a *real* anticlimax after the everlasting mountains. But isn't it good to roll along on those four wheels while you rest your legs?

The Far North

At Indian Stream in midsummer, the white-throated sparrows whistled, sweet but mournful, at daybreak from the tops of the spruces. The cool night air of the north country became warm in the sunshine. Insects hovered over the clearings, where women went to the well, to the spring, or to the brook for water. Flocks of crested cedar birds, wax-sleek, darted from the dead limbs of trees in pursuit of insects in the sunlight. Grass of the swales and meadows grew as high as a man's belt, and continued to grow in the thundershowers that came out of the northwest. Corn and wheat began to mature. Goldfinches with black wings flew across the roads and hid among the weeds of the stump fences. Chickens dusted themselves in dooryards, and hogs wallowed in the sunny muck of barnyards. Vegetation of all kinds flourished, green and heavy.

–*Daniel Doan,* Indian Stream Republic:
Settling a New England Frontier, 1785–1842

45

Mount Magalloway

Distance (round trip): 2 miles

Walking time: 1½ hours

Vertical rise: 1000 feet

Map: USGS 7½' Magalloway Mountain

Growing up in Orford on the Connecticut River, Dan was fascinated by the river's history. Later, he spent much time exploring its headwaters in the Pittsburg area, and eventually he wrote *Indian Stream Republic: Settling a New England Frontier, 1785–1842.*

During a lengthy international dispute about the boundary between northern New England and British Canada, made even more complicated by claims of rival land companies, the settlers in this area declared themselves an independent republic. For a brief golden age, from 1832 to 1834, they governed themselves with their own constitution and laws. They were rugged individualists descended from, as Dan wrote, "the wanderers and the rovers, the explorers, the footloose, the men seeking quick wealth through fur, the men defending their log huts, the men taking to the woods-life as to a drug (pounding heart of the chase and the ultimate freedom, which they could never give up)." But when a border confrontation resulted in bloodshed, the New Hampshire militia moved in, and later the Webster-Ashburton Treaty of 1842 awarded the Indian Stream territory to the United States, with a boundary at Hall's Stream. Dan wrote, "The rabbit-ear shape of the state's northern silhouette became permanent."

Mount Magalloway, elevation 3383 feet, named after the river beyond it, gives you wilderness views into Canada, Vermont, and Maine, along with New Hampshire. The hike itself is short and easy, but the trip north can seem almost as much of an adventure as it was for the Indian Stream settlers.

Donald K. MacDougall

On Mount Magalloway

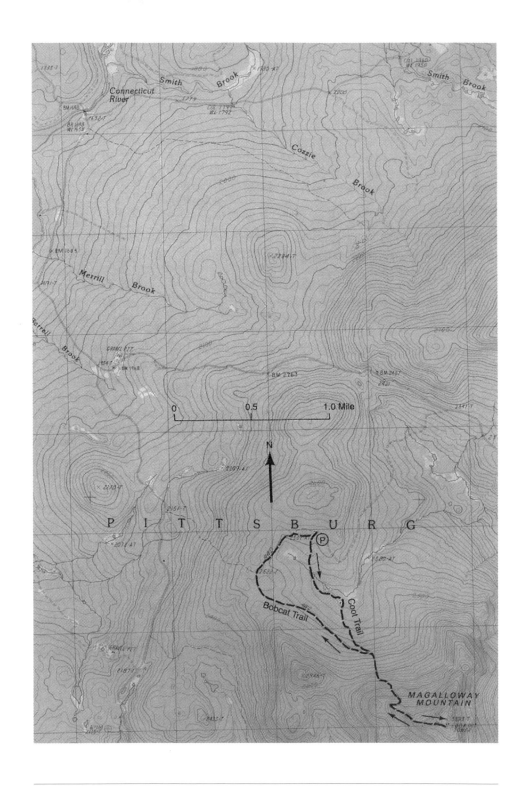

How to Get There

Drive US 3 north from Pittsburg. Note your mileage when you see the dam on First Connecticut Lake, on your right with signs for the New England Power Company and the First Connecticut Lake Park and Picnic Area. Continue on US 3 for 4.7 miles. On your right you'll see a sign for Magalloway Mountain Lookout Station. Turn onto the gravel road and reset your mileage.

Watch out for logging trucks! They have the right of way here.

At 1.2 miles you cross a bridge over the Connecticut River. Go straight, through open orange gates. At 2.3 miles bear left. At 2.9 miles bear left again. Drive on through another set of open gates. On this stretch of road I saw a fox stop to contemplate my truck, then dart into the woods. At 5.2 miles turn right. The bleak utilitarian road becomes prettier, in July abloom with daisies and buttercups that perhaps have already gone by where you live. At 6.2 miles bear right. The road ends in a clearing at 8.1 miles. Park on the right or left.

The Trail

A large sign straight ahead mentions that the Magalloway fire tower was one of the first lookouts, built in 1910; a new steel tower was built in 1933. The sign's map shows you the routes of the two trails to the summit, Coot and Bobcat. Coot is the old service road to the tower, while Bobcat is a longer, higher trail. You can do this loop either way. I have chosen the clockwise route.

Start up the trail, to the right. A sign will remind you about day use only and no camping or open fires or ATVs. You may also be reminded by moose tracks that this is indeed wilderness. You almost certainly will be seeing moose tracks farther along the trail if not immediately.

Quickly, the trail divides. Take the left branch, the Coot Trail. It passes a cabin on the right and begins rising steadily over roots and rocks, through mixed hardwoods, past ferns, wood sorrel, clintonia, Canada mayflower. About 10 minutes from the trailhead, it divides briefly, then rejoins. You climb on through birches, maples, spruces, and over loose rocks.

At 0.5 mile, glimpses of mountains begin to appear. The trail again divides and rejoins. Keep looking back. You'll get a view of First Connecticut Lake. The distances may make you think some more about the settlers here who chopped out a clearing in the forest, built a log house, planted corn amid the stumps, and faced winter. Spring was a long time coming. As Dan wrote, "April moved along slowly. It could not be said to blossom, for there were no blossoms in April at Indian Stream, save those of the swamp maples whose red tassels appeared late in the month. April did at last turn into May. The little brooks along the edges of the clearings, and the pools in the woods, no longer froze to silence and sheets of glass at night."

The trail moderates. At 0.75 mile a branch trail to the right cuts across to the Bobcat Trail. Stay on the Coot Trail, which becomes steep again. In about 50 yards the Bobcat Trail joins the Coot Trail. Turn and look down at the lake view.

In spruce and fir, the trail levels into a beautiful wide path leading to the Magalloway fire tower. The warden's cabins are to your left.

From the tower the views seem limitless. To the west you're looking at Vermont's Monadnock Mountain, Mount Hor, Bald Mountain, Gore Mountain, Brousseau Mountain, and Jay Peak; in Quebec, Hereford Mountain, Mount Foster, Mont Chagnon, and Mont Chauve; First Connecticut Lake and Back Lake are in the foreground. To the northwest and north are more mountains in

Quebec: Mont des Trois Lacs, Mont Megantic, Mont Saint-Cecile. You can see both First Connecticut Lake and Second Lake.

Maine mountains appear as you swing your gaze to the northeast and east: Rump, Merrill, Snow, West Kennegago, East Kennegago, Bigelow, Big Buck, Spaulding, Abraham, Aldrich, Saddleback, and Deer. Aziscohos Lake lies below. The mountains to the southeast and south are also in Maine: Bemis, Elephant, Aziscohos, Baldpate, Sunday River Whitecap, Slide Mountain. In the Mahoosuc Range, Maine merges into New Hampshire from Old Speck Mountain and Goose Eye Mountain to Mount Success. (See Hike 50 in *50 Hikes in the White Mountains*.) Farther on to the south and southwest you continue into New Hampshire with Mount Moriah, Mount Hight, Wildcat, Pinkham Notch, Mount Washington, Mount Jefferson, Mount Eisenhower, Mount Field, Mount Waumbek, Mount Cabot, and Dixville Peak.

For more views, walk northeast around the warden's cabin and follow the trail about 200 yards.

To descend, retrace your steps on the main trail to the junction of the Coot Trail and the Bobcat Trail. Take the left branch onto the Bobcat Trail. You pass the cross path to Coot that you noticed on the way up; stay on Bobcat. Soon another smaller path crosses to Coot, and again you'll stay on Bobcat.

There's a fine view of Second Connecticut Lake. The high trail is relaxing, leveling out at 0.5 mile, woodsy and dreamy. Then it descends through wet areas, where muddy moose tracks rouse you to alertness.

The Bobcat Trail rejoins the Coot Trail, and you walk out into the clearing.

Backpacking Hikes

He awoke before daylight. The birds were beginning to sing in the woods. One called from across the brook and another, as though just awakened, answered with half a song. Amos looked out through the front of the shelter. There was a growing light among the trees. He could see the white cascade of the brook and the gray ledges and the dark pool. The near trees stood out distinctly but he couldn't see into the woods, although even as he watched they seemed to open up. The sky was growing lighter above the pointed spruce tops. And the birds sang everywhere.

—Daniel Doan, Amos Jackman

46

Gordon Pond

Time allowed: 2 days, 1 night

Distance (one way): 8¼ miles

Walking time: 8 hours

Vertical rise: 2300 feet

Maps: USDA/FS 7½' Lincoln; USGS 7½' Lincoln; USDA/FS 7½' Mt. Moosilauke; USGS 7½' Mt. Moosilauke

The last time I hiked to Gordon Pond I saw a red fox carrying a limp hare in her jaws. Evidently she was taking dinner to her cubs. This rare sight appeared along one of the old logging roads that make backpacking so pleasant in the middle sections of the Gordon Pond Trail. The pond, 2567 feet above sea level at the north end of an interesting, swampy plateau, lies under Mount Wolf and below a rugged section of the Appalachian Trail, the southerly 3.3 miles of the Kinsman Ridge Trail.

How to Get There

Two cars are necessary. Park one at the Appalachian Trail's crossing of NH 112 in Kinsman Notch, 5.9 miles from the US 3 traffic lights in North Woodstock. With the second car, drive east to the forest service sign for the Gordon Pond Trail on the north side of NH 112 opposite Govoni's Restaurant, 2 miles from North Woodstock's traffic lights. Park on the highway shoulder west of the restaurant to avoid the area reserved for customers.

The Trail

First Day: NH 112 to Gordon Pond
Distance: 4½ miles
Walking time: 4½ hours
Vertical rise: 1800 feet
The Gordon Pond Trail first follows a driveway between cottages uphill, and then 100 yards farther in the woods it makes a right turn onto the old logging railroad grade last used in October 1916.

Watch for the blue blazes. At 0.6 mile the

Backpacking Hikes

Gordon Pond

Jacqueline Donegan

trail turns left into a power line clearing, where you may want to pause to sample the blackberries. The trail reenters the woods to the right and continues along the railroad grade at 1 mile, bearing left.

During this sweeping northerly curve past dark hemlocks among the beeches and birches, at 1.3 miles a road comes in on the right. Keep straight here, and again when another road comes in at 1.5 miles. Rose-breasted grosbeaks sing in the sunny treetops.

You near Gordon Pond Brook, but the trail takes you under the high cables of the power line again. Then, a few minutes later, you swing right to the bank of Gordon Pond Brook and cross on the smooth stones. (This crossing may be dangerous in spring or after heavy rains.)

The angle of incline increases. You have left the railroad grade behind and are on a logging road dug out of the slope years ago

for sleds. It takes you high above the brook on your left. Here's where I saw the red fox.

The trail, making for the head of the valley, turns left at 3.5 miles and crosses Gordon Pond Brook and begins the sharp ascent to Gordon Falls, which is on a tributary brook. During times of high water, you can hear the splashing as you reach the spruce woods. Gordon Falls is really a cascade down a cleft in solid rock. The V-shaped trough, after rains, contains sparkling water for 50 feet until it escapes as white spray at the rocks in the pool.

Above the falls the brook becomes darker, or seems to, where the trail crosses to the west bank. Be careful on the slippery ledges.

The brook flows through boggy, spruce-shadowed flats. You cross this tributary again as it dwindles away west, and you walk into birches high above Gordon Pond Brook on your right. One shallow crossing

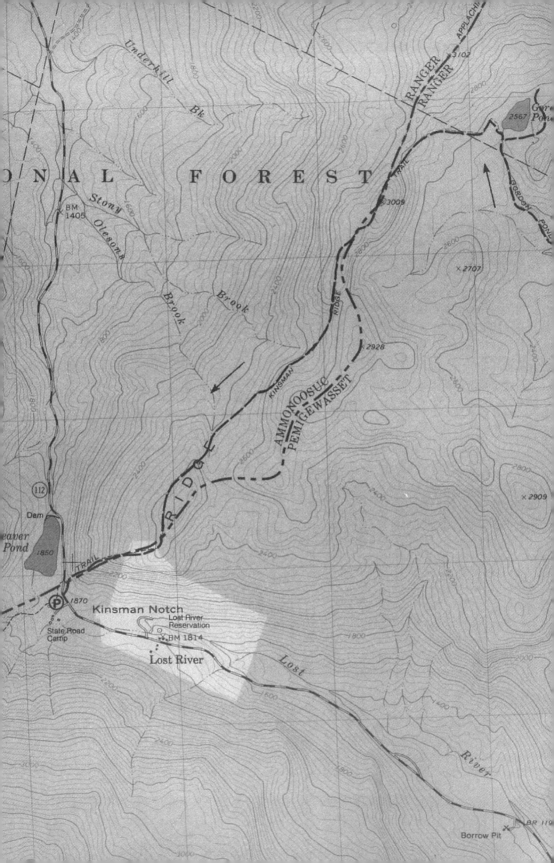

Carrying equipment and supplies for a single night or a week, your body needs some special attention, preparation, and toughening. A good conditioner for carrying a large pack is a small pack. Your daypack will train your body somewhat. Then add the extra weight gradually to your backpack. Carry it partially loaded, slowly increasing the weight until it equals what you'll need for your backpacking trip.

Such training will ensure that you're not flattened by the backpack in the first hundred yards. Actually, the only way to train for a backpack is to lug one around all day—there's just no other real training.

—Daniel Doan, Dan Doan's Fitness Program for Hikers and Cross-Country Skiers

of this stream puts it on your left for the final 15 minutes to the pond.

To reach these 3 acres of clear water and the view of Mount Wolf, continue straight beyond the trail's turn left across the outlet. Several paths wind among the trees on the shore.

Breezes blow across the water. You face the forest on Mount Wolf. It sweeps to the steep east face—a blend of spruce green and birch green. To the right of Mount Wolf, a low gap rises slightly to a wooded ridge. As in all impounded water habitats, birds enliven the scene.

Follow the shore to the left across a breached beaver dam, then to the right. You'll find campsites back from the shore under the spruces.

For your water, return to the brook at the

outlet. Filter or treat it. Another precaution: After supper, put your remaining food in a bag and hang it high on a tree branch.

Second Day: Gordon Pond to NH 112

Distance: 3¾ miles
Walking time: 3½ hours
Vertical rise: 500 feet

Retrace the route along the south shore and among the trees to the Gordon Pond Trail where it turns west across the outlet. Fifteen minutes up through spruce woods takes you to the junction with the Kinsman Ridge Trail, which along here is part of the Appalachian Trail. Turn left, to the south. (The Kinsman Ridge Trail extends north for 13 difficult miles over two summits of Mount Kinsman and over Cannon Mountain, with assorted minor summits in between, to Franconia Notch Parkway near the tramway.)

At once the Kinsman Ridge Trail leads up on rock steps over the first of six wooded knolls. This is no former logging road. The trail is rough; it twists over ledges, rocks, and roots. Along this evergreen ridge the boggy hollows beside the trail are often green with carpets of sphagnum moss, showing how bogs look when not churned by hikers' boots. Often you walk on rock stepping-stones and sometimes on split logs.

At about 1 mile a lookoff rock shows the Pemigewasset River's East Branch valley all the way to Mount Carrigain.

You may think that the uphill is over when you leave the evergreens and descend into leafy woods. Ahead, however, are two more knolls to climb over. At the first you climb past a rock face deeply spread with a tapestry of green moss. The last knoll grows from a deep hollow and descends as abruptly.

Kinsman Notch seems much lower than

when you parked your car there the previous day. Your descent to it is partly on rock steps laid slab over slab down to the asphalt of NH 112 and the noise of cars, which appear first through the treetops. The trail is so steep that you see gleaming hoods and tops but no wheels.

The Kinsman Ridge Trail ends at NH 112. Now you know one rough section of the route between Maine and Georgia.

47

Smarts Mountain

Time allowed: 2 days, 1 night

Distance (round trip): 7½ miles

Walking time: 6 hours

Vertical rise: 2860 feet

Map: USGS 7½' Smarts Mountain

This is the second mountain I climbed as a boy in Orford, after Mount Cube, north of Smarts. For Cube, when I was 10, an adult led the way. Five years later, in 1929, with my friend and contemporary Claud Sharps, the adventures of Smarts Mountain began.

We discovered the remote approach to the elongated ridge and the distant, 3238-foot summit. Our fishing for trout in Jacobs Brook initiated exploration of an abandoned settlement in the eastern section of Orford known as Quinttown. One day we followed a dirt road past the tar-paper shacks and fields of the hermit Billy Brown. The road ended at Mousley Brook. Beyond a crude logging bridge we saw a wooden arrow on a tree. The red and white paint indicated a trail of the Dartmouth Outing Club. Our first attempt was cut short by a downpour somewhere a mile or so up the mountainside. We retreated to a deserted logging camp for the night. Later that summer, however, we gloried in the summit, its tower, and its DOC cabin.

I incorporated the trail we followed in 1929 into the 1978 text of *50 More Hikes in New Hampshire.* In 1991, after trails over Smarts and Cube were relocated to improve this section of the Appalachian Trail by moving it onto land more scenic, wilder, and better suited for protection, I revised the Smarts backpack.

This loop backpack starts at the south trailhead off the Dorchester Road, also called the Cummins Pond Road, in Lyme Center. The Lambert Ridge Trail leads you up a route with extensive views from open ledges. It joins the old Ranger Trail for the

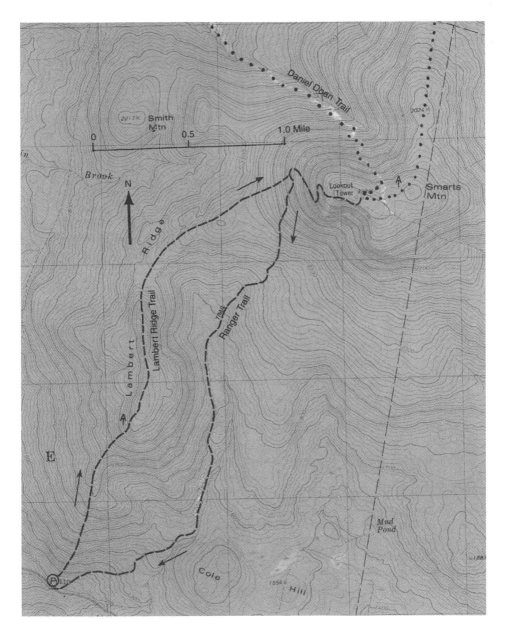

final ascent. Because both trails start at the same parking area, your return can be by the Ranger Trail all the way.

Take a tent. The board cabin beyond the unused steel tower may be occupied by AT hikers or Dartmouth students. Same for the tent platform.

Note: Dan's favorite trail up Smarts, the Mousley Brook Trail, has been renamed the Daniel Doan Trail. The Dartmouth Outing Club made the change in recognition of his efforts "to stimulate interest and involvement in hiking and the out-of-doors." For a day hike up the Daniel Doan Trail, see Hike 15 in *50 Hikes in the White Mountains*.

How to Get There

Drive east from Lyme off NH 10 on the road to Lyme Center. Beyond that village, bear left at the AT sign onto the Dorchester Road (the Cummins Pond Road) and proceed 1.6 miles to parking near a bridge over Grant Brook. You are 3 miles from Lyme Center.

Park your car. There is room for 10 or more cars. Organize your equipment and food.

The Trail

First Day: Dorchester Road to Smarts summit

Distance: 4 miles
Walking time: 3½ hours
Vertical rise: 2860 feet

Now you are all ready for Smarts, pack shouldered, eager as a leashed hound.

The Lambert Ridge Trail is your choice to the left, northwest, marked by the AT white stripes. Disregard occasional yellow blazes. You find yourself enjoying a fine example of modern trail-building. The trail rises moderately through open mature hardwoods. Some of the DOC water bars here are made of rocks and should serve hikers and prevent erosion for a generation or two. You walk steadily up to the ridge at an equable grade.

About 0.5 hour from your car, you emerge onto the first shoulder of bare rocks with a view to the southwest. The wide green swaths you see on the forested, precipitous ridge are for skiers at Dartmouth Skiway. Farther away, Moose Mountain rises east of Hanover.

Fifty yards up the trail you look southeast to Reservoir Pond. Now you are definitely on the ridge, and still climbing. The terrain slopes off on either side. More and more, your boots grip bare rock, bedrock indeed, displaying striations and an interesting "wavy gravy" effect. Cairns mark the trail.

An hour from your car offers you a view both encouraging and tantalizing: the summit of Smarts. You have surmounted about half the required vertical rise.

Beyond this lookoff the trail becomes enclosed in trees of birch, maple, and scattered evergreens. You descend into a sag and cross a small brook draining a boggy area in the saddle. There are wet and muddy spots on the Lambert Ridge Trail, and several of them are along here. An unmarked detour veers to the right, then soon rejoins the trail. Your descent into the sag from the high point on the ridge is approximately 150 feet.

But never mind that. You are about to enter spruce/fir growth entirely, which means the summit is your next objective. Also indicative, you realize that the trail is closer to your eyes. This section is the steepest of the hike, very nearly keeping to the fall line. It takes you by the most direct way to the junction with the old route, the Ranger Trail. Catch your breath. Then climb on along the upper Ranger Trail.

As you approach the summit, you come to a spur trail on the right leading to the DOC tent platform. It's the site of a former open shelter held down by cables. Previous to that, a DOC log cabin burned down. Fine views stretch to Moose Mountain and various ponds. Perhaps save this diversion from the summit for later.

Keep on toward the steel tower where it rises above the evergreens. From the tower cab you look across the Connecticut River to Vermont, where you see Mount Ascutney southward, Killington and Pico southwest, and Camel's Hump and Mount Mansfield northwest. Turning to New Hampshire, you

Smarts Mountain from Dame Hill

Daniel Doan

look north and east over nearby Mount Cube's quartzite-frosted summit. Then there are Mounts Carr, Stinson, Kineo, Moosilauke, the Franconia Range, and finally Washington. I always look northwest into Orford. I select a domed hill called Sunday Mountain (I once thought it so named because it was shaped like the scoop of ice cream in a sundae). Then I pick out the house on its shoulder, called Dame Hill, where I lived for a year.

To the south from the tower, under the steep brow of the mountain, Reservoir Pond gleams. Cummins Pond lies to the east along the Dorchester Road. To the southwest there's the Dartmouth Skiway's open slopes and lifts near Holt's Ledge and, farther south, Moose Mountain in Hanover.

For your water, proceed on the AT 0.1 mile beyond the tower to a spring on the right. Filter or boil it, of course. For your tent, if the cabin and platform are filled, you'll need to explore more of the summit for a suitable campsite. I have preferred an opening back in the spruces somewhere.

When I first saw the summit of Smarts in August 1929, the tower was a scaffolding of peeled spruce logs and poles about 30 feet high. A platform and railing accommodated the fire warden, who no longer occupied it nor scanned the forests for smoke, which he could locate on his circular map, also gone, though the table remained. A dubious-looking ladder didn't stop two 15-year-olds. Tall spruces were yet to come—they stood only about 10 or 15 feet tall at the time.

We made ourselves at home in the fire warden's cabin, also of peeled spruce, maintained as one of a string of DOC cabins between Hanover and Moosilauke. "Log hut" is more accurate than "cabin." It nestled—well, squatted—below the tower a few yards south. Even partially grown boys had to crouch to enter the doorway, and the door swung out—a dangerous feature I'll explain soon. The interior was cozy, with a stove, a wide bunk, a split-log floor, and two windows. Porcupines resided below the floor. And I should add that there was no lock.

Our explorations about the summit led to the discovery of another peeled-log tower on the East Peak, as it was called. The view from that tower included the north ridge slanting into Quinttown toward Mount Cube and ponds such as Rocky and Lamprey.

Back to the cabin door that opened outward. I must change the scene to total winter snow and ice. Battered and bent scrub evergreens topped the mountain on December 31, 1929. Claud and I, intrigued by stories of north woods trappers, decided to spend New Year's Eve on the summit of Smarts in that remote and exciting cabin on top of a mountain. All went well as we snowshoed with our packs up the trail from Quinttown. Then in the steep part the evergreens began to droop from the weight of snow and ice. Our packs weighed a ton, and we became very tired. I broke a harness. The trail vanished into nearly impenetrable snow and evergreens.

The harness repaired, a can of frozen beans opened and shared with spoons from our cook kit, we plowed around searching for the lost summit and the safety of the cabin. We were scared. One of us spotted a telephone wire draped in ice and snowy spruce branches. Glory be! The wire, though mostly buried in snow, must lead to the tower. After long slogging, we found that it did—and to the cabin as well. Warmth and shelter awaited us—beyond an outward-opening door encased in ice, especially at the bottom.

But we were well-prepared campers and had packed a small ax. We took turns using it, and you can bet with no regard for the edge of the blade and not much for the door.

Ah, the relief and security of those walls and roof in that log hovel! The crackling fire in the stove. Hot canned spaghetti, bacon and eggs, and tea, cooked for New Year's Eve supper. Then we slept soundly, wrapped in blankets on the bunk, no seeing in the New Year, and awoke to a new decade and—though we didn't know it then—50-odd years of more adventures in the White Mountains.

Second Day: Smarts summit to Dorchester Road
Distance: 3½ miles
Walking time: 2½ hours
Vertical rise: no climbing

After shouldering your pack in the morning, retrace your steps of the day before to the junction with the Ranger Trail and continue on it, leaving the Lambert Ridge Trail on your right. You descend to the south through a forest of hardwoods and conifers. There are no views. Erosion, removing thin cover on the bedrock, has left the trail on ledge along here.

You may notice head-high bushes with crimson branches—red osier dogwood. You may also be puzzled by cairns in the woods. They once supported telephone poles for the line to the tower. That was after the forest fire, when no trees remained to which the wire could be attached—probably the wire that led two boys to the cabin.

Continuing downward, you cross an upper branch of Grant Brook and soon cross it again to the west bank. You are nearing a shed of some sort, way up here on the mountainside. It's the unused shingle garage that housed the fire warden's jeep. You are 1.5 miles from the summit, with 2 miles of eroded jeep track ahead.

It takes you along the west bank of the

brook. The water sparkles in the sun or runs darkly in the shade of spruces and hemlocks. But watch for mud and puddles in the jeep road. Deer-track Vs and sometimes the cowlike hoof marks of moose indent damp ground.

Absorbed by sights and sounds of this downhill walk, you could be surprised when you step from woods into the parking area and realize you are about to be carried by four wheels—with maybe a little regret that hiking is over.

Daniel Doan fishing a beaver pond on Cheney Brook

48

Cheney Brook

Time allowed: 3 days, 2 nights

Distance (round trip): 3 miles

Walking time: 3 hours

Vertical rise: 580 feet

Maps: USDA/FS 7½' Mt. Osceola; USGS 7½' Mt. Osceola

To spend nights camped near a boggy beaver pond is to place yourself in direct relationship to the life of the wilds. Bogs are active both day and night, but their effect in darkness is downright otherworldly. Your eyes, the principal sense in daytime, are replaced at night by your ears. Instead of seeing a bullfrog's green arc into the water you hear his deep basso sound out as night descends. Birds sing twilight notes and go to sleep. The chorus is taken over by trilling tree frogs. Maybe an owl hoots from a dead stub in the bog. Or a sudden puff of wind above your tent rubs a tree branch along a smaller tree, and you immediately think that a bobcat has screeched. You turn on your flashlight and play its beam up into the branches. No bobcat, of course. But on the ground the light may reveal a deer mouse hopping lightly away, or it may catch the twitching ears of a curious hare. If you move too quickly you'll startle him, and he'll demonstrate his alarm by a thump with his hind foot.

There are other more mysterious sounds. Is that splashing caused by a raccoon foraging after frogs? Or a beaver mending his dam? A mink swimming after trout? A deer feeding on water plants? At Cheney Brook the slow sloshing of heavy hooves and body might be a moose. The last time I was there, we followed moose tracks up the steep bank beside this tributary to Pine Brook.

A primary problem in bog camping is finding a high and dry campsite. Another is insect life: mosquitoes, blackflies, deerflies. At Cheney Brook the campsite can be on rising ground north of the bog and far

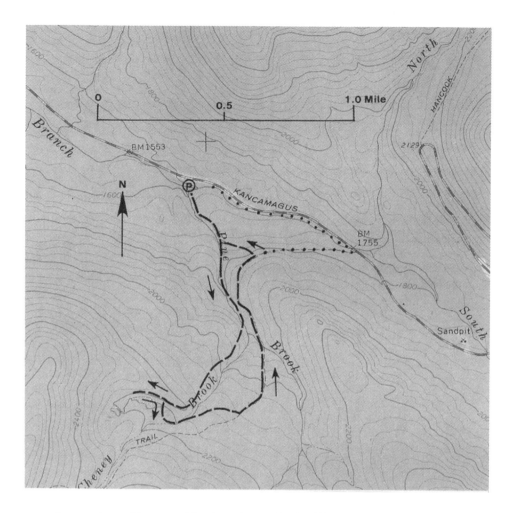

enough away to avoid some of the insects gathered along the water. But a bug-proof tent is a must.

Because there is no trail to the bog on Cheney Brook, you'll be more than ever dependent on a map. Travel by streams eliminates the need for a compass, but of course you'll have one with you if you should need it. The map to use is USGS Mount Osceola Quadrangle.

How to Get There

The Kancamagus Highway is the access road to this bushwhack. Drive east from Lin-

coln. At 4.7 miles you cross the Pemigewasset River's East Branch and pass the Lincoln Woods Trail on your left. Another 3 miles brings you to a parking area on your right bordering Hancock Branch. A sign identifies it as OTTER REST AREA, WHITE MOUNTAIN NATIONAL FOREST.

Now you'll be wise to check the water level in Hancock Branch. Walk down through the wooded rest area. Across the stream you'll see Pine Brook cascading in from spruces below the smooth ledges called Otter Rocks. Your aim is to reach the east bank of Pine Brook. Crossing at low water can be merely careful long steps across the channels in the ledges or stepping from rock to rock below Pine Brook, where the stream is broader but usually shallow. For medium-high water a solution is to drive another 0.7 mile to the East Pond Trail and follow it until you hear the sound of Pine Brook on your right; then cut down through the woods. In time of real freshets, I suggest you backpack elsewhere.

The Trail

First Day: Kancamagus Highway to Cheney Brook's beaver pond

Distance: 1 ½ miles
Walking time: 1 ¾ hours
Vertical rise: 580 feet

Following up Pine Brook on its east bank, you'll pass bivouac sites no longer allowed along the Kancamagus Highway, where the forest service's Forest Protection Area extends 0.25 mile from either side.

Your progress through the spruces, both around the trunks of large trees and through the young and clinging thickets, must be made slowly to avoid aggravation of body and nerves. At times you move faster in open woods. Generally, the route should be maintained 40 or 50 yards from Pine Brook, bypassing some of the steep bank.

But keep returning to the brook and watching for the tributary running down from the west. That's Cheney Brook. The obvious remedy for missing it is to cross to the west bank of Pine Brook, but the walking there is more difficult. You can be alerted by your watch if you've noted the time you started. I use up most of an hour contesting the way with hobblebush and admiring the falls and pools under magnificent pines, which now and then tower above the spruces.

Another indication that you should cross

I lifted my pack. If you balance a pack on your thigh, it's halfway to your shoulders while you make up your mind to swing it up for the final balance on your back.
—Daniel Doan, Our Last Backpack

to Cheney Brook may be voices of hikers on the East Pond Trail to the left, which follows an old railroad grade here and approaches Pine Brook.

Watch for a change in the brook bed from stones and boulders to ledges and sluices of yellowish rock. Then look for a big sheltering rock on the left, whose overhang could protect you from a rainstorm. It's the size of a small garage. Keep past it and climb a 10-foot bank. From the edge of Pine Brook you look for a large boulder on the west side. About 50 yards upstream and also on the west side is another imposing boulder. Cheney Brook joins Pine Brook between these. A massive log partially blocks the flow from Cheney Brook. Some years, depending on debris washed down in the spring, Cheney Brook may split into three trickles to join Pine Brook. The tributary shows the dark cast of water that has been impounded behind a beaver dam.

Cross here and head up the north bank; it's easier than the south side. Almost at once you may notice an ancient windfall with exposed roots that suggest a giant tarantula, according to one of my companions who dislikes spiders. A few minutes later, as you approach the steeper climb, you come to a great prostrate pine, which was sawed from its stump and abandoned by early loggers. Why? one wonders. It looks sound enough, without the hollow that sometimes explains left-behind logs.

Now you begin the steep climb. Spruce woods are mixed with maple and beech on which you can haul yourself up. Slow and steady does it. Keep above the brook and its ravine. A half hour should bring you to the little plateau and bog on the side of the mountain. You no longer look up to daylight but ahead at it. Mountain? Yes, you're climbing the approach to Scar Ridge and Mount Osceola's West Peak.

Swing right, along the north side of the bog, before you reach the nearly impenetrable bushes growing from wet sphagnum moss where several outlets drain from the beaver pond. This curve should take you across an old logging road through damp, semi-open ground. Here's a safe place for a campfire. I suggest you drop your pack and look around for a tent site. There's a little bank and a higher location for the tent, although a growth of spruce and fir obstructed by many fallen young trees adds nothing to the ease of selecting a space. Persevere, however, and note how the crisscross tangle demonstrates an interesting example of natural forest thinning.

Your next move should be to acquaint yourself with the pond and bog before you pitch your tent. (You may find a better place for it.) Go west a short distance through the spruce woods. The bog is on your left. Then you see the old beaver dam and an acre or so of water, along with its dead stubs, water brush, sunlight, and bird life. A breeze usually comes from up on Scar Ridge across the pond. Over there, a dominant summit, Mount Osceola, tops the range that includes its East and West Peaks.

For drinking water, keep on through the woods to the west end of the pond. Or you may walk along the shore, wet with sphagnum moss and thick with leatherleaf to your waist. Mountain holly grows higher at the end of the pond and hides the little spring holes that contribute to the western inlet. You'll need a cup to fill your kettle. Disinfect the water.

After you've made camp, there's probably not enough time for further exploration and enjoyment of the pond. Soon after the light fades on Osceola, night descends with its frog chorus. If you quiet down you begin to hear the animal splashings at the water's edge. High on the ridge night winds rush through the trees. In the pond an alert beaver may get a sniff of your campfire—or of you—and slap his tail to warn of the intrusion. The sound is like that of a canoe paddle brought down flat and hard.

Second Day: Spent at the pond

The next day can be devoted to the bog and the pond, to pastimes like admiring the tree swallows nesting in the dead stubs. Study of the bog shows many of the unusual plants that thrive in the cold, acid habitat created by sphagnum moss. Leatherleaf, the most common of the water bushes, provides a nest place a foot above the pond for redwinged blackbirds. Pitcher plant grows near a hummock under a great pine stub that hulks over tiny twinflowers. (Before visiting Cheney Brook, a reading about bogs would be rewarding. *The Audubon Nature Encyclopedia* contains a good, concise account.)

The second night you'll feel more at home. Your camp arrangements will come naturally. Familiarity with a woodland environment makes living there easier and more pleasant.

Third Day: Cheney Brook's beaver pond to Kancamagus Highway
Distance: 1 ½ miles
Walking time: 1 ¼ hours
Vertical rise: 5 feet
Your return on the third day need not be back down the brook. You may cross the bog outlet, where the various seepages and drainings join to pitch over the steep slope you climbed. On the south side bear left

downstream. Watch carefully for a faint trail east along the bank. There are ancient blazes grown almost over with bark. The trail seems to be kept open (if that's the correct word) by rabbits, deer, and moose, more than by humans. It follows a logging road grown to trees. You should look ahead for that indefinable appearance of lesser growth along the suggestion of a sled road's 8-foot width. It leads away from the brook in an easterly direction to the East Pond Trail.

Turn left on the East Pond Trail. You soon descend to Pine Brook and a crossing that puts you on the old railroad grade. If you've had enough bushwhacking, follow the grade out to the Kancamagus Highway. But remember, there'll be 0.75 mile (west) of asphalt marching, gravel-shoulder crunching, and zooming cars. I'd rather cut through the woods when I hear the traffic noise and pick up Pine Brook, to the left and west, for the return to the car.

49

The Kilkenny

Time allowed: 3 days, 2 nights

Distance (round trip): 16½ miles

Vertical rise: 3100 feet

Maps: USGS 7½' West Milan; USGS 7½' Stark; USGS 7½' x 15' (metric) Pliny Range; USDA/FS 7½' Percy SE; USDA/FS 7½' Percy SW

During this leisurely backpack into the Kilkenny region of the northern White Mountain National Forest, you will walk through forests of white birches, visit secret little Kilback Pond, camp beside Unknown Pond, and look out at vast wilderness views from Rogers Ledge and the Horn.

The excitement and anticipation of any backpack is enhanced here because of the sense of far-north adventure. The area is relatively remote, away from the more popular hiking trails.

Don't do this hike in the spring. The trails can be muddy even in late summer.

Bring along a small day pack in your backpack, to use on the side trips.

The route of this loop was suggested by Steve Smith, whose wonderful *Ponds & Lakes of the White Mountains* includes descriptions of the ponds you'll see.

How to Get There

Take NH 110 northwest from NH 16 in Berlin. At about 7 miles, watch on the left for the sign for the Berlin Fish Hatchery. Turn left onto York Pond Road.

In 1.6 miles you reach the White Mountain National Forest Kilkenny Guard Station. Bear right. As you drive past conifers, you'll see a sign explaining that in 1903, after logging in the Kilkenny, thousands of acres were burned; the forest service planted these evergreens from 1934 to 1936.

At 4.7 miles you come to the Berlin Fish Hatchery. Leave your car in the parking area on the left outside the gate, which is locked between 4 PM and 8 AM.

A crossroads in the Kilkenny

Ruth Doan MacDougall

The Trail

First Day: Gate at Berlin Fish Hatchery to Rogers Ledge Campsite; Side Trip to Rogers Ledge

Distance: 5 miles
Walking time: 3½ hours
Vertical rise: 1500 feet

Walk through the open gate. A sign directs you right to Mill Brook Trail. York Pond Road, straight ahead, will be your return route. Go left behind the hatchery building at another MILL BROOK TRAIL sign.

The wide trail curves left. Take a right and then a left. As you begin walking uphill, you notice trillium, bunchberry, and clintonia.

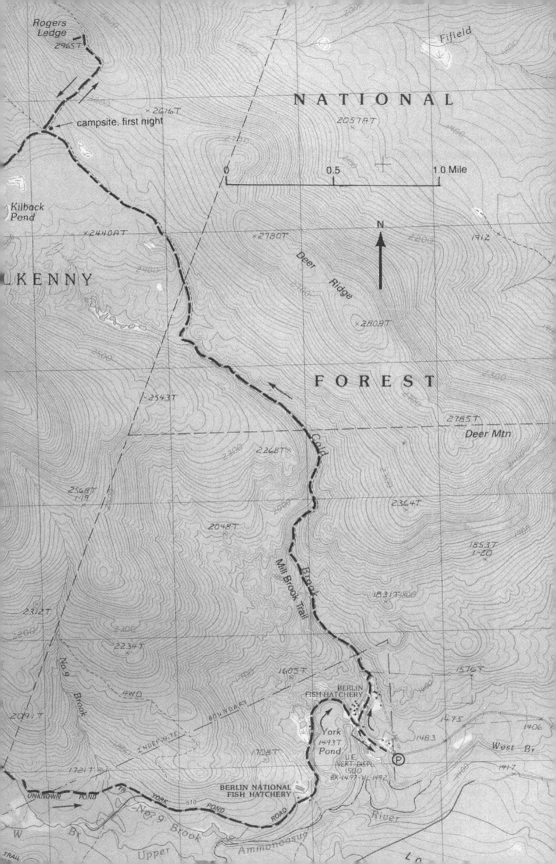

There's meadow rue, too. And probably moose tracks.

Despite the trail's name, the name of the brook it follows here is Cold Brook. You continue ascending, listening to Cold Brook's enthusiastic burble, on stone steps across muddy patches. White birches are a preview of the beautiful birch forests ahead. The trail rises high above the brook, then accompanies it again. Rocks assist in mud. You begin to climb more steeply.

Through tall grasses you cross another muddy spot. Then a series of bog bridges helps you deal with mud. Sweet woodruff appears beside the trail.

At about 2 miles, you notice spruce and fir coming in. The trail levels, dips downhill past a clump of trillium, and heads uphill again. You have now moved away from the brook.

Birches! The trail winds through a white grove, the birch leaves chartreuse in the sunlight. You stroll into a moose-browsing area where maples and hobblebush have been nipped off. You may hear or see a golden-crowned kinglet.

At 3.8 miles you come to the junction with the Kilkenny Ridge Trail. Turn right on the Kilkenny Ridge Trail toward Rogers Ledge. The trail steepens. At about 0.1 mile there is a campsite sign pointing to a path on the right. At about 4 miles from the fish hatchery, you reach your home for the night.

While you get acquainted with this campsite you may discover evidence of moose browsing. As my friend Amy exclaimed, "It's a moose supermarket!" This definitely adds to the feel of being deep in the wild.

Hang your food on a tree branch; put binoculars, camera, water, snacks, and any other essentials into the day pack you've brought, and stash your backpack. If you don't feel comfortable about leaving your backpack, shoulder it again.

Return to the Kilkenny Ridge Trail, blazed yellow, and turn right for Rogers Ledge, named after Major Robert Rogers, frontiersman and commander of Rogers's Rangers in the French and Indian War. You walk up through birches, past ferns, clintonia, bunchberry. The trail curves left around large rocks. On a rock staircase you climb toward the ledge. The trail circles under it to another rock staircase. At about 0.5 mile from the campsite, take a little path left and step out on the cliff, 2945 feet.

The view is huge and wild, including the Mahoosuc Range, the Presidentials, the Androscoggin River valley, the Kilkenny basin, the Pliny and Pilot Ranges. But you can also glimpse civilization, Berlin and its mill stacks. And there is a miniature delight, little Kilback Pond far below, which you'll see close-up tomorrow.

Return to your campsite. For water, go south on the Kilkenny Ridge Trail, past the junction with the Mill Brook Trail, less than 0.2 mile to a small brook. Of course you'll filter or treat it.

Second Day: Rogers Ledge Campsite to Unknown Pond Campsite; Side Trip to the Horn
Distance: 6¼ miles
Walking time: 4 hours
Vertical rise: 1600 feet

Return to the junction with the Mill Brook Trail and take the Kilkenny Ridge Trail south, crossing the brook where perhaps you fetched water yesterday.

Then you wend your way uphill and down, following the yellow blazes, past mossy rocks, wood sorrel, clintonia. You ascend some log steps. There are birches overhead and hobblebush beside you along the gradual incline. You walk through an enchanted glade of moss and fir. Indian pipes pop up, waxy white amid bunchberry. After a muddy patch, your feet are on pine duff again.

At 0.7 mile you come to Kilback Pond, a treasure. It's a scene in shades of green, the grasses along the shore, the conifers, the ridge beyond, all reflecting in the quiet water. There are also some high-bush blueberries. The trail passes a swamp on the right to a second spot from which to enjoy Kilback.

Then you cross rickety bog bridges, notice trillium and lady's slippers, and continue uphill and down, over more bog bridges, past asters and sheep laurel. Mud again. At about 1 mile the trail leads decidedly upward toward the sky, climbing steeply. But it levels in birches, and downhill you go.

The ascent resumes, through a moose-browsing area. You are heading uphill in earnest now. No switchbacks! After a long, steady climb to the crest of the ridge above Unknown Pond, you catch your breath on a stretch through ferns. Then the trail descends past bunchberry, clintonia, and wood sorrel. Ahead, there's a glimpse of blue. You walk down into the campsite at Unknown Pond, 2.2 miles from your Rogers Ledge campsite.

In addition to the main campsite, there are others scattered about, some nearer the pond. Be especially careful to practice "low-impact" camping. Unknown Pond is no longer so unknown as it used to be, but when you stand on the shore and look out across its serene surface, up to the dramatic silhouette of the Horn, you'll hope everybody who visits here will treat it tenderly.

That Horn up there is your next destination. Hang your food, hide your backpack, and set off with your day pack. Or, again, if you prefer, take your full load with you.

The Kilkenny Ridge Trail and the Unknown Pond Trail coincide briefly. Follow the Kilkenny Ridge Trail south, turning left at the junction. (The Unknown Pond Trail continues north to Mill Brook Road.) Bear right at a fork, following the yellow blazes through ferns and firs downhill, across bog bridges, and then uphill. A rock staircase leads you back into birches. The trail levels, dips down and up, and becomes rougher, climbing. At 1.7 miles take the side trail left to reach the 3905-foot summit of the Horn, up a rock scramble, at 2 miles.

The view to the east and southeast includes the Mahoosucs, Mount Moriah, and Carter Dome. To the south are the Pliny and Presidential Ranges. Before you, southwest, are the Bulge and Mount Cabot. You can see into Vermont on the northwest, and among the mountains on the north are Percy Peaks, Mount Magalloway, and summits in Quebec.

Retrace your steps down the side trail to the Kilkenny Ridge Trail and back to Unknown Pond.

Third Day: Unknown Pond Campsite to Gate at Berlin Fish Hatchery
Distance: 5⅓ miles
Walking time: 3½ hours
Vertical rise: no climbing

Today you are taking the Unknown Pond Trail south. It passes the shore, then drops down into ferns. Not so clearly blazed as the Kilkenny Ridge Trail, it is marked yellow, making a rocky, curving descent, then leveling for a spell along Unknown Pond Brook, which it will follow.

Here are sweet woodruff and meadow rue. After the first brook crossing, turn left. The brook cuts far below the trail. Cross a tributary and bear left. When you cross the main brook again, bear right. The lovely birches bring back memories of the birch forests you've seen in the past two days.

The trail gets muddy, the brook thudding alongside. Again you cross it, turning left among tall, pink joe-pye weed. A log takes you over one last little crossing.

Now the land opens up to mountain views. Mount Cabot is on your right, Terrace Mountain to your left. In the muddy spots you may see moose tracks. You cross a clearing heaped with slash and pick up the trail to emerge, at 3.3 miles, on York Pond Road.

Turn left. You have 2 miles ahead of you on this dirt road that becomes paved, but they are made interesting by the fish hatchery operations and by York Pond itself.

You reach the gate. Travel usually expands time, and it seems impossible that you could have seen and experienced so much in only these three days since you left your car here and set forth into the Kilkenny.

50

Wild River

Time allowed: 5 days, 4 nights

Distance (round trip): 21¼ miles

Walking time: 17½ hours

Vertical rise: 5310 feet

Maps: USDA/USGS 7½' Wild River; USDA/USGS 7½' Carter Dome; USDA/ USGS 7½' Jackson; USDA/USGS 7½' Chatham

The forested Wild River valley extends southwest from the Maine border to Carter Dome. The river is well named. In the 1890s it specialized in washing away the grade and bridges of the Wild River Railroad. Begun in 1891 by the Wild River Lumber Company, the railroad eventually transported logs from far up the valley out to Hastings, Maine. This now-vanished lumber town has grown to woods but still shows on maps. From Hastings's sawmills the railroad carried lumber to Gilead, Maine, and the Grand Trunk Railroad, running from Portland to Montreal.

The Wild River Railroad crews were tough. For 12 years they kept the trains going despite the washouts. The line was also noted for runaway trains that hurtled down the steep grades and for one boiler explosion. But a campfire of trout fishermen did what the river and its valley couldn't do. Logging ended with the disastrous forest fire of 1903.

Nine years later the remaining forest and the devastated land, known as Bean's Purchase and comprising about 34,000 acres, became one of the first three properties to be bought by the federal government for the White Mountain National Forest.

The first day of this backpack, and a short climb, places you for the night on the south ridge of the Wild River valley. The second day you climb over two rocky peaks and descend to make camp near the Wild River. The third night you spend beside the bogs and beaver ponds at the source of the river. On the fourth day the high point of the backpack at 4832 feet, Carter Dome, shows you

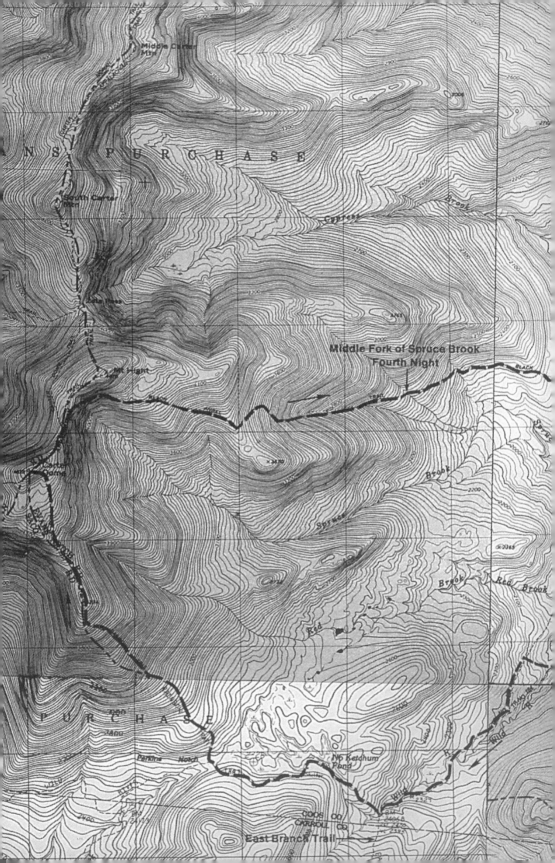

Middle Fork of Spruce Brook
Fourth Night

East Branch Trail

both the Wild River valley and the Presidential Range to the west. After the fourth night, camped at a tributary on the north ridge, you descend to the river once more and complete the loop.

How to Get There

The Wild River Campground is the jumping-off place for this backpack. The US Forest Service maintains 12 campsites on the river's south bank, 5.5 wooded miles from NH 113 at the end of the gravel Wild River Road. The turn west from NH 113 is north of Evans Notch and 3 miles south of US 2 in Gilead, Maine. The junction where you turn shows on maps as Hastings, Maine—that former lumber town.

At this corner you'll notice a bronze plaque on a boulder. Shaded now by pines, it commemorates the completion of the Evans Notch Road (NH 113) in 1936 by the Civilian Conservation Corps. Here you turn west onto the Wild River Road to the campground.

Before long you drive back into New Hampshire. The road follows the route of the Wild River Railroad with the river northwest to your right. It ends in the campground's parking area from which the Basin Trail and the Wild River Trail enter the woods.

The Trail

First Day: Wild River Campground to Blue Brook Shelter

Distance: 2 ¼ miles
Walking time: 2 hours
Vertical rise: 580 feet

Your first day's hike is on the Basin Trail to Blue Brook Shelter. (You'll return on the Wild River Trail at the end of the backpack.) This is an ideal beginning for a backpack. It's a woods trail and provides just

enough distance and effort on a backpack's first day, which often shrinks to an afternoon or less for actual hiking. Late companions, loading the car, driving, and last-minute stops always seem to accompany the beginning of a weeklong outing like this.

The Basin Trail begins as a crushed-stone path leading south up to a former railroad spur. It passes campsites and proceeds into deeper woods. The trail crosses wet ground on a plank walkway. Your boots plunk along until you're on solid ground again and ascending beside Blue Brook to a crossing at pools and cascades. The trail curves right to follow the stream. Cliffs form the opposite bank and at their base the rock slants into the clear water, through which you see a pale band bisecting the smooth ledge.

Now comes a section of trail whose easy steepness stretches your leg muscles. Big yellow birches give you shade and beeches are joined by increasing growths of spruce and fir. You climb upward to a fork in the trail. Turn right for Blue Brook Shelter. It's 0.25 mile away, and you reach it by slabbing around the slope. (The Basin Trail leads ahead 0.25 mile to Rim Junction, which you'll learn about the next day.)

The shelter is built of logs and stained brown. Its popularity may cause you to seek a tent site off in the woods. The water supply is Blue Brook, which you reach by a short path north from the shelter. The stream glides down a nearly vertical ledge. Disinfect the water.

The trail through the clearing is the Black Angel Trail. (The Black Angel Trail to the west climbs over the next ridge and then descends to the Wild River Trail at Spider Bridge and continues up Carter Dome. It will be your descent route from the Dome on the fourth and fifth days.)

Backpacking Hikes

Second Day: Blue Brook Shelter to Mount Meader, Eagle Crag, and Wild River

Distance: 6 miles
Walking time: 5 hours
Vertical rise: 1800 feet

In the morning the first destination is Rim Junction. Take the Black Angel Trail uphill from the shelter. An easy pace will best prepare you for scaling the summits south of Rim Junction. During the first 20 minutes on this trail, eager anticipation often conflicts with a protesting body.

About 0.5 mile from the shelter, open hardwoods surround Rim Junction. You're on the col between Royce Mountain to your left and Mount Meader to your right. Five trails intersect here, and the Black Angel Trail ends. These five prongs at the junction warrant careful study of trail signs and your map.

Turn right, to the south, from Rim Junction onto the Basin Rim Trail to Mount Meader.

The Basin Rim Trail leads down through spruces and across ledges, which open to wide views east into the basin, a perfect little glacial cirque. You can look beyond the basin to the Cold River valley along the Maine–New Hampshire boundary. Behind you to the northeast are the cliffs of West Royce Mountain, East Royce Mountain, and Evans Notch. Ahead Mount Meader looms more and more rugged as you approach along the rim of the basin.

Formidable little Mount Meader! Well, formidable enough for ordinary folks. There's a rock face where I and three companions took off packs and handed them up to the agile leader. At another vertical pitch we scrambled among spruce roots and rotten rock, wondering which set of boot scrapings led to the next paint blaze. We chose correctly, and the blaze finally appeared. The trail wasn't really obscure; it just

I held the frying pan over the flames till jets of smoke rose, then poured in some batter. It was too watery, so spread at once much larger than I liked. I wanted my first attempt to be small, a pancake, not a broad flapjack, on a theory of mine to start easy on all projects. Too late now.

–Daniel Doan, Our Last Backpack

reflected the various choices of individual hikers.

The trail does level out for a bit through open woods that shade thriving hobble-bushes. Then you climb steeply again into spruces along the very edge of the Basin. Views to the east are toward Speckled Mountain in Maine, identified by its long ridge and fire tower. The woods close in again, and you come to a seasonal brook. Beyond it begins the final stiff climb of 0.5 hour to Mount Meader's ledges. There you reach a good lunch lookoff, although not the true summit. The green valley of Cold River spreads out its deltalike meadows and forests from the crags of Evans Notch. Away to the north the summits are in the Mahoosuc Range.

The Basin Rim Trail ends among scrub spruce and open rock at a junction near these lookoff ledges. From the junction turn right onto the Meader Ridge Trail heading for Eagle Crag. (To the left—southeast—the Mount Meader Trail descends to NH 113 near North Chatham.)

The Meader Ridge Trail takes you to the true summit, 2782 feet. It's in the woods, and you could easily walk over it without noticing. This is 933 feet above the col that initiated the Mount Meader ascent. You may wonder at the sweat and puffing it caused.

The Meader Ridge Trail, winding up and down, passes some east lookoffs and a spur trail to a western vantage point. You descend in spruces to a rocky ravine and brook. Keep left across the brook and up a ledge and knoll. You pass along a narrow ridge where you can see the Carter Range off to the west.

Next you climb to a minor summit only to step down again so you can climb once more, this time to tree line. Eagle Crag rises above you, 3030 feet high.

As you emerge on Eagle Crag you first look to North Baldface's barren bulk and peak. Like South Baldface, it was burned over in the 1903 forest fire. You look at it across a glacial cirque. On the mountain's east shoulder a curiously contorted rock formation shows the unimaginable pressures that formed North Baldface. Turning from this toward the west, you see into the Wild River valley and beyond to the Carter Range, the Dome (appropriately named), and Mount Washington.

The Meader Ridge Trail continues a short distance across ledges marked by cairns to a junction and its end at the Baldface Circle Trail. Your route to the Wild River and to your night's tent site is the Eagle Link, branching west off the ridge.

Turn right onto the Eagle Link, which may seem tedious after those exhilarating views. It's a boggy trail at first as it leads into the spruces. It's also a rough trail. At least it's downhill. Then you climb briefly over a shoulder of North Baldface. The lower section of the trail improves when it begins to follow an old logging road. You walk down through a white-birch forest. The first crossing of an unnamed brook's tributary and the brook itself should not deceive you into assuming you've reached Wild River. You still have about 0.75 mile to go. The trail descends by an easy grade.

Then the trail turns left and presents you with Wild River, which you'll recognize by its dark bed of mossy rocks. There is no bridge. When you have made your way across, pause and consider camping for the night. The Eagle Link Trail continues ahead about 0.25 mile to its junction with the Wild River Trail. That's for tomorrow.

The likeliest site for your tent in this area is to the left upstream. If you follow indications of an old trail and explore off it to the right and toward a low ridge, you can locate a flat, dry spot in open woods, but keep it at least 200 feet away from the stream. Even that far, the soothing sound of the current should suggest early sleep after this day of good exercise and fresh air.

Third Day: Eagle Link campsite to Perkins Notch Shelter
Distance: 2 miles
Walking time 1¾ hours
Vertical rise: 550 feet

This is an easy day. Use it for settling into the forest, for rest, for observation near the source of the Wild River, for exploration.

After striking camp return downstream to the Eagle Link Trail at the crossing of Wild River. Turn left and proceed to the junction with the Wild River Trail. You are 5 miles southwest of the Wild River Campground. A left turn puts you onto the Wild River Trail as it follows up the stream, out of sight of the water. The woods have grown up since the 1903 fire. About 0.75 mile of walking brings you to a crossing of the river. Then curving south with level going, the trail swings uphill and westerly as it passes, on the left, the East Branch Trail, which leads to the East Branch of the Saco River.

Another crossing to the north bank heads you abruptly northwest, where the stream comes down through a gap in the ridge. One final crossing to the south bank precedes your arrival at the bog country that distinguishes Perkins Notch. Glimpses through the spruce and fir show you the east slopes of Carter Dome. You are above and walking parallel to No-Ketchum Pond. The name must refer to one of those days when bog-channel trout refuse to take either bait or flies.

The pond existed in 1880, and it was then long and narrow as at present. Appalachian Mountain Club hikers exploring Perkins Notch estimated its length at 500 feet and its width at 60 feet. I'd say it's narrower now due to the growth of the quaking bog that borders it. This floating mass of roots and humus contributed by sphagnum moss, pitcher plant, leatherleaf, and sheep laurel (to mention only a few) extends back from the water's edge several yards to solid though wet ground.

This long channel and source of the Wild River gathers the flowage from another 0.5 mile of bog to the west. Beavers in No-Ketchum Pond were noted as early as 1927. (Of course beavers were here earlier, before they were trapped out.) This date coincides with the return of beavers to New Hampshire from the north after their virtual extinction in the state. They add greatly to the interest of this bog country, which preserves its wild and desolate expanse all the way to the foot of Carter Dome and to the shoulder that ends at Perkins Notch. There are no cliffs or crags in this notch: It's an imperceptible height-of-land.

Just beyond No-Ketchum Pond you come to the Perkins Notch Shelter. It is built of peeled spruce logs, which formerly rose as trees in front of the old cabin used by beaver trappers in the winter and by trout fishermen in the summer. The logs, stained brown inside and out, partially close the front under the overhanging eaves. The board bunk accommodates six people. Here again as at Blue Brook you may want to camp outside the shelter.

If you arrive early, with the afternoon ahead of you, take advantage of a unique opportunity to study the plants, animals, and birds of the bog. (Also, take plenty of fly dope.) The bog country extends north to Red Brook, whose upper reaches are a series of beaver ponds plentifully supplied by water draining from Carter Dome. Bog enthusiasts and avid trout fishermen can make their way to Red Brook by crossing a beaver dam between No-Ketchum Pond and the next pond west and heading north with compass and map. The distance is only about 0.75 mile, but it's very difficult. For a landmark beyond Red Brook, watch for a rocky knob bared by the forest fire—if you can see over the bushes in which you thrash around most of the way.

Fourth Day: Perkins Notch Shelter to Carter Dome and Spruce Brook on the Black Angel Trail

Distance: 6 miles
Walking time: 5½ hours
Vertical rise: 2340 feet

The Wild River Trail continues to be your route for the first section of today's hike. It leads southwest from the shelter and up the ridge a short distance. Then you slab around the contour above the bog. This forest trail goes for 0.75 mile before a brief descent to Perkins Notch at 2586 feet. On your left, water flows into the Saco River system; on your right, into the Androscoggin. The actual dividing point, the height-of-land, lies to your right at a patch of sphagnum moss.

Here the Wild River Trail bears left, to the west. You take the Rainbow Trail on the right for Carter Dome.

You may find no trail sign. Bears have thoroughly clawed the fir trees to which the sign has been attached. Sometimes the sign lies in splinters on the ground. You'll recognize the Rainbow Trail, however, by its northerly direction and by its soon-to-be-encountered sharp ascent. After a steady northwest climb from leafy forest into evergreens, the trail bends more to the west and then heads north for the approach to the top of the barren shoulder at 4274 feet. The views prove that you've been climbing. You're almost 1700 feet above Perkins Notch. The Wild River valley extends eastward beyond the bogs, a wide forest rising left to massive Carter Dome and, on the right, to Mount Meader and the Baldfaces.

Now the trail takes you down 75 feet in elevation to the spruce/fir col before you start up the Dome's rounded green cap. You're climbing again for the final 0.75 mile of the total 2.5 miles from Perkins Notch.

There's one last shoulder and the scrub spruces open to the summit's clearing, which is rapidly returning to evergreen woods. Mount Washington pierces the horizon ahead of you beyond the Wildcat Range. The ledge around you once supported a fire tower where a lookout was killed by lightning. The elevation is 4832 feet.

The Rainbow Trail ends at the Dome's summit. Now you take the Carter-Moriah Trail in a northeasterly direction. (Left, to the southwest, the Carter-Moriah Trail descends to its terminus in Carter Notch near the AMC hut.)

About 0.5 mile from the Dome, you come to the Black Angel Trail on the right. Here, at 4600 feet, begins your route back to the Wild River valley. You may feel disappointed about the views from the Dome. If so, you can think about leaving your pack in the spruces for a side trip to Mount Hight. This rocky pinnacle is one of the great lookoffs in the mountains. It rises 0.75 mile farther along the Carter-Moriah Trail.

Time and energy will be factors in your decision. The round trip will take you 1 hour—not counting the time you spend on the crags of Mount Hight. You'll need at least another 1.5 hours to reach the night's camping place along Spruce Brook down the Black Angel Trail. You'll also need enough energy for an extra 200 feet of vertical rise because Mount Hight peaks beyond a col. If you decide in favor of Mount Hight, avoid the left-forking Carter Dome Trail down to Zeta Pass. Stay on the Carter-Moriah Trail and return on it.

As for the Black Angel Trail, the walk down it is at first gradual for 0.25 mile, dropping only about 100 feet in elevation. You have then a rugged climb downward. Certain sections are rough with ledges and roots. The trail angles down more gradually, and at times seepage wets the trail into mucky walking. The spruces become taller and older.

Before the 1903 fire, loggers never reached this high forest and somehow neither did the flames. So you walk through aisles of spruces, with mossy carpets on either side and wood sorrel spreading across alternating shadow and sunlight. Ax and saw *almost* did slash the virgin evergreens. A camp existed on the middle fork of Spruce Brook. Lumberjacks cut sled roads up the slopes from the spur track off the main railroad.

The trail enters birch woods. They change to spruces, and back to birches again. The trail jogs left off a long ridge, bears right, and then left again as it heads down abruptly. You descend to the upper branch of Spruce Brook, which trickles between steep, moss-grown rocks. Although camping is possible here, the forest floor pitches down at a sharp angle. Across the brook 50 yards and up to the left there's a site for one small tent.

You're better off to descend for another 0.5 hour to the middle fork of Spruce Brook. This mossy stream crosses the trail through ground more nearly level. You may choose your campsite, remembering the US Forest Service rule that requires you to be 200 feet from water and trails.

Maybe you should think of the careless fishermen who neglected their campfire and started the 1903 blaze. Campfires, as Ben Franklin (I think) said of freedom, require eternal vigilance. The holocaust caused by the fishermen ironically killed thousands of trout, because ashes fell into the streams. Years passed before trout once more appeared in any numbers.

Fifth Day: Spruce Brook campsite to Wild River Campground

Distance: 5 miles
Walking time: 3¼ hours
Vertical rise: 40 feet

Walking the Black Angel Trail in the morning—after erasing all signs of your camp—can be a letdown after the mountaintops and the strange environment of Perkins Notch; yet it's pleasant and relaxing for the 2.25 miles to the Wild River Trail. You soon cross the lower fork of Spruce Brook (usu-ally dry) and descend to damp areas where one or two springs cross the trail.

Then you are off the ridges and enter the valley. A backpack's end, like its start, should be simple. You swing along easily, your pack lightened by all the good meals you've eaten out of it. Watch on your left for a curiously grown yellow birch. The big stump that nursed the onetime seedling has rotted away and left a massive tangle of roots 5 feet off the ground but supporting the main trunk. You walk on through more woods of deciduous trees.

The Black Angel Trail joins the Wild River Trail as the latter comes downstream on the old railroad grade. Turn left onto the Wild River Trail. The Black Angel Trail coincides with it for a short distance until after the river crossing on Spider Bridge. Just before this footbridge, the Highwater Trail leaves left for its route on the north bank to Hastings and NH 113.

Your dry-shod crossing of the river takes you in a few yards to Black Angel's branching, on the right, toward Blue Brook Shelter. The Wild River Trail, which you follow, is now a wide way above blue pools and sparkling rapids. Beyond a mudslide grown to bushes the trail becomes a jeep road at an earthen roadblock.

There are more lovely pools in the river. They are tempting on a hot day if you have time for a dip before lunch. From Spider Bridge to your car is only 2.75 miles and requires only 1.75 hours to reach it. The rushing river and the calm pools, hot sun to dry you, a good lunch from your quickie supplies—what a way to end a backpack.

Index

Let Backcountry Guides Take You There

Our experienced backcountry authors will lead you to the finest trails, parks, and back roads in the following areas:

50 Hikes Series

50 Hikes in the Maine Mountains
50 Hikes in Southern and Coastal Maine
50 Hikes in Vermont
50 Hikes in the White Mountains
50 More Hikes in New Hampshire
50 Hikes in Connecticut
50 Hikes in Massachusetts
50 Hikes in the Hudson Valley
50 Hikes in the Adirondacks
50 Hikes in Central New York
50 Hikes in Western New York
50 Hikes in New Jersey
50 Hikes in Eastern Pennsylvania
50 Hikes in Central Pennsylvania
50 Hikes in Western Pennsylvania
50 Hikes in the Mountains of North Carolina
50 Hikes in Northern Virginia
50 Hikes in Ohio
50 Hikes in Michigan

Walks and Rambles Series

Walks and Rambles on Cape Cod and the
    Islands
Walks and Rambles in Rhode Island
More Walks and Rambles in Rhode Island
Walks and Rambles on the Delmarva Peninsula
Walks and Rambles in Southwestern Ohio
Walks and Rambles in Ohio's Western Reserve
Walks and Rambles in the Western Hudson
    Valley
Walks and Rambles on Long Island
Walks and Rambles in and around St. Louis

25 Bicycle Tours Series

25 Bicycle Tours in Maine
30 Bicycle Tours in New Hampshire
25 Bicycle Tours in Vermont
25 Mountain Bike Tours in Vermont
25 Bicycle Tours on Cape Cod and the Islands
25 Mountain Bike Tours in Massachusetts
30 Bicycle Tours in New Jersey
25 Bicycle Tours in the Adirondacks
25 Mountain Bike Tours in the Adirondacks
30 Bicycle Tours in the Finger Lakes Region
25 Bicycle Tours in the Hudson Valley
25 Bicycle Tours in the Twin Cities and South-
    eastern Minnesota
30 Bicycle Tours in Wisconsin
25 Mountain Bike Tours in the Hudson Valley
25 Bicycle Tours in Ohio's Western Reserve
25 Bicycle Tours in Maryland
25 Bicycle Tours on Delmarva
25 Bicycle Tours in and around
    Washington, D.C.
25 Bicycle Tours in Coastal Georgia and the
    Carolina Low Country
25 Bicycle Tours in the Texas Hill Country
    and West Texas
The Mountain Biker's Guide to Ski Resorts

We offer many more books on hiking, fly-fishing, travel, nature, and other subjects. Our books are available at bookstores and outdoor stores everywhere. For more information or a free catalog, please call 1-800-245-4151 or write to us at The Countryman Press, PO Box 748, Woodstock, Vermont 05091. You can find us on the Web at www.countrymanpress.com.